WHERE I'M FROM

WHERE I'M FROM

A POETIC JOURNEY ACROSS FIVE CONTINENTS

a memoir

EBONY WALDEN

SWP

SHE WRITES PRESS

Published in 2026 by
She Writes Press, an imprint of The Stable Book Group

1569 Solano Ave #546
Berkeley, CA 94707
https://shewritespress.com

Library of Congress Control Number: 2026909835
ISBN: 979-8-89636-138-1
eISBN: 979-8-89636-139-8

Interior designer: Katherine Lloyd, The DESK

Printed in the United States

Names and identifying characteristics have been changed to protect the privacy of certain individuals.

To my parents, Henrietta and Ricky,
without whom I would not be here. I believe
I am the best parts of you both. Even your faults
have made me who I am. I hope I became some
of the things you were not able to.

To my grandmothers Theola (RIP) and Anne,
aunts Suzette and Eunice (RIP), and sisters Danielle
and Natasha, thank you for being my constant support.

CONTENTS

AUTHOR'S NOTE

Where I'm From is a true story—at least, as true as memory allows. The events and experiences I recount are drawn from my memories, journals, emails, blog posts, and trip notes, and I researched facts where I could. I've done my best to present these experiences as honestly and accurately as possible, but memory is not perfect. Where my recollection faltered, I used my imagination—always guided by the emotional truth of the moment.

Most of the names of people I met abroad have been changed, except where individuals are difficult to identify. Organizational names have been either omitted or fictionalized to protect their privacy, though a few public or well-known names remain. My intention is not to misrepresent, but to honor the people and experiences that shaped me while respecting their privacy.

I cowrote "Where I'm From" poems with people across the globe. While I originally hoped to reproduce them in full in this book, tracking down contributors and securing permission more than a decade later proved difficult. Instead, I have chosen to weave their details into narrative vignettes—preserving their spirit while respecting privacy.

Some people, places, organizations, and events have been left out. These omissions are not meant to discount or diminish anyone, but to keep the narrative focused and authentic to the transformation I underwent.

Lastly, the observations throughout this book reflect what I thought and felt at the time. Nearly fifteen years later, both the places I visited and my perspective have changed. I also see the tension of writing about the Global South through a Western, privileged lens. While some of my views and the lens through which I experienced things were genuine at the time, they were also limited and sometimes naive. For example, volunteering while traveling, teaching English, and working in children's homes was impactful, but I now understand how the revolving door of untrained volunteers can be harmful to children and communities. The "do-gooder" mentality, even when well-intentioned, can sometimes be paternalistic and disruptive.

Even so, the connections I made and the lessons I learned remain deeply meaningful. The people I met mattered to me then, and they still matter to me now.

INTRODUCTION

In September of 2010, I stood defeated at a red phone booth on the side of a road in Greatham, England. I rested my fifty-pound backpack on the wall of the phone booth and let myself slide down. My strength sank with me. Once I hit the ground, my shoulders began shaking and tears flowed in parallel rivers down my face.

I looked down at the directions I'd printed from the website: two miles to walk. That was too far with my backpack. My feet hurt, and my shoulders were sore. I'd already tried calling a cab. The number kept ringing and ringing. The phone at the retreat center where I was staying did the same—ringing, ringing, and ringing. I didn't have a cell phone. After volunteering in Central and South America for two months and backpacking for five weeks through six European countries, I just wanted to be stable. I wanted to rest; not sightsee, not traipse around cities on my own, not meet random people I wouldn't see again. The burden of carrying a bag and myself had become too heavy, and the weight came crashing down on me. I wanted more than ever to be in a warm, safe place, eat a home-cooked meal, and bask in the smiles of people who might remember my name.

I sat there for ten minutes, my hands covering my eyes, legs stretched out in front of me. No cars drove by, no people passed. The air was chilly, and gray clouds loomed above. It was just me, a red phone booth, a sleepy town closed on Sunday, and my tears. Breathless and defeated, I felt the ache of my own need. I thought traveling the world would be liberating, but at that moment, I felt more lost than ever. How would I find a way forward?

I'd started my around-the-world trip three months earlier, in June 2010, feeling confident, excited, and hopeful—like I was on top of the world. A friend had given me the idea for traveling the world, and with an overinflated sense of "can do" and nine months of planning, I ran with it to craft a larger-than-life experience of my own making. I was turning thirty that year, and to celebrate my life, I planned to visit fourteen countries, volunteer, write poems, and connect with people along the way. I was going to capture the beauty and brokenness of the world—to highlight the voices of the overlooked and unseen on The Poetic Justice World Tour.

What I didn't realize was that the real story was about me.

I grew up in Jamaica, Queens, and Hempstead, Long Island, in New York during the height of the crack epidemic in the 1980s and '90s. It was a time when the media vilified so-called welfare queens and single-parent households, even as our communities were navigating the devastating impacts of poverty, a drug crisis, mass incarceration, and disinvestment. Crack vials with red, yellow, and blue caps littered the gray sidewalks. On the big screen, *Boyz N the Hood* and *New Jack City* displayed some of the toughest aspects of Black urban life in America. My family was part of that story. My mother, single and undereducated, with three young girls, struggled financially. My father, caught up in the drug economy and often incarcerated, was absent more than he was present. My home was filled with love and support from extended family but still marred by poverty—water being cut off, winters without heat, and the hum of struggle that never faded.

I wanted to be done with struggle. Being labeled "talented and gifted" in school allowed me to excel. I worked hard, got straight A's, and made my way to Georgetown University and the University of Virginia. I left instability behind and focused on building a life for myself, one where instability did not exist. I spun myself into the kind of person I could be proud of—polished, successful, responsible, and self-sufficient. The kind of person who goes on trips around the world.

In my late twenties, a friend told me that it seemed like I came from a Huxtable household, referencing the two-parent successful Black family that America loved. I laughed. My young life was more like *The PJs* than *The Cosby Show*—but that wasn't the story I wanted to tell. I never denied my upbringing, but shame made silence easy. I didn't know it then, but it was poetry that offered a small window out of shame and into sharing.

"Where I'm From" is a fill-in-the-blank poem another poet gave me months before my trip, a tool for exploring identity and belonging creatively. It was a perfect tool for a trip that was supposed to be about collecting stories from others. As a social-justice-focused urban planner living in Charlottesville, Virginia, who in 2009 fell in love with spoken-word poetry, I set out to create "Where I'm From" poems with some of the people I encountered on my travels. I'd sit with people from all over the world—children, teachers, and fellow travelers—and ask them questions: Where are you from? What foods and phrases remind you of home? What joys and struggles have shaped you? And together, we would craft a poem.

As I wrote with them, I was forced to confront my own story—the pieces I had tried to outrun. The poems became more than just creative exercises; they became bridges between me, the people I met, and myself. Along the way, memories of my childhood surfaced—raw and uninvited. My past was demanding to be seen, healed, and shared.

Where I'm From is about how I was changed by the people and places I encountered during my eight-month journey around the world and the lessons I learned. It's also about remembering—retrieving the stories I tried to leave behind. Through these stories of my past, I reckoned with the choices my parents made and the impact they had on me. They helped me learn that healing doesn't mean erasing the past; it means weaving it into the present.

This book begins and ends in North America and is organized by continent and country. Although I initially planned to visit fourteen countries in ten months, I ended up traveling to seventeen countries over eight months. Only fifteen of those are highlighted in this book. You will journey with me to experience the people, places, and foods of these countries, each offering a lesson I didn't know I needed—lessons about connection, resilience, vulnerability, and identity.

In some places, I volunteered, immersing myself in the community for several weeks. In others, I explored—backpacking for a few days or weeks. The time I spent in each place mirrors the depth of experience you'll find in each chapter. Some are long and in-depth, some short and fleeting—all transformational.

This journey of self-discovery, with its lessons and experiences, is for anyone who longs to or loves to travel (through outer landscapes and inner territories). This book is also for anyone who has carried the weight of their past and wondered how to put it down. I hope it will be a spark for you to explore your own story—not just the places you've been, but the history you carry within you. I've included journal questions in Appendix B to help facilitate your reflection.

I hope that through reading this book, you are better able to hold the beauty and the brokenness of your own story, and to find peace in both. But first, I hope you accept the invitation to go with me on a journey—to learn, to experience, and to ultimately be transformed.

That lonely road in England, outside a red phone booth with nothing but my backpack and the weight of my own tears, was one of many pivotal places on my trip that caused my cracking sense of self to eventually shatter. This is the story of how I got to that lonely road and how I gathered those pieces up and kept going. How, in searching for the world, I finally found myself.

NORTH AMERICA

1

DREAM OUT LOUD

The thing you should know about me is that I love a challenge, a big idea that will take all of my soul to make happen. When I take it on, I broadcast it to others to bring energy and momentum. I love planning and strategizing and getting people excited enough to support me. I have an entrepreneurial spirit, but instead of making money, I am usually asking for it. That is exactly how I got from sitting on the edge of my bed, pondering the idea of traveling the world, to making it happen.

It all started with my friend Fred. I met him in March of 2009, when we carpooled to Virginia Beach to see our mutual friend, Sam, run his first marathon. We talked the entire time and bonded over our mutual love of travel and adventure. He lives in Atlanta, but we decided to keep in touch.

Three months later, on a sunny June day in 2009, I was walking home from downtown Charlottesville, where I worked as a city planner. The warm breeze ushered me from Main Street down the hill on Seventh Street. I was about to cross the train tracks when my phone began vibrating. I was surprised to see Fred's number; I hadn't seen or heard from him since that weekend we'd carpooled.

"Hey, E, I have a crazy idea," he said.

I chuckled. "Let me hear it." From what I knew of Fred, he was likely getting "bright" ideas all the time.

"I want to go on an around-the-world trip!"

Over the next hour, Fred proceeded to tell me more. He was reading *The Rough Guide to First-Time Around the World*, a travel guide for those thinking of traveling the world for the first time. The book was offering him insights into the cost and logistics of such a trip.

By the end of the conversation, I was home, saying, "You don't have to ask yourself why. The question is, why not?"

We hung up, and I sat on the edge of my bed intrigued, fingering my short locs (also known as dreadlocks). I remembered the vision board I had created in 2007 as a life guidepost. It was tacked to the corkboard above my desk at work. It held images that embodied the things I wanted in the future: a brownstone with a porch—a home with outside space to connect; a toned Black woman holding weights—fit, healthy, and strong; and a pen and paper—denoting more writing to reflect and share. I envisioned the passport atop a world map I had placed there to represent my travel goals. I recalled my bucket list, which included visiting five continents. I loved the idea of adventure: doing things and going places I hadn't before, crossing off more accomplishments. I could make that happen in one trip. The idea lit a flame in me.

I was going to be thirty in 2010—a milestone into adulthood. I was single, with no children and no real attachments. I had some money saved. After three years at my job, it was a good time to transition. *Why not?* I thought. *Go for it!*

For a number of reasons I wasn't privy to, Fred didn't end up going on such a trip, but I was glad he'd dreamed out loud because from there, I was off and running.

Once the idea took hold in my head and heart, the planning was like a snowball rolling down a hill, gaining momentum and girth with the passing of time and distance. Each turn a resounding yes!

In July, I sat at my work desk, dreaming of where I might go, and made a list of my top twenty-five travel destinations. In August, I went to a burger lunch at Boylan Heights with my coworkers from the city of Charlottesville and discussed my idea with Neal. Lean, dark-haired, and particular, Neal was one of few people in the office around my age. Though we weren't close, I was bursting with so much excitement about the trip that I told him about my idea. As we waited for our burgers, engulfed by the smell of fried foods, Neal took it upon himself to sketch the continents on the back of the paper menu, a half-sheet menu that allowed you to check off your topping preferences. Though we were at a long table with about eight other colleagues laughing and joking around us, we were in our own world. With our heads almost touching, we charted the most logical route to most of the countries on my list, places like Peru, Spain, Kenya, India, and Australia.

Our orders arrived. Neal took a bite of his burger and I grabbed a handful of fries. He glanced at me, picked up the small pencil, and asked, "Where to next?" We had charted my route through Central and South America.

I pointed toward Europe and said, "Spain, por favor." He smiled and drew a dotted line connecting Peru to Spain. We globetrotted for the rest of lunch. The back of that menu became the basis for my travels. I put it up on the corner of my bedroom mirror so that it would be at the forefront of my mind every day.

By early September, I was consumed with the high I get from a new project, the thought of making things that exist only in my head a reality. I had gotten the same feeling when I started a youth leadership development program at a faith-based nonprofit in my neighborhood and when I started hosting a poetry open mic, the WordSmith Poetry Jam.

Alive with the possibility of this new project, I needed to do something to make it real. In mid-September, I drafted an email entitled "Ebony's World Tour," and after reading and rereading it for a few days, it was time to send it. I didn't know if I was ready. As a way to stall, I sat at my office desk and twirled in my chair to take a look at all of the familiar things: I saw the street outside my office window at city hall that I looked out on every day. A white orchid on my windowsill. My two diplomas on opposite walls, framed in dark wood and blue matting—one from Georgetown University and one from the University of Virginia. I thought about how far I had come from my high school on Long Island. Then I turned toward my vision board, just to the left of my computer screen. When I looked at the passport image, I got a solid feeling inside and finally pressed "send." This trip was in line with my desire to see more of the world, for adventure.

The email went to almost everyone I knew, listing the places I wanted to go and asking for information, contacts, recommendations, friends to stay with, or volunteer opportunities.

Emails came from all over the country saying, "I *love* your idea," "Go girl!" and "I have a friend in France," and "You must go to . . ." People's responses pushed me forward and gave me the encouragement and resources I needed to take the next step.

I knew sightseeing wouldn't be enough for me. To create a meaningful experience, I wanted the trip to include service learning in the Global South. I wanted to connect with real people and experience the joys and challenges the world had to offer. A friend of a friend told me about an international volunteer company that places travelers in a range of affordable volunteer programs, from teaching English to working for environmental preservation.

I structured my trip around where there were volunteer programs that interested me. I decided to volunteer in Guatemala, Peru, Kenya, South Africa, India, and Thailand. The volunteer organization would provide training and orientation to each country, which I found comforting. Everywhere in between—Costa Rica, Spain, France, Italy, England, China, Japan, and Australia—I would stay in hostels, sightsee, and connect with friends of friends. I also found an international hospitality organization, Servas, which linked travelers to people who were willing to offer their homes for two nights of free lodging. These connections would ground me. I continued to prepare for my travels by researching each country extensively to know what to expect and started to teach myself Spanish via workbooks and audio courses.

After the email, I began telling everyone I knew that I wanted to travel the world. Although I had never traveled solo before, I liked doing things I hadn't done before, and I had no trouble imagining myself going alone. What I did need was financial support. After doing research all summer and fall, I created a budget from a template I found online and estimated that such a trip would cost roughly $30,000. I had $7,000 in the bank. With that funding gap, in December I came up with the idea of asking 150 people to give me $150 each, which would provide me with $22,500. I knew I would need to develop a campaign to do it.

In February, I launched a dedicated website for what I dubbed The Poetic Justice World Tour. I hosted a monthly spoken-word open mic in Charlottesville, Virginia, and poetry was an integral part of my life that I didn't want to leave behind. I was inspired by the storytelling that happened at my weekly open mics. Thus, I planned to write and perform poetry inspired by the beauty and challenges I encountered worldwide. I wanted to encourage others to express themselves by creating poems with people from each community I visited. I developed poetry exercises tailored for children and envisioned collaborative poetry sessions with the folks I would meet in each country.

The website served as a central hub, hosting my blog and providing detailed information about the trip. It also became the focal point for my fundraising efforts. With a simple click, visitors could donate to or "sponsor" the dream I was pursuing. I maintained a regular schedule of blog posts and sent monthly updates on my trip-planning progress. In March of 2010, I wrote:

One of the reasons I decided to go to Peru was to climb Machu Picchu. I heard about it when I read Donald Miller's new book, A Million Miles in a Thousand Years. *It's essentially a book about the elements of a story. The things that make up a good story in fiction are also the elements that can make our lives meaningful, adventurous, and memorable. The protagonist (you are the main character in your life) is trying to overcome an obstacle to get to something they really want.*

In that vein, he climbed Machu Picchu (it's a pretty hard two-to four-day hike, and he was out of shape) and advocates for doing things in your life that you never thought you could do in your wildest imagination. It's your job to make your life a good story, to do things that make the readers turn the page. I kind of took this to heart and am planning on going around the world. That's kind of the point of this trip anyway, to live a good story, to go to new heights (personally, spiritually, and artistically) on old peaks (the ancient and modern world).

Plane tickets would be my biggest expenditure, and I budgeted $8,000. I requested more quotes online than I could keep up with. I was surprised when Tim, a travel agent, contacted me via email, as I didn't remember reaching out to him. He quoted $7,750 for the tickets to all of the countries I wanted to visit, with the promise of open tickets so I could change the dates of arrival and departure if needed. This flexibility was crucial, as there were bound to be some places I would want to leave early and others I would wish to stay longer.

Six months after my initial email, my general country-to-country route and time frame were set. I would leave in June of 2010 and return in April of 2011. I planned to go south, to Central and South America, and then east to Europe, Africa, Asia, and Australia. I would have to contact Tim one to three weeks before I wanted to leave each country to confirm my flight booking. Having a travel agent would take one more responsibility from my shoulders, allowing me to focus more on my experience and less on logistics.

On March 4, 2010, I stood at the fax machine in the front-desk area of my job with a pounding heart. I looked up at the big department sign above the fax machine and heard the three Black receptionists behind me at the front counter laughing and joking as usual. By then, everyone at work knew I was planning to travel. I had told my supervisor in February that I planned to resign in May.

A few days later, my department head, Jim, a big-hearted and boisterous man always bursting with good ideas, came into my office and offered to give me a year's leave of absence instead. My mouth sat open for a few seconds while his eyes widened in anticipation of my response. I didn't even know that was an option. After my initial surprise, I accepted. He walked out of my office, saying, "And if you meet someone in Tahiti and decide you want to stay, just let us know as soon as possible." I doubted that would happen. I was more interested in visiting than staying.

That day at the fax machine, my mind was swimming with caution and what-ifs, and my hands were a bit shaky. All the anxiety that I had compartmentalized by planning washed over my body. I was about to fax over my credit card authorization forms to Tim to pay for my plane tickets. I stared at the forms, looking at the numbers that would be charged to my credit card. They blurred a bit as anxiety and uncertainty began to wash over my body.

I wasn't so sure about Tim, about spending $8,000 on this trip, about traveling alone as a woman. Then I remembered how easily things had unfolded. It felt like destiny. This gave me the courage I needed to move forward.

I held my breath while I heard the fax machine crackling and then a loud beep, signifying that they had gone through. *This is it*, I thought. *I am locked in*. I stood still, flooded with fear of having made a wrong choice mixed with anticipation at moving forward. I would have to trust and rely on Tim's expertise the entire trip. I had researched the company and asked him a bunch of questions, but I didn't even know Tim's last name. I wasn't used to trusting strangers. I didn't trust most people with even the simplest of tasks, let alone with nearly $8,000 and the responsibility of managing my airline travel for almost a year. On the flip side, it felt good to depend on a person with expertise who would make it easier for me to enjoy the ride. I hoped that Tim would prove trustworthy.

Being meticulous in my planning efforts was how I kept all the moving parts of my trip together and my uncertainty at bay. A master spreadsheet kept it all in order: my to-do list, trip budget, donations, travel gear, and a Gantt chart of my travel dates and anticipated costs per country.

By April, my life was full to the brim with transactions. I received donations via PayPal online in addition to checks (in my hand and through the mail) from friends, colleagues, and associates. By the beginning of May, I had accumulated $21,500 of my anticipated goal of $30,000. I sold my car, computer, guitar, and couch. It was easy to let go of these things in exchange for getting closer to my goal. My life felt lighter and my heart fuller at the same time.

My inbox was full of receipts for travel merchandise from Sierra Trading Post. Travel gear was a world of its own, and I was baptized in its novelties. My bedroom was full of boxes of merchandise that would ultimately have to fit into two bags: a backpack, and a carry-on.

In late May, I stood in my living room with one of my closest friends, Leonette. Light-skinned, with square-framed glasses and locs, she stood with a camera in her hand. I was trying to pack all of my gear. She took pictures of me suited up for my blog. "You look ready, Eb. How do you feel?"

I looked at my black Camel daypack, the black three-ring binder with the poetry exercises I had put together for the kids I hoped to work with while volunteering, and my gray rolling carry-on. They sat near a chair by my door. My world would be stuffed into those two bags for ten months. I had thought a small rolling suitcase was a better idea than a big backpack because it was $200 cheaper than most packs. Now, I was not sure if I'd made the right decision.

"Girl, after this planning, I am ready to go. Let's just hope I am fully prepared."

I was excited about what was ahead and uncertain about what would come my way, but I also felt like I had prepared as much as I knew how. I'd tried to buy the best travel gear and had researched extensively so I would have all the bells and whistles. I chose the items for comfort, durability, and versatility. Everything was compact. For the dress-up shoot, I was wearing my tan, quick-drying, UPF 30 convertible pants from the North Face. They could zip off and become shorts or roll up and become capris. Complementing the pants was a blue ExOfficio shirt—quick-drying, moisture-wicking, and wrinkle-resistant. On my feet were blue-and-gray Merrell hiking shoes. In my carry-on were clothes, papers, and toiletries. I packed a mini-Toshiba computer, a new Nikon camera, and a compact Flip Video camera to make sure I captured my experience.

I stood posing in my doorway with all my gear on, one bag under my right foot and the other on my back, as Leonette snapped shots from my lawn. "I'm so proud of you, Eb," she said between flashes. I smiled, holding both thumbs up. I was proud of myself too.

> *"Have I not commanded you? Be strong and courageous. Do not be afraid; do not be discouraged, for the LORD your God will be with you wherever you go."*
>
> —Joshua 1:9 (New International Version)

The two things in life that seem to carry me on my journey, both to stabilize and strengthen me, are scripture and quotes. I was strengthened by them as I planned, and I placed them in my metaphorical backpack to take them out of my memory when I needed them. Joshua 1:9 was a scripture I'd carried with me since I became a Christian in college. I was always traversing new territory, so the command to "be strong and courageous" and not be afraid were words I always needed. That verse was etched in my mind and heart and highlighted in the blue mini-Bible I'd packed. Choosing to venture into faraway lands brought with it uncertainties and fears, but this scripture served as a constant reminder that I was never alone. While it didn't promise an absence of danger or challenges, it gave me hope and confidence that I could face whatever lay ahead with courage and faith.

In my planning phase, I also read numerous books written by women travelers to help encourage me. One was *Go Girl* by Marlee LeDai, a book I got for Christmas. LeDai wrote about using travel as a metaphor for the spiritual journey, and the book had some great quotes that I read over and over to place them inside myself. They reminded me that this trip wasn't just a whim—something greater was calling me forth. I wrote one down in the marble notebook that I would take with me as a journal.

> *"Travel is a calling more than anything else. And when something bigger than you calls you, grace supplies the means—be it money or gumption."*
>
> —Marlee LeDai

These quotes and scriptures provided solace and guidance while planning, reinforcing my decision to carry them with me on my journey. They were not just words but anchors of strength and wisdom, shaping my perspective and resolve.

Many people asked me why I wanted to travel the world. Was I going to search for myself? No, not consciously, although I knew every journey was a search for self in some way. Traveling more was on my vision board, and I liked to take on things no one around me had done. I felt compelled to go, and I would take it step by step. "Just put one foot in front of the other," my mother always said. That was how I had lived my life, taking the next right step. That was how I planned that trip and, ultimately, that was how I would make it around the world and back home.

On Memorial Day in 2010, almost a year after I got the idea, I stood confidently before the eager eyes of loved ones, days away from departure, with every logistic taken care of and almost every dollar raised for an around-the-world trip to fourteen countries and five continents. I was ready to embark on this adventure. I wanted to see what God was doing amidst the beauty and brokenness in the world. I would be changed. I wasn't exactly sure how, but I knew I would be.

The last hurrah before I departed was a party with my family. The bright yellow strapless dress I wore popped against my deep brown skin. At twenty-nine, I was in the best shape of my life; my shoulders shone and my arms were defined. I was going around the world and I was full of myself. In my hand was my favorite apparatus at the time, a mic, and I was glowing. I was used to being the center of attention and wearing the confident and sexy host persona after having spent a year hosting a lively poetry open mic in Charlottesville. I loved looking out into the audience, seeing a diversity of faces, hearing the dynamic stories, and even performing a few pieces of my own. I had started performing spoken-word poetry only after being inspired by the event I hosted. I'd watched others and thought, *I can do that*. And I did.

On that sunny Long Island day at my mother's house, the blacktop driveway was lined with my entire immediate family and family friends—over thirty people in total. It was a going-away party, fundraiser, and open mic all in one. They wore yellow, too, thanks to a memo my mom had put out. I guess she thought we should all shine.

As the emcee, I yelled into the mic to get the crowd excited. I had done the same thing at my past events, and it always worked.

"When I say 'make some,' you say 'noise.' Make some!" I shouted

"Noise!" they replied in unison, my mom's voice clear over the rest. Her pride was hard to contain.

"Make some!"

"Noise!"

"Make some!"

"Noise!"

To prepare for the party, I had spent an hour workshopping poems with eight people in my family, from ages sixteen to seventy-two. For the workshop, I led two simple exercises. One was an anaphoric (repetition of a word or phrase) "Where I'm From" poem, which I'd learned from a traveling poet, and the other was another anaphoric poem exercise, starting each sentence with "I am . . ." This is what I planned to do during my travels with some of the people and children I met, and I wanted to start at home.

In some ways, perhaps, I was as much a stranger to my extended family as I would be to the people I met around the world. Having left home twelve years earlier as one of few people in my immediate family to attend college, I was perceived by most of my family as fairly quiet and nonchalant. The open mic allowed them to see me in another light, as an emcee and poet.

"Now I would like you all to put your hands together for the woman who made this possible in so many ways: first and foremost, for my life, for this party, this good food, and that nice banner over there for The Poetic Justice World Tour I am about to go on." I pointed to the banner over the garage with a globe in the middle. "For her support and encouragement of this trip, you all better give it up for my mother," I said, raising my voice a notch.

The crowd roared, clapping and stomping feet, like they always did at my open mics. I loved helping people to find their voice and speak their truth, share their story. I loved providing the space for that to happen, and I loved to listen.

My mom came boldly down the back stairs to our faux stage in front of the detached garage. I held the mic for her. She was wearing yellow pants and a yellow T-shirt as vibrant as her personality, their close fit highlighting her full figure and sizable bust.

"I am from Jamaica, Queens, where the McDonald's is on Sutphin and Linden," she began.

"I am from 'if you lie you will steal, if you steal you will kill,'

"I am from collard greens and black-eyed peas,

"I am from raising three wonderful girls on my own and filling them and my two grandchildren with wisdom, love, and the knowledge of God."

She got so into that line, with finger-pointing, emphasis, and moving her head sassily, that she lost her place. We were all laughing.

"Tell them where else you're from," I interjected.

"I am from being on welfare to owning my own home," she said.

"I am from Bobby McFerrin, Jackson Five, and BeBe and CeCe Winans." She swayed from side to side in a dance motion.

"That's where I'm from."

The crowd went wild again, laughing and clapping. I was proud of them and elated that I could create a lively atmosphere for my family to tell their stories.

My mother was one of the biggest supporters of my trip, and she exuded light that day, like the yellow we were all wearing. I was still perplexed as to why she was not more concerned. One of the reasons the trip probably happened was that I got no pushback from anyone, not even my mom. One day the previous summer, after making small talk on the telephone, I got up the nerve to say, "Mom, I think I am going to go on an around-the-world trip." I winced, as if getting ready for a blow of caution. I imagined her throwing her hands up in the air when she said, "Well the Lord has been with you this long. He will be with you as you travel the globe too." And that was it.

I was used to telling my mother what I was going to do rather than asking for advice or permission. I had made all of my own major life decisions since high school. I knew she worried about me more than about my older sister Danielle and younger sister Natasha, since I was the only one of her children who did not live in New York. I hadn't returned since I left for Georgetown in 1998. I was always "doing something" and "never allowed grass to grow under my feet," as my mom put it. Perhaps my eccentricity had prepared her for this wild idea. Her peace was another sign that I should move forward with abandon.

It never occurred to me to tell my father my plans, and I can't ever remember having done so. I can't recall if he was present that day, although I doubt it. I assumed my older sister Danielle told him about my trip. I had his number but never used it. I saw him when I went home for the holidays, but there was never anything more than a few minutes of small talk. Since he and my mother had never married and broke up when I was a toddler, he'd never lived with us. He had a peripheral presence in my life at best. My sense of independence and self-confidence was born of the love and support from my mother and extended family. I knew I needed both qualities to succeed. But my mother's lack of a college education and personal struggles had limited her ability to guide me to the places I yearned to go, and although my father was around, he was absent from child-rearing. Navigating unfamiliar territory alone was nothing new. It was just how I did life.

What proved to be the most shocking and adventurous aspect of my trip to other people was my plan to travel alone. The choice was easy: I'd either travel alone or not go at all. Waiting for someone to travel with was simply not an option. I reveled in the fact that I was going to do something that probably less than 1 percent of the world's population would ever do. I liked the title World Traveler. I took it on as a new identity.

In my mother's backyard that day, I soaked up all of the love, support, energy, and familiarity I could. I knew I would not see anyone I knew for close to a year. Familiarity would escape me as I traversed from country to country roughly every three weeks. I knew it would be transformative, but I also knew it would be hard and lonely at times. I knew that at some point I would feel discouraged. For me, the planning and beginning of things was where all the excitement was; the middle was always hard, and although I always crossed the finish line, I was typically dragging myself.

After my family members finished telling the crowd where they were from—my aunt, my grandmother, two of my cousins, and my mother's two best friends—I gave them a small piece of me. I started with one of my favorites, entitled "I Am":

"I am the liquid life coursing down the river Nile,

"The rhythm of my waves will carry you miles."

I made a wave motion with my right hand.

"I am the beat of the wind, blunt, cold, and agile,

"I am the red apple from New York, giving you a taste of bittersweet with a smile."

I paused and gave them my best smile, showing my teeth.

"I am the sound of fury coming at with you determination,

"I am Queen Sheba on white wings leading a Black nation."

I flapped my imaginary wings.

"There is so much promise in this form that is short but wild,

"I am a ferocious lion, rocking my mane with vigor and style."

I shook my head, showing off my dreadlocks, which came down to my ears.

"To say that I am fabulous is putting it mild," I said with sass, and paused. The crowd laughed on cue.

"I am a hardworking woman, rich and profound . . ."

I spoke these words and my vision for travel that day with conviction. It was the same conviction I had carried all year, the same one shaping the way I lived.

I believed in myself, in my dreams, in my ability to be myself, do well, and get things done. I said these things out loud and on stage, so everyone around me believed them too. Their willingness to part with their money and their words of encouragement said so.

A line from the book *The Alchemist* perfectly captures the spirit of that year.

> *"When you want something, all the universe conspires in helping you to achieve it."*
>
> —Paulo Coelho

I raised $1,125 that day and had so much fun with my family. We got to know each other a little better, laughed, and cosigned on each other's similarities through poetry. I could travel the world by myself, but I couldn't do it alone. Dreaming out loud by broadcasting the vision of world travel allowed others the opportunity to join me in that ambitious endeavor. My entire community had conspired to send me off with courage and love. This was the beginning of saying yes on a scale I'd never known.

On June 6, 2010, I wore a big smile and my favorite pair of dark-gray jeans as a good luck charm, a blue fleece with purple stripes down the arms, and my Merrell two-tone gray hiking shoes. Alicia Keys's "Un-Thinkable (I'm Ready)" played in the background as I sat staring out the backseat window of my sister's white Mazda Millenia. I, too, was about to do the unthinkable, and I was ready.

We drove up to the international departure section of LaGuardia Airport and stopped at TACA Airlines. My first flight was to Guatemala City, Guatemala. I would be teaching English and taking an immersion Spanish class in Antigua. Eager to start my adventure after months of planning, I got out first. Then, I heard the sound of three car doors opening and shutting as I went to the trunk to get my carry-on.

"This is it," I said to no one in particular.

I embraced my sister Danielle first and then my niece Anaya and Aunt Suzette.

My mother hugged me last. My mother is a hefty woman, which makes her hugs strong and comforting at the same time. That day, it was as if all of her love wrapped around me like a warm blanket. She held on to me for about a minute then kissed me all over my face.

"Mom!" I said, frowning.

"Be careful, and remember to be aware of your surroundings. There are crazy people out there." She looked like she was about to burst into tears.

"I love you guys. Keep me in your prayers," I said gently as I put on my daypack and grabbed the handle of my carry-on. I took a few steps forward and then looked over my shoulder to take one last look at the four of them standing there, watching me leave. They all had the same uncertain look on their faces. I waved with a smile and then headed straight into the sliding double doors that opened automatically in front of me.

My heart sank as I buckled into my seat, bound for Guatemala. The weight of navigating planes, trains, and unknowns alone for months pressed on me. I tried to inhale confidence and exhale anxiety—until the two women beside me broke my spiral. They didn't speak English but were warm and hilarious. Delores, round and radiant in red, leaned in with a booming voice and bold perfume, asking why I was headed to Guatemala . . . and why I didn't have a husband. I burst out laughing. It was the first of many inquiries into my singleness, and one of many moments when a brief, unexpected connection helped put me at ease.

CENTRAL AND SOUTH AMERICA

2

GUATEMALA: RAYS OF SUNSHINE

THE FIRST NIGHT IN ANTIGUA

As I stepped out of La Aurora International Airport just outside of Guatemala City, my eyes scanned the crowd for any sign of the volunteer organization picking me up. A swirl of questions churned in my head—would I be forgotten, scammed, or safe? I gripped the straps of my daypack tightly. With no checked bags, my backpack and carry-on had become extensions of my body.

Then I saw it—my name on a sheet of white paper. I exhaled, realizing I'd been holding my breath. Someone knew I was coming. I felt seen and covered. Safe. I didn't know it then, but I'd carry my sense of safety like my backpack—close, constant, and never fully off.

I would be volunteering in Antigua, a popular location for Spanish immersion schools that catered to tourists. As the shuttle wound its way into town, the sky turned purple and gold—like a sign lit up in the dark. I enjoyed the city's Spanish colonial charm and lively, colorful streets. Cobblestone streets were lined by buildings in shades of mango, peach, and lemon, framed by volcanoes and lush green hills. Brightly painted chicken buses, a common type of local transit, zipped past tuk-tuks (three wheeled vehicles that look like golf carts) and mopeds.

Oscar's house, where I'd stay, was a pink-and-white two-story home with white iron bars on every window and a heavy metal gate. I would become familiar with the way the doors clanged shut like prison bars—reassuring and unsettling all at once. I felt safe, yet I was nervous that such protection was necessary.

When I arrived that evening, Oscar pulled up the garage door on the side of the house, which opened into his dining room. He greeted me with a friendly face and a hearty, "Hola, chica." The inside was a stark contrast to the vibrant exterior. All the walls and floors were dark brown wood, and the furniture was covered in worn brown cloth. The long dining room table covered with a red-and-white-checkered tablecloth straddled the kitchen and dining area. The eight of us volunteers would eat there three times a day.

Oscar grabbed my bags and led me upstairs. At the top of the stairs, four young white women—Liz, Candice, Rebecca, and Chelsea—sat on a couch, watching TV. They greeted Oscar and me as we passed. The upstairs was simple and camp-like: three beds to a room, a bathroom, and a small lounge area. I chose the bed near the window. My roommates were Kara and Courtney, nineteen-year-old friends from the US.

I sat down on my bed, and it wasn't long before I was giving them my travel elevator speech: "I'm Ebony, and I'll be here for two weeks teaching English." I'd have to repeat this all week. I was glad I'd arrived just minutes before dinner; it left no time for small talk. I loved conversation but wasn't into small talk.

Oscar quietly set all the food on the table and then sat on a stool at the counter, overlooking us. My first dinner was vegetable soup, bread, and beans. The other volunteers engaged in a lively chat. I heard them, but I wasn't listening. There was laughter and talk of boys, ladies' nights at local bars, and cheap drinks.

After dinner, I got the basics from Gabby, a pleasant eighteen-year-old volunteer with long, wavy brown hair. She gave me the rundown in short, quick sentences. "Meals are at 7:00 a.m., 1:00

p.m., and 7:00 p.m. The volunteer headquarters is about a fifteen-minute walk. You can walk over with someone tomorrow for orientation. You can access the Internet there. That's also where Spanish classes take place and volunteers touch base. Do not walk by yourself alone at night." She said the last sentence sternly, like a concerned mother would.

We went upstairs so she could show me the bathroom. "The shower head has an electric current flowing through it to heat the water. Touch it and it will shock you." A chorus of agreement came through the walls from a few other girls, who were back to watching TV in the lounge area.

"There are tourist trips every weekend, salsa lessons every Saturday night, and Spanish tutoring every Monday, Wednesday, and Friday. You will likely work half the day and take Spanish lessons for the other half."

I nodded.

After the tour and some small talk, I was ready to go to bed. I lay facing the wall, listening to dogs barking and the zoom of cars and motorcycles. I felt like a child before the first day of school. Doubt about how I would manage the newness balled up into a knot in my chest, and a queasiness roamed around my gut. The uncertainty I'd kept at bay during the months of planning sat as my companion that night. I put in my earplugs and wore my eye mask to block it all out so I could sleep. These would prove to be two of my wisest and most-used purchases.

THE SUNSHINE BEGINS

After a day-long volunteer orientation, which included a two-hour course in teaching ESL, I hopped off the back of a chicken bus to arrive at a white school building with a painting of two smiling suns on the side. The rectangular school complex had a grassy area with a few trees, and a sandbox in the middle. One long yellow school building took up the right side of the complex. Forty or so students from ages five to what seemed like eighteen stood in five lines. They said a blessing, heads bowed, hands in prayer. The young men and women at the head of each line, wearing white T-shirts with the same sun as the sign, were teachers.

Kate, a volunteer program staff member, led me into the main building, where she introduced me to the secretary, then left.

"Hola. ¿Cómo está?" I greeted her. After shaking hands, I sat down in front of the principal's desk to wait. Next to me sat a young, slim boy with a blue knit winter hat, which was odd since it was over seventy degrees. He looked around eleven or twelve years old.

"Hola. ¿Cómo se llama?" I asked.

"Mateo," he replied.

He asked me the same question.

"Ebony," I said, unsure what else to say. I had limited Spanish proficiency, having only started learning Spanish a few months before my trip. I'd taken French in high school.

I asked him how old he was, and he said twelve. We stared blankly at one another for a second. Then he blinked his brown eyes and raised his eyebrows a bit. "Where are you from?" he asked in Spanish.

"Estados Unidos."

"Where?" He turned his whole body toward me, intrigued.

A friend of mine had given me an inflatable globe for moments such as this. I took it out of my backpack and began to blow it up. I pointed to Guatemala. "We are here." Then I pointed to Virginia. "I am from here. Virginia." He nodded.

"I am here to teach English. I am traveling around the world." I took my finger and circled it around the inflatable globe.

His eyes widened. He leaned in, as if I was about to tell him a story, but I couldn't. My Spanish vocabulary was exhausted. I looked at the door. The principal was nowhere in sight. I tried to recall some questions or conversation starters I had studied before the trip. My mind drew a blank. I looked back at Mateo and at the globe in my hands. I knew how to say hands in Spanish—*manos*—but didn't know any other body parts. *Perhaps Mateo could help me*, I thought.

I began to point to my own body parts, asking him to say them in Spanish. "*¿Qué es esto?*" I repeated. Within two minutes, I had him singing "Head, Shoulders, Knees, and Toes" in English while I provided the Spanish equivalents. That moment solidified our friendship for the rest of my time there.

Ms. Ana, the school's founder and principal, arrived a few minutes later. She was a middle-aged, Guatemalan woman with bangs, a pink shirt, and a bright smile. She clasped her hands and then enveloped me in a hug. She was short, so although I am only five foot three myself, I towered over her.

Ms. Ana put her hand on my shoulder to usher me into the classrooms—five of them, all themed. The galaxy room had a wall painted black and dotted with stars and the moon. In the metamorphosis room, a mural depicted tadpoles in a pond and a huge frog on a lily pad. Each room held five to ten smiling students, eagerly shouting "Hello! Hello! Hello!" as we entered. Despite their initial shyness, the children's greetings warmed my heart. The young teachers looked on with enthusiasm as Ms. Ana proudly introduced me as their new English teacher.

Each mention of my role heightened my nerves. I had minimal ESL training and a library of resources from the volunteer center. Would I be able to handle this? My only reassurance was knowing I had more English proficiency than anyone else at the school.

We walked to the end of the rectangular yellow building. Straight ahead were the bathrooms, housed in a cement-block building with a red roof and two red swinging doors. When a chubby five-year-old girl with a bowl haircut emerged, a faint whiff of urine drifted out. I made a mental note to drink little in the mornings so I could avoid using the school's bathroom. Bathroom and shower conditions would become a part of my growing list of things to pay close attention to during my travels. They could make or break an experience.

"Tell me about the school. How did you all get started?" I asked, standing beside Ms. Ana at the end of our tour.

She spoke with a thick accent and switched between English and Spanish. "In Guatemala, there were very few schools for children with disabilities or students with special needs. They are often left at home alone, without access to education," she said somberly. She explained that the students' needs ranged from autism to deafness, physical differences, and struggles that showed up in learning, emotions, and behavior. This was my first time hearing that I would be teaching at a school for children with disabilities. I was surprised, and my anxiety immediately grew. I was untrained and felt ill-prepared.

She continued, "Children in our community weren't being served. I wanted to help, so I opened this school. Initially, the school was small, but with the support of friends, we rented this land and constructed these buildings. I trained the teachers."

"Wow," I said, looking around again. I was saddened, though not shocked, by the neglect of children with disabilities. But I was also moved by Ms. Ana's courage in the face of harsh realities. She carried an air of peace and compassion; her words were full of care, but there was also a persistent strength and clarity in her mission. She had seen a need and chose to do something tangible about it. I loved that!

Looking at me with a smile, she said, "Thank you for coming here to teach English. We are glad to have you." She touched my shoulder, and we walked toward another classroom. She told me that I would teach three to four classes a day for thirty to forty-five minutes each. The strength of her presence eased my nerves about teaching English with minimal ESL training. Standing before my first class, I gazed into the curious eyes of five-year-olds, wondering what lessons this place would teach me.

A few days later, I awoke to my bed inching away from the wall, along with some rocking and stirring motions and a looming rumbling noise. It took me a second to remember where I was. *Guatemala, volunteering, Oscar's house, around-the-world trip*, I reminded myself internally as assurance.

I would later learn it was a small earthquake—my first, and quite a startling way to wake up. I was shaken and couldn't return to sleep. This was the beginning of being shaken. In some ways, I would become more fragile as my trip went on, and in other ways more solid, more human.

My mornings were a series of small hurdles. The first hurdle was the shower—mostly cold water. By the time it warmed up a bit, I was just about finished. The electric showerhead, if moved or touched, would send a jolting zip through my system. Then there was navigating breakfast, switching back and forth between English and Spanish. I made it a point to try to arrive early, to chat briefly with Oscar, my host dad, before all of the noise and chatter began. There was usually some drama within the larger volunteer community from the previous day.

"Did you all hear what happened?" Gabby said to the seven of us one morning.

"What?" we said in unison.

She leaned in a little closer to the table. "Kelly and Grace were walking home last night, and their purses were stolen."

"Are they okay?"

"They are fine. Just shaken up." Gabby took a sip of coffee.

"Man, they weren't even alone," I said.

"Yes, ladies," Oscar interjected from across the counter in the kitchen. "Always take the tuk-tuk after dark. It's not safe to walk after dark."

The constraints of being a woman traveling were always apparent. We couldn't be out after 6:00 p.m. alone—not even with another woman. I knew how fragile my existence was as a woman traveling abroad, but I refused to be scared. I'd be aware and take precautions, but I stepped out daily believing I would be okay.

Later that morning, I jumped off the back of the chicken bus ready for the waves of laughter that would greet me. The children were in line, praying. I said a prayer for myself that I wouldn't botch the lessons I'd prepared. After the prayer line broke, Mateo rushed over to hug me. "Hola, Evony." All of the Guatemalans pronounced my name with a *v* sound instead of a *b*. He put his hand out for me to grab and led me to my first class. On our way, three other children ran past me, saying, "Hello, nice to meet you," and waving and then putting out their hands for me to shake. They had absorbed yesterday's greeting lessons well.

My day began in the virtues classroom. It was a small room of middle school students, four girls and one boy. This was by far my toughest class. They were rather rambunctious, so I liked to visit them first thing in the morning, when I had my wits about me. We had been reviewing colors, food, and greetings, but I started this day a little differently.

"Let's make a list of words you know in English," I said, turning toward the green chalkboard. "You can just shout them out, and I'll write them."

While the four others were shouting hello and goodbye, one student begin shouting "fuck you," over and over. The rest of the group laughed uncontrollably and joined in. I was a little frustrated but was also trying to hold in my laughter. I wasn't sure what to do with that except say, "Bad word," shake my finger, and then pick up my chalk and turn around to continue to write. "What are some other words?" I said.

"Fuck you!" More laughter rang out behind me. I could tell it was going to be a long morning.

I pulled out my Spanish/English dictionary to look up the two words I would use incessantly with this class: *stop* and *listen*.

"*Alto, alto!*" I shouted, trying to get them to quiet down. "*Escucha, escucha!*" To get their attention, I started singing "Head, Shoulders, Knees, and Toes" in Spanish over their laughter.

"*Cabeza, hombros, rodillas, pies.*" I gestured to body parts as I sang.

Then I sang it in English and gestured for them to stand up and join me. One by one, they stood up and began to sing. After a few rounds of singing, I started to draw fruit on the board and asked them to identify it in Spanish. "*¿Qué es esto?*" I said, drawing a banana. I said "banana" in English. They repeated after me, and we continued until there was an apple, banana, pineapple, and orange on the board. "*¿Qué color es?*" I asked and then we ventured into colors, pointing to the fruit on the board and then to colors around the room. When we got to brown, I pointed to my skin. I had been really surprised that no one had reacted to the fact that I was Black. My hair, however, was another story. In another class, I had been asked if it was a wig and had responded, No, *es naturale*." They had smiled and touched my hair gingerly.

When I moved toward one of the desks to pick up a sheet of paper to denote the color white, Lucca, the same little girl who had yelled, "Fuck you," touched my hand and rubbed my skin. "Brown," she said, moving her hand softly back and forth over mine. Despite the profanity and some uproar, what I felt most at the school was gentleness.

The next day, the entire school was testing, so I went into an empty classroom to prepare my lesson. Walking into an empty classroom felt nice. Quiet was not something I'd gotten much of in Antigua, with the bustling city, the rambunctious children, and the seven other volunteers. It stretched my introversion. I took a deep breath and sat at a desk.

Camila, one of the children of middle-school age, walked in. She had curly hair pulled back in a short ponytail. Camila could not hear. She immediately went over to the glitter station. I thought she wanted to maybe paint a picture, so I searched the room for some construction paper. As I was deep into my search, she tapped me on the shoulder. Startled, I turned around, and she stretched her arms straight in front with her palms up, gesturing for me to do the same. I did. She then proceeded to rub pink glitter on the insides of both of my arms. I hesitated at first, but then realized the only things I had to do later that day were to eat lunch and take Spanish lessons. What did I have to lose? Camila massaged the glitter in figure eights, slowly and methodically, her head tilted to the side. She was deep in concentration, humming softly and occasionally looking up to meet my gaze. I was her human canvas, her art project for the day.

I was happy to be in Camila's presence in the quiet, connecting without words, through facial expressions, touch, and gestures. I preferred it to constantly telling people about my trip, who I was, and what I was doing around the world. The spiel had gotten old in the first few days. It was also a struggle to be both the only Black person and one of the few people over twenty-five in the entire community of over a hundred volunteers. I felt alone, with few people my age and race to relate to. Though I loved the children, teaching was exhausting. It was nice to receive this gift from Camila. With tenderness, she moved her glitter-covered fingertips toward my face; I retreated and pointed her toward my eyelids. I could handle eye shadow. I closed my eyes as if I was getting a facial, with my head tilted back, chin up. It could have been one minute or twenty; I'm not sure.

I sat, smiling and be-glittered, until a bell rang for snack time. Camila hugged me, and with her in my embrace, I gazed down at my pink-glittered arms and let out a laugh. Though I tried to wash the glitter off that afternoon, I kept finding it on me for the next five days—sparkling reminders that the children were determined to stay with me.

On Friday, while the children were at recess, I decided to take a moment away and wandered into one of the classrooms where Isabela, one of the school's teachers, and José, a student, usually met. José was about twelve years old, tall for his age, with shoulder-length hair, bangs that nearly covered his eyes, and round cheeks that flushed easily. I never heard him speak. Isabela was the only teacher assigned to work closely with him, and she met him with patience and care.

Isabela, on the other hand, was fairly small and youthful-looking, likely in her twenties. She had long, curly, brown hair and a smile bigger and brighter than anyone else's there. Isabela was gentle and patient with José. When I walked into the classroom, she was painting the bottom of his feet purple so he could make footprints on a piece of beige construction paper. They both seemed content in the quiet classroom, its walls lined with stuffed animals, charts, paper, abandoned computer screens, tubs full of learning supplies, and toys.

"Hola," I said and took a seat.

Isabela was one of the best English speakers there and had seemed open and friendly, so a few days earlier I'd asked her to do a "Where I'm From" poem with me.

"Is it okay if we start the poem now, while the others are at recess?" I asked. "If we don't finish today, we can continue tomorrow. I will write, and you can talk and finish painting with José." I pulled out my red Spanish/English dictionary, just in case I needed it.

I began by asking her what she remembered from her house growing up.

"Flowers. There were many flowers in my house," she replied.

I asked if there were any sayings she'd heard growing up. This one took a few tries. I had to look up the word *sayings* in my dictionary.

A lightbulb of recognition lit up her eyes. "Si, yes, 'you must keep your room clean.'"

I laughed. "I think that one is universal."

Next, we moved on to the names of friends and family members. "Lucho, Pato, and Nina. Andrés, Chelis, and Mario," she replied. Then we talked about tragedies, which I knew could open a can of worms. I took a deep breath and had my pen ready to scribe in my marble notebook with the words SPOKEN SOUL on the front. A friend had cut those words out from a magazine for me before I left, and I'd glued them on the cover. It was a reminder, in moments like this, that I was inviting people to speak about their lives and the truth about who they were.

"Losing my friend Mario in a . . ." She paused. "How do you say it—*secuestrar*?"

I opened up my small but thick red Spanish/English dictionary and began flipping through the pages to the *s* words.

My eyes fell on the word. "Hijack?" I said out loud in disbelief.

"Si, secuestrar," she said with a nod.

She had been involved with the wrong crowd, selling and using drugs. A drug deal went bad, and her friend was killed right in front of her.

I sat back in my chair and said, "Wow." After a moment I asked, "How did you get involved in that lifestyle?"

Between her broken English and my limited Spanish, I was able to get bits and pieces of Isabela's backstory. Her mother had left her at an early age, and she and her father had a rocky relationship. She'd left home in her teens.

It was a bit hard to follow, but I gathered that she had experienced assault, deep loss, and betrayal over the years. I ran my hand across my forehead, as if it would help my brain compute.

"Oh," I said solemnly. I took another deep breath, feeling as though I was in way over my head. She had experienced so much pain in her short life, yet she spoke about it matter-of-factly. That lingered for a moment, and Isabela spoke again. "My boyfriend left me for my best friend, and I went a long time without speaking to my dad." I was struck by how young she was and how much tragedy she had overcome. She seemed to have so much joy within her when I saw her on campus, always smiling.

"How about things you are proud of? Joyful moments."

Her small hand moved to the side of her face. "Drug rehabilitation, reconciliation with my father after many years, and finding a special person who loves me very much."

"Oh, a special someone?" I inquired with a playful tone, wiggling my eyebrows.

"Si. Christian," she said, blushing. She touched José on the head, as if the love that she and Christian shared was overflowing. "His love healed me."

Love does have that power, I thought.

Then, almost as if to remind me of her other joys, she brightened and told me about her favorite music—salsa, rock, *románticos*—and about foods she loved: lasagna, papas, pizza.

So much of her life was distilled into these fragments—flowers and sayings, betrayals and violence, recovery and love. I was impressed by how she had come out on the other side of pain. She was not harsh, but hospitable. I am sure she had scars, but her attitude and outlook seemed generally positive and hopeful.

I was grateful for how deeply she had let me into her life through this poem—how, in seven lines, I was able to see some of her soul. In the simple act of remembering, she showed me not only where she was from but also the strength it had taken to still be here.

OSCAR'S KITCHEN

Oscar's kitchen always smelled of black beans, whether he was cooking or not. Oscar was a medium-height Guatemalan man in his fifties who'd decided to make money by being a host dad for up to ten young women. After growing up in a single-parent household, I felt it odd to be living in a place with a dad present—and a dad as the primary caretaker, at that. Oscar cooked our meals, answered our questions, and looked over at us from the kitchen counter with something between bewilderment and amazement. He usually sat at the counter while we ate meals at the table. Sometimes his wife Rosa joined us, but she wasn't present most of the time.

The opposite was true for my life: My dad wasn't a daily presence growing up. It is hard to remember any meals with my father. My family is primarily matriarchal—men are around, but are not intimately engaged in the lives of children. My father was in and out of jail until I was about ten or eleven years old. After that, he was physically present at my grandmother's house but not involved beyond giving me lunch money and buying me clothes. I can't remember many real conversations with my father as a child, and none that allowed us to see and know one another well. This cooking, present, available, and attentive father figure felt as new to me as Guatemala.

Yet there was something safe, familiar, and at ease with Oscar. He was like background music that the other ladies ignored. For me, he was soft jazz I paid attention to and enjoyed. He probably spoke as much English as I did Spanish, but that didn't stop either of us from trying to communicate a little each day.

I relished mornings in the kitchen with Oscar, practicing my Spanish while he cooked and answered my questions. I'd wake up a little early and go downstairs just to speak with him and have him all to myself before all the other volunteers arrived for breakfast. I was happy to talk to an older adult and glad to have someone to practice Spanish with, free of embarrassment and consequence.

One morning, as he was preparing eggs, I began asking him questions about his life, hoping to craft a "Where I'm From" poem.

"How did you end up doing this?" I asked. "Taking care of volunteers, I mean."

"I lost my job," he said without emotion.

Oscar went on to tell me about how he used to work fixing old typewriters. When they became obsolete and his children had grown, he decided to use the extra rooms to house volunteers. He was always smiling, so I figured he found joy in hosting us and liked our presence, our excitement and curiosity about Guatemala.

After a few warm-up questions, I asked him more penetrating questions. "What was one of your most tragic moments?"

He stirred the eggs in a pan, thinking. "The earthquake in the seventies that destroyed my home and much of this neighborhood."

After a moment of silence, I wanted to lighten it up a bit. "What were some of your happiest moments in life?"

"That's easy. I played basketball in high school, and I still remember when we won our championship," he said with bright eyes, as if it had just happened. "Oh, and the birth of my three children, of course." He tapped the side of his head, as if chastising himself for not saying that first. From the way his eyes lit up when he spoke of his children, I could tell that Oscar was a good dad. I felt more fathered for the two weeks he was my host dad than I'd felt by my real father in my whole life.

We crafted his poem together. He answered my questions, and we discussed his answers, both of us speaking a Spanish/English hybrid. I had a template of the poem activity in Spanish, just in case I needed the directions in Spanish, but wrote Oscar's answers in English. When we finished, I asked him if I could videotape him reading his poem. I wanted to create a minimovie of all the people reading their poems when I returned.

"Si, chica," he said.

I hurried upstairs to get my Flip camera and returned quickly. "This is only going to take a few minutes."

We did three takes. I had to remind him to look up at the camera once or twice while reading, instead of staring at the paper the entire time.

"One last time," I urged.

"Okay, chica." He still looked a little sheepish but more confident than the first time. I could tell he wanted to please me. Maybe he was flattered by all of the attention.

"Here we go . . . In five, four, three, two, one, go!"

"I am from Antigua, Guatemala," he began. "From 'life is not easy' and 'always do better.' From the earthquake of 1976 and from winning basketball championships in the city. From *música ranchera*, rock and roll, and the smell of enchiladas and bacon in the kitchen."

When he finished, he looked up and grinned, proud.

I had to remind him to say the last line.

"That's where I'm from," he said with confidence. He was claiming the story of who he was, and I loved it.

"Cut! You did great!" I was glad that we had a few good takes but sad that our exercise was over. Getting to know the details of Oscar's life had been a treat—a treat I'd never tasted with my father. Oscar had humored me and let me get to know him; he'd made me breakfast, lunch, and dinner. He'd answered my naive questions about the city and culture. He'd offered fatherly care I never knew I was missing. It was only through encountering Oscar that I realized its absence in my life. I was grateful, overcome by the beauty of the experience, while an emptiness also filled my chest, as I grieved the reality that I had gone my entire life without such moments.

My earliest memory of my father, Ricky, is not of his presence but his absence. My first memory is that of a Polaroid picture from the early eighties. In it, Ricky looks young. He's wearing a navy blue leisure suit and Adidas, with a small Afro surrounding his dark brown face and a gold rope chain around his neck. He's sitting on a black milk crate in front of the black door of his "office." The black door led up to an apartment on Sutphin Boulevard in Jamaica, Queens, amidst two-story brick storefront buildings. In the Polaroid, my sister Danielle and I, aged around seven and five, respectively, stand on either side of him. I wear a red warm-up suit with a puff on top of my head, and she wears a blue warm-up suit with a Jheri curl. Ricky has a smirk on his face; my sister and I stare blankly. We stand next to him, but there doesn't seem to be much affection going either way.

This picture is the only real memory I have of my father until I was ten or eleven years old. I remember him through pictures and word of mouth. I recall walking along Sutphin Boulevard in Jamaica, Queens, with our mother, who would stop and talk to neighbors, proudly proclaiming us as "Big Black's kids." Big Black was my father's street name, and he was known and respected in our neighborhood—even revered. She always said it loudly and with a big smile, affectionately touching our heads or shoulders. When I was a child, I would ask where he was, and I was told, "He is at school." I must have visited him with my father's family—my grandmother Theola, aunt Suzette, and grandfather

Buford—when they went to see him. I faintly remember bus rides but never recall actually seeing him. He seemed famous in our neighborhood, as if having him as my father was something to be proud of. But to me, he felt like a ghost. I've always called him Ricky; Dad never seemed appropriate.

I was about eleven when he came home from prison and stayed at my grandmother's house—or at least he was there a lot, maybe too much for my liking. For Danielle and me, his arrival marked the tail end of our four-year stay with our paternal grandmother. One day, we were having spaghetti for dinner. My sister and I sat at the round kitchen table in the corner, between the back door and the stove, deeply focused on our spaghetti and meatballs, our mouths forming *O*s as we slurped. Our father walked in, searching for his separate pot of veggie spaghetti sauce—Ricky didn't eat meat. Eunice, a longtime family friend, and our quasi-live-in caregiver and aunt, had left a medium-sized pot on the stove just for him.

"Hey," he acknowledged us. We nodded, engrossed in sucking up our noodles. He grabbed one of the golden, stone-like plates—the good ones—from the mahogany cabinet across from the stove and headed for the pot that held his special sauce.

"What the fuck?" he exclaimed, eyebrows furrowed as he poured some sauce over his noodles. "I know there ain't no meat in here," he said in disbelief. "Look at this shit!" Agitated, he dipped his fingers into the sauce and flung it, hitting the microwave, splattering some on the stove, the floor, and a bit on the wall.

Danielle and I froze, exchanging wide-eyed glances before returning our attention to him.

"What y'all looking at? Eunice knows I don't eat meat. Why would she do some shit like this?" He slammed his plate onto the stove and stormed out of the kitchen, muttering.

We remained seated, waiting to hear the confrontation between him and Eunice.

"There ain't no meat in that sauce, Ricky! It's chunky tomato sauce," she yelled as their argument escalated. "What's wrong with you, boy?"

"I know, right?" my sister whispered to me. We resumed eating our spaghetti. For a long time, I could see specks of that spaghetti sauce on the wall, a lingering reminder of bad behavior.

I accepted Ricky as an erratic person and a sporadic presence. I never yearned for his company; it always brought disruption. It wasn't until eighteen years later and worlds apart that I became aware of how much I yearned for a father. Though Ricky and I had a few good moments over the years, my kitchen experiences with Oscar gave me the first taste of what nurturing and present fathering could be like. It was lovely and unfamiliar.

GOODBYES

In between my first week and my last day of volunteering, I taught ABCs, colors, numbers, food, greetings, and more. The students were fascinated by my hair, often calling it *muy bonita* (very beautiful). There were moments of cursing, rambunctiousness, and new lessons for us all. Every morning, two or three more kids would run up to me to say hello and give me hugs. Double that number walked me to the gate when I was leaving. During recess, I handed out bagged drinks with straws and chips or fruit. They relished in the goodness, the reprieve from learning, the novelty of my presence, and the company of one another. After only nine days, I felt like I was part of a family.

My final day was a love feast. One class drew pictures of Antigua on construction paper, gave me flowers, and made me a farewell sign. They gave me the drawings—the mountains of

Antigua—to take with me, so I would remember them. Nothing could make me forget them.

During recess, I sat down and pulled my marble notebook out of my black backpack, which was already showing signs of wear from the dust. I glanced around the campus, taking in the environment—the yellow building, the bathrooms, the sandbox—and the familiar faces of Camila, Mateo, Isabela, and others smiling in front of me, eager to write their names in my book. I handed it to Camila first to sign, and it was swiftly passed from hand to hand as I watched. The entire atmosphere buzzed with energy.

Isabela said, "Friend me on Facebook."

"Okay, I will."

Ms. Ana approached me and said, "I felt such chemistry with you. You were a good English teacher."

I hugged her.

Another teenager approached me, grinning. She held out a red flower.

"Gracias," I said, placing the flower in my hair.

After much bustling and chatter, Mateo returned my book to me. I glanced at all the names and turned it around to read some of the messages written upside down and sideways in Spanish. I could make out most of the words: *love*, *thank you*, *teacher*.

"Picture, picture!" someone shouted, and suddenly, a crowd surrounded me, chanting, "Photo, photo, photo!"

"Let's take it over there." I pointed to the courtyard, and we moved like a fluid organism of smiles and laughter. We posed for a group photo with me at the center.

As my time came to an end that afternoon, sadness flooded my body, and my stomach dropped. I would truly miss this place, these people.

I walked toward the exit and the others dispersed, returning to their conversations and games. Mateo kept pace beside me.

"Where are you going next?" he asked.

"Costa Rica," I replied.

He looked at me with sadness. "*Bien viejo*, Evony."

"Gracias, Mateo. You're my favorite student," I said as we crossed the threshold.

Midway to the bus stop, he lifted me off the ground and swung me around. After he set me down, I looked him in the eye and rested my hand on his shoulder.

"Goodbye, Mateo. I'll miss you the most." I hugged him again, then turned and walked away, my eyes misty. I glanced back several times to wave. Each time, he was standing in the same spot, waving back, wearing the same blue knit hat as the day we'd met.

My experience in Guatemala taught me that connection didn't require perfect Spanish or the best training, but presence. Mateo's hug, Camila's glittered hands, and Ms. Ana's courageous leadership showed me that I could belong, connect, and be inspired daily if I stayed open. *How will I do this five more times at my other volunteer placements?* I thought. I could only hope for experiences as fulfilling as this one. The suns painted on the side of the school smiled at me one last time, and I smiled back.

3

COSTA RICA: PURA VIDA

PURA VIDA!

Leaving the community and purpose of Guatemala was bittersweet, but I was excited to trade routine for rest—and Costa Rica. On the plane, my upgrade to first class felt luxurious after two weeks of modest living. I sank into the plush seat, vodka cranberry in hand, staring into the clouds and wondering what adventures lay ahead.

Costa Rica was vibrant, friendly, and surprisingly touristy—I barely needed Spanish. I quickly learned that fried chicken was big, Imperial beer was everywhere, the coffee was divine, and the people were warm. The scenery? Stunning.

Each day in San José, I woke up at 5:00 a.m. with no agenda except exploring. My life felt *pura vida*—a Costa Rican phrase my tour guide said could mean "it's all good," "this is living," or just "cool." A greeting, a vibe, a state of mind. It is an expression of a leisurely lifestyle and friendliness. If we were at a poetry jam, I would do a little call and response, asking my audience to say "pura vida" after anything I said. It would be fun.

The beauty of backpacking is waking up, deciding to go somewhere new, and just going. In San José, everyone was in motion—two girls headed to Coco Beach, one guy to Panama, someone else to Monteverde. Like most travelers, on my third morning, I decided to leave San José and head to the west coast.

By evening, I was at a beach hostel in Manuel Antonio. The hostel wasn't much to look at—white walls, empty rooms—but the hammock, pool, and FREE BREAKFAST sign gave me hope.

I wandered across the street and devoured *casados*—a plate of chicken, rice, beans, plantains, and slaw—for four dollars, paired with a smoothie-like fruit juice. I tracked every expense in my notebook, transferring it to my budget spreadsheet at night.

That evening, I walked to the beach and watched the sky turn purple, pink, and gold. Couples strolled hand in hand. I realized I'd never watched a sunset with someone I loved—and wondered if I ever would. I looked up at the sky and hoped I wouldn't always be alone. As it got dark, I asked a nearby couple to snap my picture standing atop a sand mount, wrote *Ebony was here* in the sand, and headed home.

"Guess what fell into my lap?" was the very random code phrase I would use in my blog to alert my girlfriends that I had a love interest, either emotionally or physically. This is what I had told my friends Hope and Jillian to watch out for in my blog.

"Guess what fell into my lap?" I repeated on Hope's backyard deck over a glass of wine, months before my trip started. The three of us laughed.

These things did not need to be broadcast to everyone, but I wanted somebody to know. I supposed everyone believed that an around-the-world trip would not be complete without a love interest, or a few. People had seen *Eat Pray Love*, and even my boss had said to just let them know if I fell in love with somebody and decided not to come back. It felt like an unspoken expectation by others and a hope of mine. I wasn't expecting to fall in love, but I did want a little excitement—I wanted to at least meet someone and share a few good memories.

I hadn't had a substantial love interest since high school. I was not a boy magnet in college, when I weighed fifty pounds more than I did on my around-the-world trip. My high school boyfriend had liked me more than I liked him; I think I dated him because I was bored. He was different, and I liked that. He had emigrated from Sierra Leone, wore wide-legged jeans, and had a muscular body and an *s*-curl atop a round, mahogany face. Everybody else had a boyfriend, or at least someone they liked, so he and I dated. I strung that along for four years, never really in the relationship, but never out. I needed something to do when I came home from college, and he would be available to make out with and take me to the movies.

One night, during my freshman year when I was home for Christmas break, we had been making out in his room. I lay on his bed with my head turned sideways so that I could watch television. He was going to town, kissing and touching me, and I was bored. *Seinfeld* was on. I loved the show, and that is where my attention was. My boyfriend kept turning my head toward him; I'd engage for a minute and then turn back to the TV. When I finally realized I was more interested in seeing the rest of the *Seinfeld* episode than having sex with him, I asked him to take me home.

"Close but no cigar" is how I would describe my love life in general. Always dates, maybe even a bunch of them but nothing had developed into a serious relationship. I wasn't sure if it was me or them. I just thought I was supposed to be doing something, but when I did, I never felt right. I was open to love but not in a rush. My life was so lively in college and afterward with friends, service, and work.

Besides, I found most guys fairly boring. What were their passions and goals? How did they want to change the world? If their hopes didn't mesh with mine, I wasn't interested. It saved me a lot of bullshit, which I witnessed my friends experience, but it also left me alone. Most of the time, I was fine with being single. I got used to that being my reality. Other times, when I was bored or when others were aglow with the energy of new love, I wanted to know that for myself.

The first romantic encounter of my trip came in the form of Raj. On my fifth day in Costa Rica, I was just planning on being a beach bum. I woke up and had a cup of free hostel coffee and made myself some free pancakes. I'd eaten more pancakes in the previous two weeks than in the past two years, but I could say that about a lot of other things, too, like sugar, coffee, black beans, and juice.

I sat down at the white picnic tables with a few others and said, "Good morning. What are you guys up to today?"

A handsome Indian guy with manicured hair and square, black-rimmed glasses responded, "Hey, I'm Raj." He pointed to the others around the table, all women. "Febe, Trish, Kacie, and I are going to Manuel Antonio in a bit. Do you want to come?"

I was unsure if I wanted to spend the day with random people. "Maybe. I'm Ebony, by the way."

I shook hands with Raj and Febe, who was a petite Asian woman, quiet and shy. Trish and Kacie were two slim young white women with blonde hair from California and Florida, respectively.

After breakfast, I decided to go with them. I'd have enough time by myself during this trip.

That afternoon, Raj and I barely spoke directly; we were just travelers, all five of us, enjoying having companionship as we explored the four-mile trail and the wildlife in the park next to the beach. We saw monkeys, a bat, lizards, crabs, and raccoons. The most interesting animal we spotted was a sloth. We stared up at the top of the tree next to a tour guide and her group and listened to tidbits from the guide. "Sloths are these slow, monkey-looking animals," she said. "They sleep almost all day and only come down about once a week to poop."

Must be backed up, I thought. *That is why they move so slowly.* I laughed to myself.

Later that evening, I went to meet Sofia for the first time. She was a friend of some friends at home who'd visited Costa Rica a year earlier. She was practicing and improving her English as their conversation partner.

I hopped off the bus and dashed across the street toward a small, white-brick building. Through the windows, I could see a woman at a desk. I went inside and said, "Sofia?"

"Ebony?" she said. "Nice to meet you," she added in careful, accented English, her smile warm and friendly. Sofia's bright eyes and wavy black hair gave her a welcoming presence. She wore tan pants and a brown shirt with her agency's logo.

We went over the usual script: where I was from, where I was traveling to, why I was in Costa Rica, and how long I would be there. I'd get tired of those questions, but at this moment they were fresh. I was happy to connect with someone who was actually Costa Rican.

We went into the town of Quepos to eat dinner. Quepos is a quaint downtown about fifteen minutes from the beach. We sat on the second floor of a fairly nice Costa Rican restaurant and talked until the sun went down. I have a propensity to either allow people to open up or to ask enough questions and show enough interest until they do. We ate *casados* and I sipped an Imperial, a Costa Rican beer, while we talked. Sofia was intense, boisterous, and jovial—quick to laugh and easy to get to know.

"So tell me about Costa Rica," I said. "What is it like to live here?"

"I am actually Colombian. I was adopted by a family, but I have been here for most of my life. It's pura vida," she said and then laughed.

"Yes, that phrase was the first thing I learned here. It's on T-shirts and everything."

"It's very common, very Costa Rican."

As we talked more about Sofia's life, I learned that it had been anything but pura vida. She had been left by her parents, adopted, and then left by her first husband. So many people she loved had left her life, but she remained open.

By the end of the evening, she was beaming with excitement as she told me about new love. "David" was a name I was becoming familiar with. They had found one another on the Internet and she was in love—the light of it was beaming off her. He, however, lived in Florida.

I was skeptical, always thinking about the practicality of things. I was not a believer in love conquers all. "How will it work? Will you move there, or will he move here?" I said.

"I am going to visit soon. I hope to move there and get married," she replied. "At this moment, I am very happy. He loves me very much."

Though I had doubts, I was excited for her. Her ability to find and believe in love again amidst heartbreak inspired me. She reminded me of Isabela from Guatemala as she'd spoken about her boyfriend, Christian. Something about their new love was redeeming for the both of them; it delivered new life and hope to their faces and their very beings. I wanted what she had. Maybe she could be this happy because she was "in this moment," a phrase peppered throughout her speech.

After we ate, Sofia took me to see her family. We walked through Quepos in the dark, past small, one-story buildings with not much light, but I trusted her. Her family was sitting outside. A few men were present, but her grandmother stole the show for me.

"Hola," I said with a wave as we stood in front of them. Their house had a store at the front, with a window similar to that on a food truck.

"Hola, *morena*!" her grandmother shouted and then laughed.

Sofia introduced me to everyone. "*Esta mi nuestra amiga*, Ebony."

"*Yo soy de Estados Unidos*," I said.

"Ohhh. Welcome, welcome," they all seemed to say in unison.

"*Muy bonita*." The grandmother raised her beer bottle toward my hair.

"Gracias," I replied.

Grandma Sarah and I hit it off. She was eighty-four and spunky, with silver hair, wrinkled skin, and no front teeth. She asked the infamous questions I'd hear everywhere in Latin America: first, was I married, and second, did I have a boyfriend? People were always disappointed when I said no. I found their obsession with romance a bit annoying. I was fine with being single and was rarely lonely, even though I was often alone.

I asked Sarah if she had a boyfriend. She said, "Si." He was younger than her too.

"In the US, we would call you a cougar."

We all laughed.

I had been a little nervous when Sofia said we were going to her house. My Spanish was not good. But I quickly learned that it was easy to connect if I was generally interested in people and allowed them to get to know me. It was easy to joke and to laugh. Laughter is the great universal language.

Back at the hostel, a bunch of travelers were sitting in the common area, discussing "ladies' night." I was so over ladies' night, which had been the outing of choice among volunteers in Guatemala. There was one almost every night of the week and drink specials that averaged fifty cents.

"Who wants to go?" someone said. Nine hands shot up, as if we were in an elementary classroom. Mine was the only one down.

"Oh, come on," Raj said to me. "It will be fun. What are you going to do here, anyway? It's only nine thirty. Are you just going to go to sleep?"

He had a point. I could see for the first time that he was attracted to me; something in his eyes conveyed personal reasons for wanting me to come along. It was then that I realized he was more handsome than I realized, with bronze skin and black hair, his white linen shirt and pants fitting his body nicely. *Ohhh, maybe I should go*, I thought.

"Yeah, come on," said Trish and Kacie in unison.

I looked at them and shrugged. "Okay."

There were ten of us, and we packed five into each cab, each car a pack of laps and legs and arms on top of one another. It was reggae and salsa night at the club, and from the moment we entered, I had so much fun. I can't salsa for a lick, but I had strong partners . . . mostly two handsome Black guys—one from Limón, which is the Caribbean side of the country, and one from the States. The one from Limón whispered in my ear, "We miss Black women . . . there are not many here." I was reminded of Livingston, the little Black town on the Caribbean side of Guatemala where I had stopped in for lunch when a few volunteers went on a side trip to the ruins of Tikal. It was the only place I had seen Black people so far. Seeing them made me happy.

We twisted, twirled, gyrated, and grinded, and I sashayed in my long blue tie-dye dress until we were a sweaty mess. I went back and sat down with the few people from the hostel group at the table, the nondancers. Raj was one of them. We sat shoulder to shoulder.

"Can I buy you a drink? What do you want? Get whatever you like," he said eagerly.

"I'll just have an Imperial. Order for me. I'll grab it when I get back."

"I'll be here waiting," he said.

I went back a few times until my drink was finished, and our flirting moved up a notch each time. We ended the night under the dark, cloudy sky, swinging in a hammock at the hostel, Raj's arm around me. It was almost pitch black, except for a few lights around the pool. My eyes had adjusted, though, and I could see. At the lower pool deck, a few people were singing. Their voices and the strumming guitar became background music. It felt good to be that close to someone and to feel desired. It had been a long time since anyone was that close to me.

Listening to Sofia talk earlier that day had increased my desire to have someone to love. I was envious and wanted a taste of what she had, even if for a brief moment. So when Raj interrupted a moment of silence between us with "I really want to kiss you right now," I didn't bother to reply. I just pressed my lips against his. Kissing quickly turned into more, and while it was nice at first, the thought of being close to him was better than the reality.

Walking by the front desk on our way back, I realized that the area we had been sitting in was on camera. We looked at each other at the same time with wide eyes, and I said *oh shit* inside.

Raj burst out laughing. "You just got 'felt up' on camera," he blurted, teasing me before walking off and leaving me to stew in humiliation.

I didn't think it was so funny; his mocking felt immature and insensitive. I may have lost interest in him at that very moment, although I didn't know it until much later. I went to sleep worried that my grainy image would end up on the Internet. I was supposed to be doing poetry around the world. I tossed and turned in my uncomfortable bunk, finally drifting off to sleep.

The next morning, Raj missed his flight. I had mixed emotions about him staying. I appreciated the interest and attention, but his flippant comment had rubbed me the wrong way. Still, we went to the beach with Febe that morning.

After buying a coconut, he sat in the beach chair next to me and took a sip.

"I was thinking, would you want to come to San José with me?" He touched my thigh lightly, as if we were closer than we really were. I felt ambivalent about his proposal, annoyed from last night. Still, the idea of a rendezvous intrigued me. I wanted to have a good story to tell my friends back home.

"Hmm, let me think about it," I said.

At that very moment, a man appeared in front of us with a live lobster, trying to sell it to us. *Who does that?* I thought, but I was happy for the interruption.

"Hey, New York," the man said. I'd encountered him the day before and had told him where I was from.

He was a short, tanned Latino man in his forties or fifties, wearing sunglasses. I said, "No, thank you," to the lobster.

"Pura vida, New York, pura vida," he said, walking away.

With that encouragement, I turned to Raj and said yes. Later that day, I emailed my closest group of friends the code phrase for a romantic encounter: "Guess what fell into my lap." I told them I'd send an email with more details later.

Sofia and I were supposed to have dinner and hang out that evening. I walked into the travel agency, smiling, and said, "I met a boy." When I explained to her that I'd be leaving with him and would miss dinner, she was sad but happy for me. I did ask for one last favor though. I explained the poem and poetry project. She nodded, saying, "Si, si."

She wrote her poem, then we talked through the answers and she polished it quickly. About half an hour later, she stood in front of my Flip camera, a little shy but willing.

She began by naming the places that shaped her: Soda El Puente and Sugar 2000, the backdrop of her daily life in Costa Rica.

When speaking of her hardships, her voice softened. "I am from being left by my father, my mother, and then my husband." The words hung heavy between us.

But she also spoke with pride about her accomplishments: finishing theological school, owning her own restaurant, and falling in love again. Her face lit up as she spoke of "David."

She added her favorite foods with a smile. "Rice and chicken, Chinese food, and ceviche."

Then, she lifted her chin, her voice steady. "That's where I'm from."

In that moment, she wasn't just reciting lines. She was holding the pieces of a life that had shaped her into the woman standing in front of me. I felt honored.

That day, I left with Raj for San José. At first, we sat next to one another on the bus, but when I saw that there were empty seats, I grabbed my things and said, "No offense, but I want to spread out." He just looked at me over his sunglasses as if he were trying to decipher my true intentions. I don't know if I knew my true intentions. I just knew I wanted to sit alone. I didn't want to have to talk to anyone, and I didn't want him touching me with familiarity. Each moment with Raj was getting more and more strained, less and less a fun-loving adventure. Whatever he said, I would reply with the opposite.

When we got to the hostel, it was the same. At the registration desk, Raj pulled out his wallet and began looking for his card. "Private room for you two?" asked the attendant. At the exact same instant, Raj said yes and I said no. We looked at each other, bewildered. A group dorm room was decided. We went upstairs and dropped off our things. Each of us chose a dorm bed at the opposite end of the room. I went to grab some food from the café downstairs and took it upstairs to the movie room. It was a pink psychedelic room with a bunch of pink beanbags and a widescreen TV. Raj joined me a few minutes later. We began to kiss. It was fine, but no sparks were flying for me. I realized that I wanted to feel something more than I actually did. So, when he whispered, "Let's get a room," while rubbing my thigh, I quickly replied, "I don't want to." I felt a pang of guilt, as if I'd led him on by coming this far. But I wasn't going to take it back. We both went pretty stiff after that. I could feel the disappointment and annoyance fuming from his body. I didn't really care.

Back in our dorm room, I put my pajamas on in the bathroom. When I came out, he was in bed, turned away from me.

"Goodnight," I said. "Have a safe trip tomorrow."

When I woke up, he was gone. I was glad to get rid of the dead weight, but sad that we didn't have a better parting . . . that my first male encounter hadn't gone better. I had wanted to like him but didn't. His jerkish comment had rubbed me the wrong way, and I couldn't get past it. Randomly hooking up was just not me, overseas or at home. I valued deep connection and wanted more than what was on the surface. My heart sank, but I preferred sadness to superficial. I sent my friends a follow-up email, entitled "Close but no cigar."

The next day, I was lost. I had taken a three-and-a-half-hour, seven-dollar bus ride from San José to La Fortuna. I'd been looking for my hostel for an hour since getting off the bus. Despite following the directions I'd printed from the website, I'd gotten nowhere. My daypack was getting heavy, my back sweating under it, and my shoulders were aching as I gripped my carry-on. Suddenly a scraping sound was coming from behind me. I turned and realized that the wheels had broken off my carry-on because of the rocky road. I didn't stop. I kept walking, and the scraping noise continued. I shook my head, thinking, *Why did I bring a carry-on on an around-the-world trip? What was I thinking? It's only been three weeks and it's already broken. Sometimes it just doesn't pay to be cheap. This is what I get for being cheap.*

Just as despair began to settle in, I spotted a group of white people walking in the distance. With renewed energy, I followed them, assuming they might also be backpackers. Relief washed over me as the sign for Arenal Backpackers Resort came into view—a "five-star hostel," complete with a pool and a bar. Finally, I could drop my bags, have a drink, and take in the view of Arenal, the volcano that towered over us like a watchful giant. Arenal is one of six active volcanoes in Costa Rica, a country that has over two hundred.

The next morning, I joined a tour led by William, our lively guide with impeccable English. He regaled us with stories about Arenal, a volcano he had climbed eight times, and its history. As our bus approached, the volcano rumbled, spewing rocks and smoke into the sky. One side was deceptively green and lush, while the other was gray and scarred, streaked with lava trails. William shared the chilling story of a nearby town that once stood by the volcano, unaware of its danger. When the eruption came, it claimed nearly eighty lives. Now, only the church steeple remained visible from a man-made lake—a haunting reminder. Arenal was like life—a striking combination of beauty and destruction.

MARGARITA'S HOUSE

Servas is an international hospitality network that costs under $100 to join and lets registered travelers stay for up to two nights for free with hosts around the world. Both hosts and travelers go through an interview process—I did mine and was approved as a traveler. I had contact lists for fifteen countries, including Costa Rica, and although I'd reached out to a few people in San José for my final two nights, only Margarita was available.

From the moment she opened the door—big smile, warm "hola," strong hug—I knew I was in good hands. She was about five feet tall with short brown hair, probably in her fifties or sixties. Her pink row house reminded me of similar ones in the US.

Inside, the walls popped with colorful paintings of Black women in royal blues and reds—unexpected and deeply comforting, as if pieces of home were looking back at me. I'd seen so few Black people in the past month and had connected with even fewer. Out on the patio, an older man in work clothes was tiling a mural of a whale. He waved brightly, then went back to work.

Margarita led me upstairs to a suite—its walls covered with pastel beach scenes and more images of Black women. A queen bed, my own bathroom, a sitting room with a TV. Heaven. I dropped my bags and sat on the bed, facing the door.

She stood there, smiling. "Dinner at six?"

"Yes, I'd love to," I said. "Mind if I shower and relax a bit?"

"Si, si," she said, slipping out and leaving the door slightly open. Giddy to have my own room, I flopped back on the bed, arms outstretched, eyes closed. "Yes!"

After I showered and took a short nap, I found Margarita in the kitchen in front of a large pot, stirring what I assumed would be our dinner. I stood next to her and inhaled the aroma-filled steam. "Mmm, that smells good. What is it?"

"It's a staple here, *arroz con pollo*, and we will have some *gallo pinto* to go with it."

"It's nice to have a home-cooked meal to end my time here." It smelled spicy.

"Please, please have a seat," she said and pointed to the small table against the wall, only a few short steps from the stove.

I was ready for the delicious meal and some conversation. I could now tell within five minutes whether I'd click with someone, and Margarita had the click factor. Since she'd opened the door, we'd felt like friends.

She offered me *tamarindo*.

"What is tamarindo?" I said.

"Tamarindo is a drink made with tamarind. How do I describe it? . . . It's like a root." She went to the refrigerator, pulled out a plastic pitcher holding liquid the same color as iced tea, and poured two glasses.

"You speak English well, by the way. Where did you learn?" I asked.

"Well, I am a retired ESL teacher," she said as she sat down across from me. "That is originally why I became a Servas host twenty-nine years ago. I wanted my children to keep up their English, and it was a good way to practice with guests. I loved it so much I kept doing it. I've probably had over one hundred travelers."

She sat down, crossed her arms atop the table, and got comfortable. I took a sip of my tamarindo, which had an interesting flavor I can't really describe, something between juice and tea. I folded my arms and leaned in.

Over the course of dinner, I learned a lot about Margarita. She was sixty-two and from Limón, the Caribbean side of Costa Rica. She *loved* Limón and described herself as being "Costa Rican with a Black heart." The Black art began to make sense.

"It reminds me of home," she said. "I grew up on the coast, around Caribbean people that were Black. It's a part of my childhood. So is the beach. I want to move back there before I am too old. You would love it. I wish you could have visited. Maybe next time."

I would have loved to visit Limón and be among Black people too.

She was a painter and so was Louis, her boyfriend, whom she'd met at a painting class. As we spoke, Louis was crafting a beautiful oceanic tile mural on her backyard wall. He waved occasionally.

She went off on monologues I loved to follow—so free, as if she were just waiting to be asked. She talked about Limón like it was her lover, with a half-smile and a dreamy look in her eyes.

"I love calypso music, I love to dance, and I love the food native to Limón, like ackee and saltfish, rice with coconut."

"Oh, I love ackee and saltfish," I said. "A good friend of mine is Jamaican. I eat it at her house. I also grew up in New York and there are tons of Caribbean people there, so I got a taste of the culture growing up as well. A lot of rice and peas and curry and roti."

"Yes, all very good," she replied with a surprised but satisfied look in her eyes.

We talked about her three children and four grandchildren, how she met her husband, how he died, some of her joys and victories. We were working our way through a "Where I'm From" poem without the prompts. I told her about the activity and asked if we could do it tomorrow. "Of course," she replied.

I was amazed at what continued to happen to me: I'd just ask, and people would willingly give me their life stories. It was as if they had been waiting to be listened to, for their voices and perspectives to be honored and cherished. The poem was a gift to both parties. Although the constant change of scenery was hard at times, I loved just getting to know people; their hospitality and their stories were priceless.

After our plates were clean and our glasses empty, like a good mother, sensing my tiredness, Margarita sent me off to sleep. I didn't put on my eye masks and earplugs that evening. I had the upstairs all to myself and the room was silent. I fell asleep with a full belly and a smile.

My time with Margarita reminded me of kitchen conversations with my Aunt Eunice at my paternal grandmother's house. I loved asking her questions and was mesmerized by her stories and sayings. She was my caretaker and confidant from the ages of eight to twelve, so talking to older people was something I'd always enjoyed.

When I was about eight, I went to live at my paternal grandmother's house in Hempstead, Long Island. It was about twenty-five minutes from where I had grown up in Jamaica, Queens. It was the burbs to me, a two-story brick cape with a large front yard and backyard. This was where my father had grown up. My sister and I had often visited with my father's family on holidays, weekends, and summers before we moved there.

My mother had lost her job a few years prior to us moving in with my grandmother, and my Aunt Mary, who shared that house with us and her two sons, was often pulled away by her own struggles. For a few years, we had periods with no lights, heat, or water. Running extension cords from our neighbor's house, hauling pails of water from next door, and not having a working bathroom had run its course. The house was uninhabitable. One day in the fall of 1988, after we'd been staying with our mother's friend for a while, my sister told me that my mother had called my paternal grandmother from a phone booth near our house. I don't remember that phone call, but I can imagine my baby sister Natasha, only a few months old, held in my mother's arms; Danielle and me stuffed next to them in the phone booth; and a black plastic bag with our belongings resting on the floor.

"Theola, this is Henrietta." My mother began to sniffle. "I-I-I need help. We don't have a place to stay, I need you to come and get Danielle and Ebony for a while, until I can get on my feet." I imagine that tears streamed down her face. Whenever my mother cried, I cried, so I am sure tears were streaming down mine too.

My sister and I got picked up soon after that call, and my mother and little sister stayed in Queens. We didn't see her again for a few months. I cried every day during those months, uncontrollably. Then, I don't remember crying much anymore as a child, with the exception of the first days of school.

A few months later, my mom had a stable place to live in Queens, but Danielle and I were enrolled in school and continued to live for four years with our grandmother, Theola. We visited my mother and younger sister, Natasha, in their one-bedroom basement apartment in Ozone Park on the weekends, holidays, and summer vacations.

Life was smaller, harder, and leaner at the Ozone Park apartment. Though I loved my mother dearly, my trust in her ability to take care of us was tarnished. My life at my grandmother's house was more spacious and full of plenty. My grandmother, a nurse, was a tough woman, dark brown, with shoulder-length hair. She barely smiled, had a mouth like a sailor, and was always fussing at somebody, but she loved us fiercely and we knew it. We had everything we needed and most of the things we wanted. I posed in front of the wall of mirrors in the living room each time I passed. Her house felt like luxury. It was full of family, with Sunday meals every day. Though my grandmother had plastic on her beige living room furniture, which no one was allowed to sit on, all were welcome at the house.

A staple at my grandmother's house was my Aunt Eunice, a friend of the family who had helped raise my father and Aunt Suzette. She had lived with my grandmother for over twenty years. She'd started out as a friend and boarder and became family. Her room was across from the one Danielle and I occupied.

Eunice was in her early fifties, medium brown, with large breasts in pointed bras. I was fairly quiet and didn't talk much, but I spoke to Eunice. I asked her ten million questions, and she taught me old sayings and showed me how to do things. Among the things she taught me was how to clean up the kitchen, play spades, shuffle cards, and fry an egg. I helped her with cooking, folding clothes, sprucing up the backyard—anything domestic. I was her sidekick.

One day, she was teaching me to clean the kitchen (we did so every night after dinner with a house full of family). I had a broom in my hand and was sweeping fairly indiscriminately. I brushed over her white Ked shoes and she jumped back quickly. "Giirrrrlll, don't sweep my feet. You do that, and I'll go to jail."

I laughed out loud; it seemed like pure nonsense.

She stared at me sternly and then said with a smile, "Just watch that broom. I don't have time for jail, Ebony. Who would take care of you?"

My grandmother took care of us financially but worked a lot. Eunice was like our nanny.

I asked her some of the same questions over and over again, especially when she was doing my hair—either giving me a relaxer, or curling it, or both. She was my personal stylist during our time there. We'd sit in the kitchen, me in a chair, Eunice standing close to the back door, her hands in my thick hair. I had nothing to look at but the stainless-steel appliances in the small kitchen. These, not being as common in the late eighties, made me think my grandmother was rich.

"Eunice, how did you come to live here?"

"I came to New York from North Carolina when I was young, about eighteen. We all did. Everybody wanted to come to New York. I started as a domestic worker and cleaned houses for white people, you know. I met your grandmother and her sister, Bet, in the streets. Everybody hung out at bars after work. Well, I actually met your Aunt Bet first, and then I met your grandmother. I came over one day to watch your Aunt Suzette when she was a baby. We fell in love with each other and I never left."

Satisfied with that answer, I would skip to another question. "Eunice, what happened to your back?" I already knew that answer too.

"Here you go with these questions again. How many times have I told you this? My house caught fire when I was about ten. My back was burned."

"Okay then, why don't you have any children?"

"I do have children—you and your sister. Hell, I helped raise your father and aunt and most of your cousins. And stop moving your head."

"I mean kids of your *own*."

"I never got married. I almost did—ran off with a man when your aunt and father were young. I got a letter from Suzette saying, 'Come home, silly Eunice, come home.' And I did, like a fool. I guess I wasn't too into that man anyway. Ha ha."

"You are funny. I'm glad you came back. What was his name?"

"Funny yourself. You are one nosy little girl. That is enough for today. Now sit still and stop with all these questions you already know the answer to."

I'd sit up in the chair, wiggle for a second to find a comfortable spot again, and launch into another subject—school or something else.

I don't think I talked that much to many other people in my life then. Maybe my mother. My father's family was a bit gruff. I knew my grandmother adored me, but she would say, "Stop asking me all these damn questions!" I'd laugh and walk away. No one took her cursing seriously; her meanness was like niceness. I learned to be a little more tough there, though, like everyone else; quiet and a bit nonchalant, as I was called. I saved my warmth, questions, and jokes for Eunice.

Margarita took me shopping for a new backpack, to no avail. On our way back, I was reminded of how I'd had to zip and unzip my luggage three times to get it fully open that morning.

I started laughing and shaking my head. "When it rains, it pours," I said.

"But it isn't raining," she replied.

"It's just a saying, meaning bad things happening all at once, my wheels and zipper breaking."

"Oh, okay. Yes, pouring rain on you."

"Something like that." I chuckled.

I reminded her of the poem activity she'd promised to do with me. "There is a place in the poem about sayings. You can teach me some of yours."

"We have a bunch of these here, serious ones and funny ones too. First one I learned was from my mother: You must treat others the way you want to be treated."

"Yes, that must be universal, I think," I said.

We pulled into her garage and made our way inside to the kitchen table. I soon had another glass of tamarindo in front of me and pulled out my camera, paper, and pen, which were always in my daypack—an inseparable part of my travel uniform.

I had already gotten a story from a Costa Rican person, but I wanted to capture the lives of people I fell in love with, people I felt close to who seemed willing to talk about their lives. I wanted to cook up a poem with Margarita and put in the details of all the stories and seasonings she had shared with me over the previous day.

When we finished crafting, she stood next to her dining room table in a yellow shirt with pictures of the beach behind her while I videotaped her.

She spoke of "an extremely loving family"—her mother, Mariela; her father, Álvaro; and six siblings. She remembered her mother's presence and the art books that shaped her imagination. Then her tone shifted: the day her brother Tico fell from a bridge in Moín and came home with fifty stitches, and the terrifying moment Manuel, the love of her life, stopped breathing.

Her face brightened again when she talked about Limón and the music she loved: calypso, boleros, and merengue. She gave a little smile and swayed, as if the rhythm might pull her into dancing right there in the room. Her love for Limón reminded me that place is more than geography—it's memory, music, and the people who hold us together. I vowed to visit Limón the next time I returned to Costa Rica.

4

PERU: CRAFTING COMMUNITY OUT OF THIN AIR

LIMA: A GASTRONOMIC EXPLORATION

By the time I landed in Lima, Peru, my suitcase was falling apart. Wheelless, it scraped noisily along the airport floor as I dragged it behind me. "This is what I get for being cheap," I muttered, shaking my head. The topsy-turvy cab ride to the hostel didn't help matters. The driver zipped through dark streets, dodging cars and honking wildly, all while singing along to the 1970s version of "Ladies' Night." I focused on the week ahead, eager to explore the culinary capital of the Americas before heading to Cusco for five weeks of volunteering. Lima promised ceviche and a fusion of flavors that had my taste buds ready for adventure.

When I arrived at my hostel in Miraflores, a hip and swanky neighborhood, my room was empty, but soon a fellow traveler joined me—a white woman with a tired smile. She'd been on the road for eight months. As I struggled with my broken suitcase zipper, she chuckled and offered advice for my journey: "Just remember to say, 'this is making me a better person,' when things get tough." Immediately, I thought, *This zipper is only making me a madder person!*

The next morning, determined to replace my carry-on, I ventured to Larcomar, an outdoor mall perched on a cliff overlooking the coast. In under ten minutes, I found a sturdy blue-and-gray backpack with compartments galore. Well worth the $250, it immediately felt like an upgrade for my journey. With my new backpack taken care of, I explored a nearby park and savored a shredded chicken sandwich stuffed with matchstick fries from a food vendor. Jazz music filled the air, cats roamed freely, and I spotted a bodega selling *chicha morada*. The deep-purple drink—a mix of boiled purple maize, spices, and pineapple—tasted like an elevated grape Kool-Aid. Sitting alone in the empty café, sipping slowly, I relished the stillness and freedom. No conversations, no to-do lists, no volunteers or hosts—just me, soaking in the moment. Likewise, I savored every variation of ceviche I would find that week—fish, shrimp, octopus, and mixed. Each time, I leaned back and relished in the abundance.

TO REMEMBER

A COUNTRY THAT DOES NOT REMEMBER ITS PAST DOES NOT HAVE A FUTURE, the opening sign of the exhibit read. I was in the National Museum of Peru at a photo exhibit entitled *To Remember*. Produced by Peru's Truth and Reconciliation Commission, the exhibit documented their twenty-year civil war, which raged from 1980 to 2000 and took seventy thousand lives. Black-and-white photos showed bombed-out buildings, people in the midst of struggle, faces in anguish. One was of a little boy about seven years old with a scar from his eye down to the top of his lip. The most memorable photo was of the back of an Indigenous woman with two long braids coming out of a rounded top hat. She was standing in a doorway, legs spread, shoulders tight, holding a shotgun about three feet long.

I was impressed that the Peruvians were willing to lay bare their painful history in the same building that celebrated their ancient past and Incan culture. It reminded me that facing your own truth could be a path to moving forward, to healing.

Outside the museum, I looked up to the hills on the horizon and saw the *pueblos jóvenes*, the informal settlements I had read about. From a distance, the hillside was a panorama of small, colorful homes of greens, blues, and yellows huddled together, softened by the gray haze of the sky. Like in many cities, there were neighborhoods beyond the tourist districts where resources were limited and daily life carried heavier struggles. I knew I wouldn't see this side of Lima, but in Cusco, while volunteering, I might. *To really understand a country*, I thought, *you have to glimpse the lives of people living at its margins.*

Although my life did not start or remain in its clutches, I knew a bit about poverty myself. As I looked up at the yellow houses on the hill, I thought back to my own yellow house in Jamaica, Queens. It was a two-story, three-bedroom house in the middle of 113th Avenue. Everyone on the block sat out on their front steps, or stoops as we called them. Most of the children my age had parents who'd grown up there as well. My mom had grown up in that yellow house, and my grandmother had passed it on to my mother and aunt when she remarried. I remember sitting on the stoop, people-watching, looking across at boys jumping and back-flipping on a discarded mattress in the vacant lot across the street. This yellow house was a home for us—my sister Danielle and me and our two cousins—until my mother lost her job and my aunt started drifting in and out of our lives, pulled away by struggles none of us fully understood. Slowly, the house became what I imagine those shacks on the hills were—no lights, heat, or running water.

My mother moved to Hempstead after four years of coming back and forth between Queens and Long Island to see us while we lived with my grandmother. That reunion, while joyous, brought with it instability. We were on welfare and used food stamps. My mother, two sisters, and I moved into a modest two-bedroom apartment on the ground floor of a duplex. It had dusty-pink aluminum siding outside and peach-painted paneling inside. My mother's room was the size of a large walk-in closet. Natasha, my younger sister, slept on the couch, and my older sister Danielle and I shared a bedroom. Over the next six years, we would go from shaky bunk beds to box springs atop crates and finally, with elation, to beds on rails. At one point, the wood on one side of my box spring broke and I was constantly taping it up so that one side of my bed did not sink to the floor. My heavyset mother would come and flop down on my bed once a week. It would break, and I would be livid—livid at my broken bed, at the fact that she broke it, at the fact that she was the reason our lives seemed broken and on the fringe. She hadn't finished high school, had lost one of the only jobs I remembered her having, and we had lost our house in Queens. After she'd leave our room, I'd get on the floor and go to work repairing my broken bed, with my sister laughing and shaking her head. She was always laughing; I was always trying to fix things. "Why don't you just leave it?" she would say. I couldn't.

Watching *The Cosby Show* and *A Different World*, with their images of successful Black families and college life, gave me hope that a life beyond struggle was possible. Education was my ticket out of poverty and into prosperity. But since my story included both, I always wanted to see both sides of a country—the touristy places and what was hidden up in the hills, behind the haze and in the shadows. I nodded to the pueblos jóvenes, the hillside settlements, as I left . . . remembering.

CUSCO: PEOPLE ARE BETTER THAN NO PEOPLE

In Cusco, Peru, which was once the center of the Incan Empire, I lived in a three-story stone corner house with a host family. My host parents, Luis and Rosa, had two sons, Patrick and Diego, and a little terrier named Runi. On one of my first days there, Runi got into my room and chewed up the handle of my water bottle. Diego, with straight black hair that almost covered his eyes, was adorable, and though he was eleven, he looked eight. Every morning, like an alarm, Luis, a slender wearer of sweater vests, yelled "Diego!" all morning for him to get up and "Runi!" so he would stop barking. Runi was a puppy, so we had to step over puddles of pee and packages of poop daily.

Ten volunteers, including myself, lived in that house—quite full, fun, and diverse. There were seven folks from the US, including Ivy and Tasha, who felt like twins, both medium brown with long braids, and Tiffany, the quiet one. All three of them were Black premed students. Of the two Canadians, one was white and the other Indian. Because there were three other Black women, I felt a level of comfort I hadn't experienced in Guatemala. There is often this inexplicable connection to other Black people, like we are in this together. They talked and laughed loud like me, used their hands in the same expressive way, gesticulating often. We often began our sentences with "Giiiirrlllll . . ."

Like a little family, all of the volunteers ate breakfast, lunch, and dinner together at 7:45 a.m., 1:30 p.m., and sometime after 7:00 p.m. We always had yogurt for breakfast. Lunch and dinner were usually a rice or potato dish. We'd guess what we were having before Rosa, our ever-smiling host mom, brought it out. Many nights, we'd sit waiting for our dinner for long periods of time, hungry, hoping to eat by 7:00 p.m. but sometimes not eating until 9:00 p.m.

One day, while we were waiting, John, who had a boyish smile and a good sense of humor, said, "How about I guess what we are having for dinner?"

"Potatoes," everybody said in frustrated unison, rolling our eyes and throwing our hands up. Then we laughed, knowing it was either a potato or a rice dish, as always.

But for dinner that day, we had something that looked like a two-layer cake, very yellow, with what looked like white icing in the middle. We all looked at each other curiously, as if to say, "What is this?" Then we smiled sheepishly at our host mom. It was *causa limeña*—chicken salad layered between cold yellow mashed potatoes, topped with mayonnaise, a slice of boiled egg, and an olive. Served cold, it looked like cake. I was not a fan. Our dessert was *mazamorra morada*, a hot-purple, gelatinous dish. I mostly played with it by spooning it up and letting it slowly drip back into my clear bowl.

We went out a few times a week for drinks as a reprieve from our unfamiliar food to "get trashed," as Ivy, Tasha, and John liked to call it. I called them the get-trashed crew. Cusco had quite the nightlife. I hung with them sometimes, and when I did, it felt like I was in college again since they were all under twenty-three. Both at home and when we were out, we operated as a group and moved like an amoeba, checking on one another, making sure everyone was all right, similar to a buddy system on a field trip.

One night we walked toward Plaza de Armas to see what club was popping. Plaza de Armas, in the center of Cusco, is a Spanish-style public square, each side lined by two-story arcade buildings. There were also two large Gothic-looking cathedrals on the plaza, which had four streets paved with stone. In the daytime, it was bustling; at night, it was much the same.

"Ladies are free," one of the club recruiters yelled as we approached him. "And so are drinks."

We all looked at one another, nodded in approval, and went in. Inside, large dark rooms were packed from wall to wall with white people grooving to loud music. We squeezed through the crowd of bobbing heads and moved with our arms in a straight line, our hands on the shoulders of the person in front of us, trying to make our way to the middle of the floor. As soon as we got to the center of the room, Beyoncé's "Single Ladies" started blaring through the speakers. Every time I and the three other Black volunteers entered a club, the DJ would start playing hip-hop and R&B.

"The party just started," I said. The seven of us begin dancing in a circle and singing "whoa-oh-oh, oh-oh-oh," with Beyoncé. We attracted looks, and other dancers quickly came to join our circle. Whenever we went, people took notice of a group with four Black people, a few white people, and an Indian person moving together. We bumped hips, waved our hands in the air, and slapped high fives, having a good time and giving our onlookers a show. I felt more comfortable being stared at in a group than alone. We were in our own bubble.

At some point, Tasha, with her long braids swinging behind her, led the movement toward the bar counter. "Let's dance on the bar," she yelled with a mixed drink in her hand. We raised our drinks as an affirmative. The rest of us followed like a trail of ants. We were now the multicultural seven who had gone further into the spotlight. With them, I had become one of those girls dancing on the top of a bar—something I'd never do by myself. I looked out at the crowd of people dancing and having a good time. Some cheered us on and adopted our moves. I felt powerful, light, and free together with my volunteer crew. I danced to one song, and that was all I needed. I jumped down into the crowd and we resumed our dance circle. Dancing on a bar abroad: Mission accomplished!

A STRUGGLING SPECTACLE

Although I loved my fellow volunteers, my weeks in Cusco, Peru, were a struggle. The first week, I had altitude sickness; we were a good eleven thousand feet above sea level. I was tired and dehydrated, with headaches and dizziness. All of the starchy foods were slowing down my digestive system too. I did not even attempt to take a brisk walk or go upstairs faster than a snail's pace because I felt like my lungs were on fire. The daily half-hour walks to the volunteer headquarters on dirt roads full of billowing dust that clogged my already puttering lungs, and the cramped forty-five-minute van ride to my volunteer placement while Indigenous Quechua women sometimes held live chickens, made life a little challenging.

On my first day volunteering, I met my two co-teachers, Emily and Ralph, at the volunteer headquarters. Emily was a brown-haired, kind young woman from the Midwest, and Ralph was a near-bald, skinny, and nerdy guy in his late thirties who reminded me of Pee-wee Herman. Emily and Ralph had been working together for a few weeks.

The van we took up the mountain to the village school was packed, but we squeezed in. An old woman carrying cartons of eggs in a blanket tied around her back was nearly seated in my lap, but I didn't protest. She cursed the bus driver because he did not stop when she wanted him to, screaming and pointing her fingers angrily. I looked over at Emily, who spoke great Spanish. She said the woman had told the driver to go to hell. I laughed out loud. I was even more amused by the llamas, donkeys, and pigs out in the streets of the school's mountain village.

We walked through the eight-foot-tall blue metal gates into a dusty brown courtyard where at least one hundred elementary school children were gathered. Boys played soccer, and girls congregated on the bleachers, all in blue-and-white uniforms.

When I entered, a hush ensued. Heads turned, eyes bulged, and fingers pointed at me. Perhaps I was their first Black volunteer. Eyes followed my every move. We were welcomed by a few teachers, who shook our hands.

"Once recess is over, we will take you to your class assignments. In the meantime, just have a seat," said the principal.

As we took our seats on the nearby bleachers, about twenty children surrounded me, laughing and pointing. Hands grabbed at my skin and yanked my hair. Ralph and Emily yelled, "Stop!" But the kids just laughed more. I became a spectacle. Everything slowed as they closed in on me. I wanted to scream, but I was too busy dodging fingers and pushing back pairs of hands. A few minutes later, the school bell rang and the children dispersed.

Emily said, "I'm sorry you had to experience that."

"I am too," I said. A storm of shock swirled around in my chest. I took a few deep breaths to calm myself.

During the next few days, most of the children followed me, laughing, but others who were generally curious got up enough courage to say hello. I tried to engage. They were children; I was probably the first Black person they had seen. I was an anomaly and their reaction understandable, though not at all comfortable.

One precious little boy who was in my class of kindergarteners stopped me midsentence while we were going over ABCs and said, "It is really hot where you are from?"

I thought about it for a second. "Sometimes, about three months a year. Why do you ask?" I said in my limited Spanish.

"Is that how your skin got like that? Was it burnt in the sun?"

I looked at Emily, who translated for me. My furrowed brows relaxed into a bellowing laugh. "I was born this way."

I got slow nods all around.

I held the back of my hand out toward him. He rubbed it gently.

"It's the same as your hand, but different," I said, and he nodded. I relished the few moments of connection breaking through in an otherwise challenging situation.

While the school placement was never great, each day I made a few new friends amidst the pointing and staring frenzy that followed me. But my three weeks at the school, a combined elementary and middle school with around seven hundred students, was challenging. We had over three hundred students in our rotation. With each class meeting just once a week for thirty to forty-five minutes, it was hard to connect or learn names. Emily,

Ralph, and I tried to prepare lessons together, but the schedule was overwhelming, and Ralph's approach grated on me. He insisted on reading the same kindergarten book about a dog to every class, regardless of their ages, and his soft voice failed to hold the children's attention. One day, a fight broke out while Ralph was reading. Despite Emily's and my efforts to intervene, Ralph continued reading in his whispery tone. Frustrated, I told him I couldn't handle his style and opted to work alone. When the placement closed for two weeks, I was relieved.

My next assignment was at a boys' middle school. There, though I sometimes taught up to fifty twelve-year-olds at once, their energy and respect made the whirlwind of the classroom bearable. They called me *professora*, stood when I entered the room, and thanked me after each class, often with kisses on the cheek. My favorite student was Roberto, a curly haired, middle school boy obsessed with excelling. When I marked "excellent" on his perfect worksheet, he hugged me, beaming as he returned to his seat. Moments like that made the mayhem worth it.

In addition to the school situation, my Cusco days were full of uncertainty and questions. Every morning as I stepped into the little white closet that was the shower room, I wondered if there was going to be hot water for none, part, or all of my shower time.

When I was too sick or tired to walk to the volunteer headquarters and needed to take a cab, I never knew how much it would cost: two-and-a-half, three, or four soles? Each cab driver had a different price. I'd nod in annoyance and slap the coins into their leathery hands.

If I wanted to buy something from the market or a street vendor, I wondered what the actual price of merchandise was. Would it end up being 25 percent of the first quote, 50 percent, or 60 percent? I bargained everywhere and hated it. When I wasn't bargaining, I shook my head in frustration at how many times I got hounded to buy something from vendors selling goods on the street. "No, gracias," I said, rolling my eyes, between five and fifteen times a day.

On my way to my volunteer placement, I wondered, *Will the school be open today? Will the classes be on a regular schedule, or will this be a holiday or random cancellation? Will there be a strike in town or a parade that closes down the streets?*

Finally, when I arrived back home, tired from a day of unknown variables, I never knew what time dinner would start. Some days, it was after nine.

An oasis in the midst of uncertainty came from my Spanish conversation partner Nicolás. Most volunteers took Spanish classes during the day and were matched with a Peruvian conversation partner. I sat in front of Nicolás a few times a week and talked about simple things, like the weather and how old he was, because those were the only things I knew how to say— comfortably, anyway. I was usually stumbling over Spanish words and asking him to repeat himself, but Nicolás never grew impatient. His square face always held a blank expression, but there was kindness behind his eyes and he had an easygoing personality. He spoke softly and slowly. After our first weeks of getting-to-know-you questions, the list of the things I could talk about and understand were quite limited. I'd try to cheat. "Can you just tell me in English?" I'd say. He'd smile and comply. And that was how most of our sessions went: a few choppy minutes of me speaking and asking questions in Spanish and then switching to English. I was just glad to have a friend. We weren't particularly close, but we were consistent.

I took as many chances as I could to remind myself that Cusco was a beautiful place, with beautiful people and culture. I found quite a few things to love. There is quite a mix of history, tourism, and nightlife. The Incan ruins were all around, and the admiration was so present. There was even Inca Kola—a yellow soda that tasted like Mountain Dew and came in a glass bottle. Walking down the street was a lively scene. I often saw Quechua women, sombreros on their heads, two braids hanging down, and a colorful fabric sack on their backs carrying either a baby or some products to sell. The streets were colorful with Incan murals, colonial architecture, and old Catholic churches. Indigenous people sold cuisine, snacks, and clothes.

My favorite thing about Cusco was the sky—so blue, crystal clear, and present. I was reading *Here on Earth* by Alice Hoffman, where she described skies so vivid—lemon-colored and so clear—that other places seemed to vanish. Her writing reminded me of Cusco. In Cusco, I felt like I was in the sky, its bright blue arms wrapped around me. When I was alone, the sky kept me company; the moon, sun, and stars were familiar. They helped me remember that one could be in the midst of so much beauty and also be struggling to breathe.

NICOLÁS—WHERE I'M FROM

We'd been meeting for a month before I asked Nicolás to do a "Where I'm From" poem. I was sitting at one of the café tables in the large lounge area of the volunteer headquarters when he arrived, wearing a red shirt. He had his usual calm demeanor and a smile. I stood to give him a hug. I had only a week in Cusco to go, and I was going to miss our time together.

He smiled and took a seat as he greeted me, "Hola, *mi amiga*, Ebony."

I reminded him that we were going to do the poem, explained the process, and instructed him to sit in front of the camera. We used a globe mural as the background for his video.

"Okay, Nicolás, tell me a phrase or saying that you have here in Peru. Maybe something you heard a lot growing up."

He gazed up at the ceiling as he thought. "Don't believe a mountain sky, a woman's tears, or a dog's limp."

I laughed and he looked at me, tilting his head as if confused.

"That sounds funny," I said. "Tell me what it means."

"Things that look real may not be real, or they can trick you."

"Have you been tricked by any of those before?"

I said it in jest, but he responded, "A woman, once. My first girlfriend. I was in love, and she cheated on me."

"Well, I see you have jumped straight in. One of the questions is about tragedies you have faced." I figured I might as well go with it.

He put his hand under his chin. "My parents, their separation, it was very hard, and I lost my job teaching in Lima. I really liked teaching, and now I am back here in Cusco looking for work. That is not going so well."

"Not good at all. But, it's given you some time to hang with me and perfect your already great English."

He smiled.

"Speaking of Lima, I had some good ceviche there. What are your favorite Peruvian cuisines?"

"I love ceviche too," he said. "I like guinea pig and *rocoto relleno*."

"I've had guinea pig here—not bad, tastes like chicken with a lot less meat. But what is rocoto relleno?"

He lit up as if it was sitting in front of him. "It's a spicy red pepper, called rocoto, and inside is meat and cheese, and it tastes so good. Very, very good. It's popular here in Peru."

"I might have to add it to my must-eat list," I said, raising my eyebrows. "While we are on the good stuff, do you have a favorite festival or celebration?"

He sat up in his chair. "Oh, very easy. Inti Raymi." He sat back and folded his arms.

"Tell me more, please," I said.

"It's called the Festival of the Sun. It happens every year at Saksaywaman. Have you been there?"

"Oh, of course, during my first week." Saksaywaman is an Incan fortress and was on all the major Cusco-area tours. It has massive gray stone walls made with boulders, some over eight feet tall. Its pronunciation, close to "sexy woman," made it hard to forget.

"Every year, June 24, there's a big festival—many Cusqueños, locals of Cusco, and tourists dress up in colorful Incan clothes. There's so much food and music, it is very nice and exciting." He was smiling again. This was the most worked up I had seen him all month. "We like to have festivals here," he added.

"I know. It seems like there is a parade every week—something closed, people dressed up and celebrating something." I shook my head. The festivals were kind of overwhelming.

In Cusco, I experienced Incan history, celebrations, and Catholic churches—alive and colorful in so many ways, some that were not appealing to my need for stability. Nicolás was consistent, though, always open and kind. I was grateful for his steady companionship through quite a few rough spots in Cusco.

With a smile and surprising confidence, he read his poem aloud in front of the camera, closing with his love of roasted guinea pig, ceviche, rocoto relleno, and the music that carried him: *romántica*, rock, and pop. When he said the words, "That's where I'm from," I suddenly felt sad. I gave him a hug, knowing we had only a few more sessions left together.

A WEEK OF MISHAPS

I decided to leave Peru a week early, because I was ready to go on the next adventure. Despite some good moments, it was hard for me to have a positive view of my experience overall. My last week was the perfect hailstorm to end a challenging experience.

It began with a frantic search for the immigration form I'd received upon arrival but lost. I needed it for my departure. After searching every pocket and luggage compartment in vain,

I learned that replacing it required an obstacle course, including a trip to the volunteer office, escorted trips to the immigration office and the national bank (with a hundred people in line) to pay eight soles, and back to the volunteer office. The process was exhausting, but after hours of navigating long lines and forms, I finally held the precious yellow replacement slip in hand.

Meanwhile, my persistent cough worsened, turning into bronchitis. The volunteer rumor was that I was coughing up blood (not true), but a trip to the pharmacy with Nicolás resulted in a green syrup from Portugal that offered temporary relief. Just as the cough subsided, a throbbing toothache emerged. A local dentist—operating out of a large, white, nearly empty room in the back of her home—diagnosed inflamed gums and prescribed Sensodyne and an anti-inflammatory medicine. Her professionalism was a relief, despite the unconventional setting and low price. It cost fourteen dollars.

Machu Picchu was another crazy adventure. Our driver's car had damp seats. We sped along treacherous narrow roads, hugging cliffs, taking occasional short stops until we were brought to a sudden halt. Residents of the surrounding area had laid a tree down in the middle of the road to protest something I didn't understand, and we had to negotiate our passage. After the four-hour car ride came a train ride, an overnight stay in the town of Aguas Calientes, and then a bus ride to the top of Machu Picchu before dawn.

When Ivy, Tasha, Tiffany, and I finally arrived, Machu Picchu was breathtaking. The peak was full of stone terraces overtaken by a blanket of green, peppered with llamas and alpacas grazing peacefully. On the horizon were more mountainous peaks. It felt like we were in an ancient village in the heavens as we watched the sun rise, covering our faces and bodies in light. I found a red flower growing out of one of the stones and knew that my experience in Cusco, though it was rough, had not been in vain. There were many redeeming moments, like flowers growing out of gray stones.

On my second-to-last day in Cusco, I walked through the front door of our volunteer home. *Grey's Anatomy* was on TV. It was always on. During my first week there, all ten of us had packed into two taxis and gone to El Molino, the indoor flea market, to buy black market copies of *Grey's*. Binge-watching it was our collective pastime. It was how we bonded and coped with the vicissitudes of volunteer life in Peru.

That evening, we sat huddled in the living room on chairs, the couch, and some on the floor. This particular episode, "Elevator Love Letter," was about a woman who kept almost dying. Each time, her family from across the country would show up to be with her and then she would not die. They were frustrated. After she had survived another near-death situation, the sick woman said to Alex Karev, one of the doctors, "It's been a long time, but they always come. They're my people. People keep you going. People are better than no people."

It was like something hit me over the head. I had missed that memo. I remembered having a conversation with a few friends in Charlottesville. We had started as a Bible study group but became something in between group therapy and a wine club. I remember saying, "I don't need people. You ladies are good to have around, but I don't *need* you. I don't feel like I *need* anyone." At the time, I believed it.

But in Cusco, I needed almost everyone in my life. My fellow volunteers kept me company. They were comic relief, companions, and reminders of home. Ivy, Tasha, and Tiffany were Black women, which so far had been an anomaly while traveling and volunteering. I was comforted by their nourishing presence. I needed host parents to cook for me and provide a home during my stay. The volunteer office helped us get around—troubleshooting, booking tours, and learning Spanish. Nicolás helped me improve my Spanish and decode and navigate Cusco's life and culture.

I looked around the room at Luis and Rosa's house, at the other volunteers in my presence. Community sustained me, and there was no way I could forget it. I had made it through being a spectacle—two overwhelming volunteering placements, sickness, mishaps, and navigating life in yet another country—and I had not done it alone. People *are* better than no people!

During my last day in Cusco, I sent my monthly e-newsletter to my supporters, always keeping them abreast of my travel adventures. I mailed my mother a box of the refrigerator magnets I had bought for her so far (I'd done that for every new country or city I'd gone to in the three years before my around-the-world trip began). I also mailed postcards. I sent my mother a postcard from every country I visited, and one postcard to each of my trip supporters throughout my travels, so they could experience a little memento for their investment. I was happy to send them off and happy to be leaving.

After five weeks in Peru, I was excited about my upcoming six-week backpacking adventure through Europe. I was looking forward to a bit of luxury, like hot showers. Armed with a guidebook to Western Europe; a two-month Eurail pass that allowed me to choose fifteen days of train travel across up to twenty-eight countries; and a plane ticket into Madrid, Spain, and out of London, England, to Kenya six weeks later. I generally knew the places I wanted to go—Spain, France, Italy, and England—but was also open to seeing more if I felt like it. The only thing I had scheduled was six days at a retreat center outside of London and a visit to some friends of friends outside of Paris.

EUROPE

5

SPAIN: HIGH ON LIFE

RAPHAEL IN BARCELONA

Raphael was thin, toned, and shirtless, with a tan derby hat atop brown hair and a ponytail that hung down his bare chest. A piece of blue cloth was wrapped around his waist, defined by a perfect six-pack. A fanny pack hugged his lower back, although it was way more fashionable than the ones I remembered from the eighties.

"Hello, welcome to Barcelona Backpackers," he said as I walked into the hostel. He spoke with an accent I couldn't place and moved his hands with an effeminate flair. I felt comforted by him from the moment we met.

I sat my daypack and backpack on the floor near the front desk, introduced myself, and began unzipping my backpack to get out my passport and credit card.

"Where are you from, Ms. Ebony?"

"Guess."

"You must be from a beautiful place. You are beautiful. I love your dark brown skin. It goes with the name," he said.

I blushed at the unexpected compliment. "I'm from the US, New York." I flashed my passport and handed him my credit card.

"Okay, Ebony from New York. I'll have you checked in soon." He gave me the rundown of the rules of the hostel and suggested I start my sightseeing with La Rambla, the port, or the beach.

I hopped on the subway to visit La Rambla, a tree-lined outdoor pedestrian mall full of cafés and boutiques that stretched from Barcelona's city center to the port. It's an attraction to Barcelona residents and tourists alike. I meandered all afternoon, entranced by the grandiose feel of the city's old buildings and stately boulevards.

Then I made my way to the beach, which was full of men in red Speedos, topless women, and vendors trying to sell things like massages, food, and drinks. One guy had a wooden board balanced on his head with stack of donuts on it, and he was running all around the beach selling donuts. I walked the boardwalk lined with palm trees, enjoying the near-perfect eighty-degree weather and marveling at the nearly royal blue ocean that ebbed in front of me. It all felt so luxurious. The W Hotel was big and blue at the end of the boardwalk, curved like the fin of a whale. I was pumped and eased at the same time.

When I returned to the hostel, Raphael invited me to join him for dinner. He held a plate of pasta and brownies in one hand and a glass of water in the other. "I also have some space cakes, if you want some dessert."

I shrugged. "Sure." I had eaten, but I had also spent the day alone, so I welcomed the company.

"Follow me," he said.

We climbed three flights of stairs and then went up a ladder to a trap door at the top. The trap door opened onto a small rooftop deck with a good view of the city. I had the feeling that few people had access to this area.

"After you." He pointed toward the picnic table and chairs.

We sat across from each other. "Raphael, I hear an accent that doesn't sound Spanish. Where are you from?" I asked.

"Brazil."

"I visited there last year and loved it. How did you get here from Brazil?"

"I took a plane. How else?" he said with sass and ate a mouthful of pasta.

I chuckled. "I gathered that. But what brought you here—why Spain?"

"I came here backpacking, loved it, and stayed. I grew up speaking Portuguese, so Spanish wasn't hard to learn." He took a sip of water. "And I *loved* this hostel, so I asked if they needed any help, and here we are. That was a year ago."

"I'm not staying, but I like what I've seen passing through. La Rambla was great, and you are not too bad on the eyes, so that is a start," I said.

Blushing, he said, "How can I get you to stay, beautiful Ebony from New York?"

I told him I'd stay if he turned into one of those beautiful deep brown Afro-Brazilian men I had seen when I went there. We laughed and joked like old friends. Soon we were talking about my trip and my poetry.

"Can you recite some poems for me?" he asked. "I need to be serenaded by a poet; it would be the perfect ending to a day."

"I usually do not recite on command, but I like you," I said, standing up.

I rarely mentioned poetry to people I met because invariably, they would want me to recite poems on command. I didn't like performing for sheer entertainment, but at that moment I wanted to share a piece of myself with Raphael. We felt like old friends, and Spain felt extravagant. I stood with one knee on the bench I had been sitting on, bowed my head, and put my hands in prayer to center myself. Since he did not know me well, I began with my "I Am" poem:

I am the liquid life coursing down the river Nile,
The rhythm of my waves will carry you miles.
I am the beat of the wind, blunt, cold, and agile,

I am the red apple from New York, giving you a taste of
bittersweet with a smile.
I am the sound of fury coming at you with determination,
I am Queen Sheba on white wings leading a Black nation . . .

I recited two more of my favorite poems, "Super Wonderful Woman" and "Speak," which made me feel strong and sound powerful.

When I finished, Raphael sat with eyes wide and mouth open. After a long silence, he began to clap with excitement. "Beautiful, beautiful!" He gave me a high five. "I have goose bumps, and it's not because it's getting chilly out here," he said.

I sat down and folded my arms.

"I am high off you. I do not even need these space cakes," he said.

"What exactly is in a space cake?"

"Marijuana in a brownie. You want one?"

"I'll pass." I waved my hand in affectionate dismissal, as I often did with friends. I didn't think getting high abroad was the best idea. "I haven't touched marijuana since college," I added. "And even then, it wasn't me. I smoked weed for a summer and then I stopped. I was about to be a senior and had to prepare for graduation. I didn't have time to become a weed head. Plus, I think it's a weak high. I prefer alcohol and being tipsy."

He took a bite of a brownie. "I wouldn't have taken you for such a straightedge. You are missing out, Ebony from New York."

I wasn't into drugs. I'd seen too many people in my community use them, and it never did them any good. Growing up in the midst of the drug crisis in the eighties and nineties, I wasn't a stranger to their reality. Walking to school, I often saw empty crack vials. Little plastic capsules with red or blue caps riddled the sidewalks, streets, and parks. Many people I knew had folks struggling with addiction, or what we in our youthful ignorance casually called "crackheads," in their family—strung out, gone for days or weeks, stealing from the family members they'd left in the wake of their destruction. I wasn't interested in getting high—or, more importantly, getting addicted. It felt like a ticket to nowhere.

I am not sure how I came to know about my father's drug business. Perhaps, it was the listening in on adult conversations, but it was something I always knew but can't pinpoint the exact moment of knowing. At some point, that drug business became a drug habit. Later, when prison prevailed and the business failed, he was back at my grandmother's house. I figured drugs were the reason behind what seemed like erratic behavior. I accepted it as a fact and tried to interact with him as least as I possibly could.

My grandmother, gruff and truthful, when she got mad at my Aunt Eunice would refer to Eunice "putting that white lady up her nose." I figured out that it was cocaine, but it didn't matter to me; I loved Eunice. She was always kind and caring to me.

I do remember being crushed when my sister told me of my mother's drug use. It was the summer before I started high school. I was walking to Hempstead High School to take the "talented and gifted" exam. Danielle, then sixteen—with fluffy bangs, a mushroom haircut, wearing baggy jean shorts and a T-shirt—was walking with me. She was going to her boyfriend's house. We were walking past a neighborhood park when she told me my mother was back doing drugs. This wasn't a new thing, she explained.

"Really?" I said with furrowed brows, trying to make connections that were sparse. My memory was foggy, and my head was beginning to hurt. I stopped and looked at Danielle. Stupefied. Heartbroken. Confused. I opened my mouth to say something, but nothing came out. Then I resumed walking, but more slowly. The questions swirled in my head. Was that why things had fallen apart in Queens? I struggled to put together the puzzle pieces that painted my mother as someone who used drugs.

"Maybe that is how she lost her job at the health department? A failed drug test?" I said.

"Maybe?" Danielle shrugged.

"Remember Mommy used to work for the health department when we lived in Queens?" I didn't want to talk about this anymore, so I tried to go back to good times. I remembered going to McDonald's every other Friday when Mom got paid, as a treat. I remembered taking a bite of my first Big Mac and most of the lettuce, sauce, and burger coming out on the other side.

We stopped at the corner of Franklin Street, cars buzzing past. I stared across at the corner store where I usually got chips and a brownie. My appetite was gone.

Danielle's voice got louder, more frustrated. "She's back at it."

I was standing still, but my head was spinning. I looked down at our matching white Reebok sneakers. Only two years apart, we had grown up like twins, but she had seen and carried far more than I knew, more than I cared to know.

"How do you know all of this?" I lifted my head and put my hands on my hips.

She went on to give me details I could not hear, though I saw her mouth moving. I shook my head. My heart was in my throat, and I could not say anything.

Once the light changed and the coast was clear, we ran across the street. When we reached the other side, I finally found my voice. "I don't want to hear anymore. I need a clear head to pass this test."

We walked for a while in silence until Danielle turned off toward her boyfriend's house and I kept straight ahead. I put it all out of my mind. Knowing of my mother's drug use was of no value to me; it was yet another disappointment. Getting a good education was my destination.

Now I know drug use is more complicated than I saw it then. Back then, there were people who seemed to function well, like Eunice, and others who were clearly strung out. I wasn't sure where my mother fell on that spectrum between recreation and addiction or if knowing would have helped me at all. What I did know was that the only thing I could control was my own path, and that's where I chose to focus my energy.

I locked that conversation away, too heavy to share and too painful to remember. Years later, Danielle told me she confronted our mother not long after our conversation—and, she soon stopped. I never wanted the details of how and why. Still, the weight of that knowledge, carried in silence, shaped how I understood my mother and myself for years to come. My trust in her cracked, but my determination to shape my own life solidified.

I didn't explain all of this to my new friend, Raphael. Instead, I sat watching him chew his space cake and said, "I'd rather get high on life." We laughed, but my mind was still walking through Hempstead, holding the weight of my sister's revelation.

The next day, I stood before the Sagrada Família, awestruck by its grandeur. Designed by Antoni Gaudí over a century ago, this Catholic church was a marvel of stone-colored Gothic architecture, its five massive pillars soaring behind me. I tried snapping a selfie, angling my camera to capture both the intricate details of the building and a glimpse of myself. The church was monumental—unfinished even after a hundred years, surrounded by cranes and scaffolding. The sheer scope of the project made me think about legacy. What work of mine could endure beyond my lifetime? *Or perhaps*, I mused, *the lesson is to be at peace with leaving things unfinished, trusting others to carry them forward.*

Gaudí's designs were like nothing I'd ever seen—old but elaborate, whimsical, almost futuristic, with curves and bright mosaics replacing traditional straight lines and gray stone. Very *Cat in the Hat*-ish. On a Gaudí walking tour, our guide, a young man with dark hair, shared snippets of the architect's quirks. "He was always over budget," he said with a grin.

Casa Batlló, another Gaudí building, looked like it was made of skulls and bones, but they were balconies and pillars eerily shaped from stone. The roof, shimmering cobalt blue, resembled bathroom tiles. Gaudí may have been extravagant, but he had transformed Barcelona, coloring and reshaping the urban landscape. *That's what an artist does*, I thought, *changes their piece of the world.*

Later, at Park Güell, once Gaudí's residence and now a public space, I admired the vibrant tile mosaics and petted a turquoise lizard sculpture at the entrance. Gaudí's work was everywhere, a lasting testament to his vision. I reflected on my own journey—spreading poetry, gathering stories, seeking meaning. Over ten days in Spain, I had explored Madrid's grand plazas, savored tapas in Seville, watched flamenco in Granada, and sunbathed in Barcelona. It was fleeting, but standing beside the lizard, I wondered, *What from this journey will last?*

6

FRANCE: THE COMPANY OF COMPIÈGNE

MEDITERRANEAN BLUE

Equipped with my Eurail pass, I made my way to Nice along the French Riviera. The streets were packed with summer crowds, and navigating with my backpack and daypack was a challenge. I walked along the palm-lined Avenue Thiers, its pale yellow-and-white buildings boasting balconies above bustling cafés. The smell of pastries pulled me along.

At Hostel Villa Saint Exupery Beach, I'd hoped for luxury but found a lobby smelling of sea salt and cluttered with beach mats. The rooms were modest—gray metal bunks with lockers big enough for my backpack. After dropping my things, I got directions from the front desk and headed to the beach.

The rocky shore was unfamiliar, the smooth gray stones awkward underfoot. I settled on my pink beach towel; pulled out my book, *The Girl with the Dragon Tattoo*, and my water bottle; and let the waves lull me into calm. Amidst the topless moms and kids with wave boards, I tuned out the noise and soaked in the Mediterranean blue—a rich mix of navy and royal hues. For the first time in weeks, I felt like I was on vacation. At the hostel, I was a penny-pinching backpacker; at the beach, I felt like royalty.

Later, I climbed Castle Hill's two hundred steps to a waterfall. Standing close, I let the cool spray refresh me. The terrace offered sweeping views of terracotta rooftops, the curving beach, and the deep blue sea. The crowded beach below looked like ants swarming.

The next day, I continued my odyssey and boarded a speedboat to Monaco. The wind blew my hair back as water sprayed my skin, and I was lulled by the sound of the engine. In my dark sunglasses, I felt like a character chasing adventure. For a few moments, I was carried away by the breeze.

THE COMPANY OF COMPIÈGNE

I had already been to Paris with friends during my senior year of college, so on this trip I was more interested in staying with a friend of a friend outside of Paris in Compiègne. I made it my business to connect with local residents and expats when possible. A friendly face and a home-cooked meal was priceless. I was to meet Nathan at Paris's central station, Gare du Nord, at 4:15 p.m. We had confirmed my stay months ago, but I'd emailed him a reminder while I was in Spain. I'd be the Black woman with short dreadlocks, a blue-and-gray backpack, and a purple sweatsuit. He'd be a white male with cropped black hair, a full beard, and black-rimmed glasses.

Gare du Nord was huge and not particularly English-friendly, but I easily found the train to Compiègne. I waited on a bench, looking at the faces of almost every white male that came my way. One face wore round, black-rimmed glasses and looked as searching as I did.

"Ebony?" he said.

I stood up. "Nathan?" I said as he came closer. With big smiles, we shook hands.

"The Black girl with a backpack was an easy way to spot you. Good description."

"It usually works."

Our train was to leave in a few minutes. He gestured for me to follow him.

When we found our seats, we settled in across from one another and chatted the entire time. This train reminded me of the Long Island Rail Road, the commuter train that went from New York City to Long Island. As we talked, the landscape went from tall gray buildings bundled together to greener scenery, with lawns and two-story homes. A pastor friend of mine in Charlottesville had referred me to Nathan, who was an American finishing up his PhD in theology and who did work for a Christian arts organization. Nathan was supposed to set up a performance for me in Paris, but it didn't work out, he informed me on the train. He was going to gather some friends in their home instead. That was fine with me: less pressure and more relaxation.

We arrived at a brown, two-story home, and a rush of three children came toward us as we walked into the door. "Daddy!" we heard along with the racing of little feet. His kids were five, four, and two. The two eldest were brown-haired boys with a striking resemblance to Nathan, while the youngest was a blonde, round-faced little girl with a pink shirt. Nathan grabbed her up into his arms.

"Say hi to Ms. Ebony. She is our guest. She will be visiting us for a few days."

"Hi," they said in unison, staring at me for a second. Then the entire entourage seemed to just float into the kitchen. I followed.

Nathan's wife, Amanda, wiped her hands on a towel and walked toward me with her hand extended. She greeted me with a warm welcome.

"I'm so excited to be here," I said. "I've been backpacking for three weeks, so it's wonderful to stay at a home." The place felt so cozy.

"The kids will probably make it eventful." Amanda showed me to my room so I could put my bags down.

For the rest of the weekend, I was a guest, but I felt like a member of their family. That first afternoon, we sat at their dining room table and cracked nuts from the hazelnut tree that grew in the middle of the small backyard.

"Ms. Ebony is traveling around the whole world," Amanda said to the kids as they watched me crack nuts at the kitchen table. They were all either sitting or kneeling in their chairs, looking at me as if I was about to do a magic trick.

"Don't you guys want to ask her where she has been so far?" she said, touching the oldest son on the head.

I put the nutcracker down and rubbed my hands together. "Wait a minute, I will show you. Let me go and get my globe."

I ran to my room and went straight for the top compartment of my backpack, where I had put the inflatable globe. I grabbed it and began to blow hard on my way back down the hallway. I sat down in my seat and blew until it was nice and full.

"Okay! We are here." I pointed to where France was on the map. They nodded and the youngest touched the place my finger had been.

"I am from here." I pointed to the US, where Virginia is. "It's a place called Virginia, in the United States." Their eyes followed my fingers.

"I've been here, here, here, here, and here." I pointed to all of the countries first and then went back and said their names.

"Wow," their eldest son replied. "Did you fly?"

"Yes, on some very big airplanes," I said.

"What has been your favorite so far?" Amanda asked.

"Guatemala. I loved Antigua. It's a small Spanish colonial city, very colorful, with lots of old cathedrals but surrounded by volcanoes."

"Volcanoes?" said the middle son, astonished.

"Yes, I've been up close to a few, even been inside one."

"Ms. Ebony does poetry too. She is going to do some poems for some of our friends tomorrow," said Nathan, walking over to the table from the sink and standing behind his wife.

"Oh, I have a fun one. The kids will love it. Do you guys want to hear it?"

"Yeah," they said in unison, clapping before I'd even started.

I stood up in the middle of the kitchen, was still and quiet for a second with my hands in prayer position, and then started:

Sometimes I feel like Superwoman
Even Wonder Woman.
You may ask,
What makes me super?
What makes me so wonderful?
Are you fast, powerful, or bulletproof?
And most importantly, can you fly?

Well, all of the above,
But not in the ways that you are thinking of.
See, I'm supernatural in a spiritual sense,
Meaning something inside tells me that I am supposed
to be great.
I'm just living in agreement with the truth.
Each time I am me, there is a gathering of power that
gives me strength.

And of course, everyone wants to know where on earth
did I get my might?
I am telling you the truth when I say I prayed one night,
"I want to be wonderful. Oh, Jesus, make me wonderful."
His response, not a moment delayed,
With words cutting my need like a blade,

He said, "Ebony, don't be silly or dismayed,
I crafted you with my own hands.
You're already fearfully and wonderfully made."
And since that day I have been a Super Wonderful
Woman . . .

When I finished the rest of the poem, clapping erupted in the kitchen. I bowed and said, "I will do some more tomorrow. I don't want to give away my whole show."

I went back to cracking hazelnuts with the kids, even going outside to watch them play while Nathan and Amanda made a simple but delicious dinner of chicken, potatoes, and green beans. That night I slept in a full-sized bed. I was happy to have an empty room by myself and to be in someone's home. I was a guest, but the Carvers made me feel like family.

The following evening, I stood in the middle of the living room reciting poetry in front of five of Nathan and Amanda's friends over red wine and chocolate cake. I felt like a griot, telling my story through poetry for thirty minutes. I was glad for a bit of depth, even if it was quick and fleeting—anything to get past chitchat, which I hated. Poems were probably as good of an introduction to me as I could give. I was glad they were interested and listened. Glad to hear their stories afterward.

The rest of the weekend was full of family fun. I played in the backyard with the kids, watched one of them ride a skateboard, and cracked more nuts. While the kids napped, Nathan took me to visit the campus of a famous old castle, complete with round stone towers on the corners.

"I'm sorry this is not really entertaining for you," he said in the car on the way there. "There isn't much to do here like in Paris."

"Oh no, I love being with your family in this small town away from all the people and attractions. It's simple, ordinary, and lovely. Thank you for having me."

The Château de Compiègne was a gray stone presence looming on a hill surrounded by green countryside. I was beginning to like small-town settings better than sightseeing in cities.

On Sunday, we went to their small gray chapel with stained glass windows and hard wooden pews to attend church. Nathan tried to translate, but I told him to stop, happy to just take it in as is. After church, we strolled through the cobblestoned streets of the town, sharing ice cream and laughter, savoring the kind of simple, sacred moments that make goodbyes hard.

After we finished our ice cream, I stood up so I could take in all five of them.

"I have loved our time together. I am sad to leave, but I have to keep traveling. I have ten more countries to go to."

They all looked a bit sad. I was too.

I said goodbye to them Monday morning. After breakfast, I rode the train into Paris with Nathan in silence. I'd miss the ordinariness of their lives. The warmth I found with the Carvers taught me that hospitality, when it was offered freely and generously, was the gateway to belonging. I'd never been a part of a nuclear family, so even their ordinary days were a novelty to me. Though it was an unfamiliar experience, they made me feel at home.

My family was anything but nuclear. It was always woman-led and extended. I lived with women: first my mother, aunt, and cousins in Queens, and then my grandmother, aunt, and cousins in Long Island. When my mother found a place in Long Island in 1992, I lived with her and my two sisters.

I remember my father banning my mother from my grandmother's house so that she couldn't come and see Danielle and me there, which she'd done almost every weekend before. No one was sure why this was. I assumed, similarly to the spaghetti situation, that he was being an ass for no particular reason. We seemed to have to beg him every week for ten dollars for lunch money—two dollars a day. Danielle spent her ten dollars quickly. I rationed mine out to last the week, but every week it was an ordeal to get that ten dollars. So much so that we didn't like asking him for anything.

One winter, about three years after we moved out of my grandmother's house, we needed new sneakers. We asked Ricky. It was February, and my sister and I got matching purple-and-white Nike Huarache shoes. We were sneaker- and urban-fashion-crazed New Yorkers. We liked Levi's jean suits, baggy jeans, Tommy Hilfiger shirts, and Nike sneakers. Our Aunt Suzette took us to buy the sneakers that day, as she was often the one who would take us shopping. We were giddy with our new purchases when she dropped us off. Later, a knock came at our back door.

Danielle opened the door, puzzled to see our father in the doorway. I stood behind her.

"Give me the sneakers," Ricky said.

"Huh?" We spoke in unison. He was still in the doorway, the door partway open.

"Give me the sneakers. It's February. You will get them back in the spring when the weather breaks. Otherwise, you will want a new pair of sneakers in the spring too."

Almost with tears in her eyes, Danielle left him in the doorway, went and got the two boxes, and handed them to him.

When the door shut, we looked at each other and said the same thing: "Asshole!"

Our grandmother made him give the sneakers back a few weeks later, but the damage was done.

My relationship with him was a blur after that. When I was seventeen, I remember him coming to my high school awards ceremony, at which I got a bunch of awards. I was fourth in my class. Everyone in my family was proud. I remember him there with my stepmother, whom he had been with for years. I remember taking a picture with both of them smiling proudly. One of my father's arms was around me, the other around his wife. That may have been one of my few memories of affection. Maybe he was getting older, or maybe it was because he was sober.

It was my mother's boyfriend at the time, Sal, who helped with all of the logistics for the huge graduation party my mother threw in our backyard. It was Sal who packed up all of my college stuff to ship to Georgetown. I didn't know where Ricky was. I was used to his absence in the details of my life, so I expected nothing more.

After I graduated from Georgetown, Ricky paid for my first car—a plum 1992 Saturn coupe. My mom's boyfriend Sal found it (he was a mechanic). Ricky paid $900 for it. I was happy and grateful. That had been much of the extent of our relationship: He would provide clothes, shoes, and some necessities; I saw him on holidays and at family functions. But he felt more like an emotionally distant uncle who was always around than a father. That is why I'd always called him Ricky. Dad or Daddy just didn't feel right. I avoided saying anything real or major to him, because what was there to say?

7

ITALY: THE PEARLS IN THE PASTURES

After staying with the Carvers in Compiègne, my return to a hostel in Rome felt jarring. Sharing a room with strangers and sleeping on bunk beds was getting old. Even the best-rated hostels were a gamble—sometimes funky, sometimes rowdy, usually full of young white travelers. Yet, standing under the magnificent ceiling of the Sistine Chapel in Rome, with its vibrant biblical scenes and intricate details, I reminded myself how fortunate I was to be in Italy, savoring its wonders. My days were peppered with pizza, pasta, gelato, and wine. I allowed myself small treats daily to accommodate my strict backpacker budget. I recorded every cost in my notebook and spreadsheet.

In Venice, the canals and gondoliers felt almost surreal, like stepping into a storybook. Saint Mark's Basilica—with its domes, mosaics, and bronze-fashioned doors—stood at the center of the busy piazza like a monument to another era. Pigeons descended on the square, disrupting the grandeur—a reminder that even the most beautiful places have their intrusions.

Tuscany, however, left the deepest impression. In Florence and Tuscany, I learned that the pearls are in the pastures. I had always been a city person, but sipping wine at a Tuscan vineyard overlooking rolling green hills bordered by a distant mountain range was better than any museum or monument. What man built in cities was remarkable, but what God created in the countryside was unmatched. To complement the scenery, I dressed up for a winery tour, wearing a red bohemian shirt that flared at the bottom. I swished and sipped red wine from a glass so large it touched my eyebrows. I felt fancy. I liked feeling fancy.

The next day, I planned a day trip to Siena—a small town outside Florence, just an hour's train ride away. I stuffed €20 in my pocket, put my sunglasses on my head, and packed my Eurail pass in the most accessible part of my daypack. I had paid $1,000 for that pass, which allowed me to travel through twenty-eight European countries over two months—but only for fifteen travel days. Each train ride was a day of travel, so all I needed to do was record the date. On my way to Siena, I didn't really want to waste a travel day on such a short trip, so I decided to gamble. If the conductor came through, I'd quickly write the date on the ticket and act innocent. If not, I'd save a travel day. Backpacking was a constant hustle—trying to make a euro stretch as far as possible.

I sat by the window, watching the bucolic landscape blur past—red-brick buildings and green hills smudged together by speed. My days in Italy were running together too: pizza, pasta, gelato, the Colosseum, the Sistine Chapel, gondolas in Venice, wine tasting in Tuscany. I had packed so much into a single week.

Suddenly, a stone-faced white man in a blue uniform hovered over me, his hand extended. "*Biglietto*," he barked.

Startled, I flinched and began fumbling through my bag.

"Biglietto!" he repeated, his tone sharper this time.

I handed him the ticket and realized too late that I hadn't written the date.

"Sorry," I said. "I forgot to write the date. I can do it now."

He stared down at the ticket, then back at me. "You were trying to ride for free," he said, his heavily accented English cutting through the air. "This is not legal. I will call the police."

My stomach dropped. I held up my hands in a gesture of surrender. “That's not necessary,” I said. “You can just write the date now.”

Images of me in an Italian jail flashed through my mind. How would I explain this to my mother?

“Fifty euros or I'll call the police,” he said, planting his fists on his hips.

“Fifty?” I repeated, stunned. “I only have twenty. I need to eat lunch when I get to Siena and get back to Florence. My money is in the hostel.”

“Where is your passport?”

“At the hostel too,” I said quickly. “But I have a copy.”

I pulled the copy from my bag and handed it to him. He rolled his eyes and stomped his foot in frustration. “You will be arrested,” he said, taking out his phone.

I jumped to my feet, my hands raised, trying to calm him down. “Please, just write the date now,” I said one last time.

He sighed, pulled out a pen, and wrote the date before stamping the ticket.

“Don't do this again,” he said, dropping it into my hand.

“Thank you, sir. I won't.”

I collapsed back into the seat, my heart racing, as the train pulled into Siena. I stepped off with shaky relief. Being cheap was not worth my freedom.

After that, I decided I needed to release the reins of my budgeting a little. Being cheap and the constant tracking of expenses was a response to the scarcity of my youth. I remembered the food stamps running low at the end of the month and having to buy the cheapest things. The cheapest laundry detergent, Trend, with its blue-and-red box, flashed across my mind. I remembered rationing my lunch money to make it through the week. Always on a budget. Even in adulthood, I never wanted to have to go without because I wasn't a good steward of my finances. I wanted to keep what I had and make it go as long and as far as it could, just in case. So, I pinched pennies and, in this case, stretched euros.

As I walked off the train, still shaken, I realized that this way of being was detracting from my experience. It had caused me to skimp on my backpack and get a wheeled suitcase—which is why it broke in Costa Rica. Now it had caused me to try to cheat the system and could have cost me a fine or a night in jail. Was it worth it?

As I walked onto the wide expanse of the Piazza del Campo in Siena and saw the red bricks and the medieval bell tower, I resolved that it was time to let go, if only a little, of the death grip on my budget. I didn't just want to visit beautiful and expansive spaces; I wanted to be more expansive with myself, my time, and my money. Scarcity had shaped me. I knew how to survive, but I was learning that survival isn't the same as freedom. Yes, I'd splurge a bit more and trust that there would be enough—maybe even more than enough.

8

SWITZERLAND: TRUST IS FREEDOM

TRUST IS FREEDOM

I decided to add Switzerland, Belgium, and Holland to my trip before heading to London. I started with five days in Zürich. A boat ride on Lake Zürich revealed the city's clean, crisp beauty. From the back of the boat, I watched white swans glide across the deep blue water, framed by clock towers on the city's adjacent hills. The scene was refreshing and I felt secure, although it was the most expensive view I'd enjoyed so far in my trip. Even McDonald's value meals were fifteen dollars. Still, I made it a point to try an ice cream cone, my go-to one-dollar treat worldwide. I was already over budget because of all the European tours I'd taken, but I wasn't too worried. I'd shaved a week off Peru and could shave a few days and weeks off here and there to stay on budget.

I am not sure what made me stop in Interlaken on my way to Bern, Switzerland—maybe the desire for a little adventure amidst the order. Interlaken is a small town tucked in the mountains, with stunning views of the snow-capped Swiss Alps. Nestled in a green valley between two lakes, a turquoise river runs through its center. It was a getaway. I felt underdressed for the beauty that surrounded me, but my hiking shoes were welcome.

On my first day, I took a lone half-day bike ride around the city. Deep into my ride, I stopped and thought, *Why am I out here alone again?* In front of me was what seemed like more trail, with very few people passing by. *What if I get hurt or kidnapped? No one will find me.*

Eventually, I hit a clearing that butted up against a lake. I breathed deep and biked over to a picnic table, where I leaned my bike against the table, sat on the top, and pulled out a banana. It was around 4:00 p.m. and the air was foggy. *A ripe place to get whacked*, I thought, then I laughed out loud. Safety was always on my mind.

The next day, I walked straight out of the hostel doors across a large, open, grassy area with picturesque green mountains in the background. This was where I was to meet my guide, Peach. Butterflies floated around in my stomach with each step. In less than an hour I would be floating through the air, paragliding with Peach directly above this exact field. I caught sight of him: tall and muscular, with brown hair that curled around his ears. He was sporting a five-o'clock shadow and what my friend would call a "flavor saver," a small square patch of hair below his lower lip. He was standing with a bunch of equipment next to a truck and a motorcycle, untangling things. He looked up with a smile when I was a few feet away.

"Ebony?"

"Peach?"

We shook hands.

"Are you ready?" he asked.

"Ahh, yeah, as ready as I am going to get. I'm a little scared, to be honest."

"No need to be! You will love it, I assure you, I've done this hundreds of times, so you are in good hands. It's a beautiful day for it too." He looked up at the sky and said, "We will have fun. Trust me."

"I'm in your hands," I replied.

Then he looked me up and down, and his eyes landed on my shoes. I was wearing my blue-and-gray Merrell sandals.

"I am going to have to let you borrow my boots. They will work better than those." His dusty brown boots were a few sizes too big, but he laced them up tightly for me.

He packed up and we got on a motorcycle. I grabbed hold of his waist, and we were off. I had never been on a motorcycle—two firsts in one day. I was getting more and more excited.

We wound up and around the mountain. It was chilly, and the wind was whipping against my face, so I tried to look to the side, with my cheek on the back of Peach's shoulder blade. I settled in and trusted in the ride itself. I trusted that the driver knew where he was going, and I felt safe. My life was in someone else's hands for a change, and it felt good. I held on tightly—less from fear and more from savoring the moment. Ahead was a winding road, the mountains loomed on all sides, the wind blew in my face, and the motorbike pulsed against my legs.

"Are you okay back there?" said Peach, glancing back.

"Just fine." I held on more tightly as he sped up.

When we got to our destination, a grassy knoll on the side of this mountain, a red-and-white paraglider was waiting for us in the center, like a large bird with its wings spread for takeoff. We walked over to the apparatus, which looked like a parachute with a bunch of attachments. Peach was in front, with me trailing a few steps behind. He turned toward me and said, "Stand in an *X* so we can get you all set up."

I stretched my arms out toward the sky and widened my legs. He clicked this and strapped that and double-checked to make sure things were secure. Once I was all strapped up, he strapped himself up and then strapped us both to the paraglider. I stood in front, with him behind me. I could feel his breath on my neck.

"Okay, so you are going to have to leap off. Just do what I tell you. You will need to run to the end there, right before the cliff, at a nice, fast pace, and I will take care of the rest."

I turned my head toward him. "So, you just want me to run and jump off the cliff?"

"Exactly! Only the wind will pick us up before you get to the end. Trust me."

I was a little skeptical, but I did as I was told. I ran toward the edge of the cliff and before I could jump off, the paraglider just rose up into the air and we were off, floating from left to right. Peach steered from the back with two handles.

Unlike skydiving, we went up instead of down. I could see the teal waterway below and the ridges of the Alps ahead, a few clouds in the distance. It was a weightless feeling of flying and gliding that felt simply divine. I begin giggling, oohing, and ahhing.

"How do you like it? It's awesome, right?" Peach yelled in my ear.

"Yes, you were right, this *is* awesome"

"Watch this!" He did something, and we began to twist and turn and dip and dive through the air. I yelled, "Aaaaaaaahhhhh," in surprise and delight.

He took us back up to a nice steady glide and pulled out a camera fastened to a stick. We took snapshots from all angles, including selfies of us laughing and making silly and serious faces.

"You are so fun, Peach. This is so fun." I was surprised at how much I was enjoying it, how unafraid I felt.

"I love paragliding and just want to make sure other people love it too."

The weight of my backpack was forgotten. The weight of my life was in Peach's hands, and that sense of trust felt like freedom.

I am not sure when I came to trust in myself, in my ability. As a child, I started to focus on controlling whatever I could, given my instability growing up. My mother was festive and decorated our Section 8 apartment (paid for by a government voucher), trying to make things nice, but nothing was ever good enough for me. I knew that my life would be different only if I made it different, if I did things differently from those around me. I would not struggle, would not put myself at the mercy of others and have to wait or not have enough. That was the goal. No one but me could achieve this for me. So I learned to ultimately trust in myself, in my smarts, and in my ability to make things happen.

Trusting friends came slowly. In high school, I was not happy with our living situation, so I never invited friends over. I probably could have—no one I knew was rich; some were middle class, but many were working class or came from families with limited means. I had friends, but I mostly engaged with them at school, their houses, or during extracurricular activities.

College was different because friendships were twenty-four seven. The summer before I started Georgetown, I went to a three-week program for incoming first-generation college students, especially students of color. The writing class we took—expository writing—along with being on the campus early with twenty-plus incoming freshmen was supposed to make our transition easier.

It did. I made a primary friend group that carried me through college. There was a New Yorker from the Bronx with sharp style and a sharper attitude—always in name brands. A Southern belle from Washington, DC, was deeply religious and Afrocentric, with a grown-woman style that could swing from leather to business suits. And a mixed-race Latino from Washington State, was always on the move. During our three-week summer stay at Georgetown, he managed to land a restaurant job, showing up at night with wraps, brownies, and stories of the day's adventures. Around them was a crew of smart, dynamic, and hilarious classmates from places like Brooklyn, Connecticut, and Maryland—each with their own unique personality.

These are the people I practiced trust and closeness with. I was rather stoic at the time, as Angie told me. I didn't even know what that meant. I had to look it up.

They were there, day in and day out; we became intricate parts of each other's lives. For notes, for laughter and trips to the dining hall or to Domino's to get wings, or to go shopping on M Street, the Georgetown thoroughfare full of restaurants and upscale shops like BCBG. A few of my friends sang in the gospel choir, and that is how I began going to church. In our second semester most of us went to church together, did Bible studies together, and did all of the other fun college stuff in between.

Alicia and I became inseparable. When people saw me, they would ask where Alicia was, and vice versa. She was also popular, beautiful, and had a great personality—so on occasion, I'd get calls from people looking for her. Her dating life was also far more eventful than mine, so I loved living vicariously through her.

I've always had this proclivity for questions, and while we were in Alicia's room at night "fake studying," I'd pull out this red book of questions she had. It was a bathroom book you get from Urban Outfitters or somewhere. The book was called *If*, and each time we got too tired of not studying and were falling asleep, I'd get out the book and nudge Alicia with my elbow.

"Get up, it's time for *If* questions."

"Oh God, here you go again—not tonight! You and these questions. You are killing me." She'd grin and turn over as if to go to sleep, but be totally in.

I'd flip through the book, looking for the right place to start. "Okay, I found one. Here we go. If you could go anywhere in the world, where would you go and who would you take with you?"

"We could go to Jamaica," she would say with her Jamaican accent. Alicia is Jamaican.

"No fair, you have been there a bunch of times," I said.

"But you haven't. I could show you around," she said, turning over to look at me. "You like curry chicken, right?" she asked.

"Yeah man," I said, in a bad Jamaican accent.

We laughed.

"Okay, next question," I said.

"Last question, Eb. It's two in the morning. You and your questions." She shook her head. "Always asking, but you never want to answer."

On and on it would go: my questions, our laughing, her dragging me around to go shopping, or to a friend's house in Maryland, or to Houston's to get her favorite spinach dip every other day, or to help her wax her underarms. At Georgetown, I learned to let people in.

Alicia and Nadine came home with me and met my family. My mom and sisters got a kick out of them both, together and separately. My mom had gotten a steady job by then at Dime Community Bank, her first consistent and well-paying job that I could remember. We had moved maybe half a mile from where we lived before to a nice brick cape-style house that was all ours, with four bedrooms and a nice lawn. My home life was finally stable. While I was away at school, my mom was moving up to the middle class and would soon become a first-time home buyer. I was happy to bring them home. I was slightly more at home with myself, this person I was becoming and creating at the same time.

9

ENGLAND: LOVE, LAMENT, AND A SOFT PLACE TO LAND

LOVING LONDON

London was great—a city of neighborhoods like New York. I saw many of the sights the first day I arrived: London Bridge, the Tower of London, Big Ben, red phone booths, and red double-decker buses. I looked forward to performing at an open mic night and going to see the Alvin Ailey dancers later that week.

My first few days, I learned that:

- Trash was called rubbish.
- Restrooms were simply called toilets or the loo.
- The British pound was worth one-and-a-half times the dollar, which made life expensive for me.
- The subway was called the Underground, which I thought was a great name for a bar or club and probably the best-named metro system I have seen. It's also known as the tube, which sounded less sexy. In the stations, the exit signs said WAY OUT instead of EXIT. The transportation card was called the Oyster.
- Taxis were cars that resembled those made in the early to mid-1900s.
- An English breakfast included baked beans.

London was the one city where I really didn't feel like a tourist. The attractions did not necessarily overwhelm life there. It felt like more of a cultural center. I loved the free museums. I visited the Tate Modern, the British Museum, and the Victoria and Albert Museum. In every new city, I asked the hostel receptionists where I should go or picked up an alternative weekly newspaper to see what was going on. I also stayed aware of advertisements for things I might want to see.

I saw an advertisement for the *Skin* exhibit on a subway. It showed an image of a man with tattoos covering his face. *The* Skin *exhibition invites you to reevaluate the largest and probably most overlooked human organ. We consider the changing importance of skin, from anatomical thought in the sixteenth century through to contemporary artistic exploration.* I was intrigued and decided to go.

The exhibit began from the biological or medical perspective, but it wasn't until the images and relics began to discuss race that I got really interested.

Race was always at the forefront of my mind and experience. Since college, going back and forth between Black and white worlds always highlighted the differences between them. Going from studying at Georgetown to working with what was then called "at-risk" Black youth in southeast Washington, DC, gave me whiplash weekly—they were racially and economically worlds apart. After Georgetown, I landed in Charlottesville, Virginia, for graduate school. Charlottesville is a small, mostly white, upper-class college town in central Virginia. Though I had a solid group of Black friends when I first moved there in 2003, they slowly moved away. Thus, my relationship circle became mostly white. I was often the only Black person in many rooms, so I always took note and was happy to see other Black people.

At the *Skin* exhibit, a handsome, dark-skinned Black man came into my peripheral view. He was about five foot seven, with neatly cropped hair and smooth skin, nicely dressed in a shirt and pair of jeans. I was beginning to stare, so I turned back to the picture of enslaved Africans before me. But I felt his eyes on me. When I turned, our eyes met. Time stopped for a millisecond. Our eyes smiled, and then so did we. I blushed.

"Hello," we said at the same time.

"Are you enjoying the exhibit?" he said, taking a few steps closer to me.

"Yes." We began walking through the exhibit together, as if we were friends.

He said his name was TK, which I supposed was a pseudonym. I asked where he was from.

"I'm from Nigeria," he said with pride. "I am studying here. I actually need to register for graduate school later this afternoon."

I asked what he was studying as we walked slowly ahead, stopping to look at each other between photographs.

"Theology. I'm interested in the Black church in England, the role the church is to play in community life, in social justice."

I started to laugh. He looked at me, confused, his eyebrows raised.

"Sorry, sorry. I am laughing because that is such a coincidence. I've been interested in the same things for the past few years. You should read this guy named John Perkins." I started walking again, gesticulating in excitement. "He is from the South in the US and was active in the civil rights movement. He was nearly beaten to death but has this model for how the church can get involved in justice, in community development. I've been a follower of his for a while. It's called Christian Community Development."

"I wonder about the similarities and differences between the Black church in the US and the Black church in the UK, in Nigeria even," he said.

"I'm sure the racial dynamic would be slightly different in each place. Racial reconciliation is one of Perkins's three tenets," I said.

"That sounds like a longer conversation."

We had finished walking through the exhibit and were lingering in the foyer. I found him intriguing. We were interested in the same things; he was beautiful and a man of faith. I rarely came across the three combined.

I asked him if he wanted to talk more over lunch or a cup of coffee. A smile stretched across his face, showing bright white teeth in exquisite contrast to his smooth dark skin.

"Sure, that would be great." He shifted nervously from foot to foot.

We walked out of the lobby onto a bustling street. He pointed diagonally across the street toward a park, noting that there were a few restaurants nearby.

I nodded and followed him into a café. I ordered some coffee, he ordered black tea, and we sat outside at a small metal table.

He told me about his studies and experiences in London, and I revealed a little about my trip and poetry. We were suspended in a cloud of unexpected goodness and energy—smiling, laughing, and mostly connecting to one another's passions and story. It felt like only a few minutes passed, but it was actually close to an hour.

He looked at his watch, worried. "I have to go do some stuff for grad school. I have to register this afternoon. What are you up to this evening?"

"I am going to perform at the London Underground." I had looked up a poetry spot and was proud that I had plans. I invited him out.

"I will be there." There was a surety in his voice.

"It starts at seven." I fumbled in my bag for the address.

We both seemed unsure of what to do next. We extended our hands, going for a handshake, but then I opened my arms for a hug.

"See you tonight," he said with certainty.

I was skeptical as I watched him walk away. I hoped to see him again.

I arrived late at the poetry spot, about twenty minutes after seven, and the café was packed. Most of the faces were white people ranging in age from twenty to sixty. I spotted his face immediately. He sat next to one of the only empty chairs in the room. He waved with excitement and beckoned me to come and sit next to him. I put my name on the open mic sign-up sheet and edged past a few people to take the chair he'd saved for me. He had brought a male friend, white, with dark, wavy hair. TK introduced us.

"TK has told me a lot about you," his friend said with a sly smirk. "I hope we get to hear some of your poetry tonight. I am excited."

The evening was full of pretty good poetry, but it was long. I was at the end of the open mic list and his friend had to leave at 10:00 p.m. I was surprised when TK stayed. We just moved closer.

When I performed my "I Am" poem, I got blank stares for the most part. Most people had done straight poetry; most were about more interesting topics than themselves. I didn't really care; TK was smiling and so was I. After I finished, I sat down and leaned closer to him, whispering, "Are you ready to go?" He nodded and we left quietly.

Outside, a nice summer breeze and dark night sky made everything seem more romantic. We meandered through the streets with no stated destination in mind. I touch people when I talk. With TK, it was no different. I was just more aware of it, because I was more aware of him, his person, his presence, his body. We talked about life, growing up, the differences between the UK and the US, our spiritual background and passion for the Black church. It began drizzling as we walked, so we hopped on a bus headed toward my hostel.

Well after midnight, the bus dropped us off near my hostel, the Waterloo. We sat waiting for the next bus to get him home. We didn't want to end the night, but I was leaving the next day for another city in England, and he had to get up early to finish registering for school.

"Well, I guess this is it," I said as the red double-decker bus came noisily down the street.

"Yes. So nice to have met you, Ebony." He stood up, looked me in the eyes, and gently rubbed my arms.

"Me too." There was a long lingering hug and then the bus was immediately in front of us and he got on. I watched it drive away before I walked in the door of my hostel.

I slipped into bed that evening, grateful, smiling and tingling with excitement. I only wish we had kissed, but we'd had such a connection and that is what I valued most. We'd followed it until our lives led us different ways. I turned over and was soon fast asleep, though I felt like the entire night was a dream.

L'ABRI

I was at a red phone booth by the side of the main road, perpendicular to the train tracks. I rested my fifty-pound backpack on the side of the booth and let myself slide down. My strength sank with me. Once I hit the ground, my shoulders began shaking and tears flowed in parallel rivers down my face.

I looked down at the directions I'd printed from the website: two miles to walk. That was too far with my backpack. My feet hurt, and my shoulders were sore. The alternative, calling a cab, was unsuccessful. The number kept ringing and ringing. The number to the organization I was staying with, English L'Abri, did the same—ringing, ringing, and ringing. I had no more coins to call either back. So, there I was, crying. After five weeks of backpacking through seven countries, I just wanted to be stable. I wanted to rest, not to sightsee anymore, not to traipse around cities on my own, not to meet random people I wouldn't see again. The burden of carrying a bag and myself had become too heavy, and their weight came crashing down on me. I wanted more than ever to be in a warm, safe place, with a home-cooked meal and the smiles of people who might remember my name.

I sat there for ten minutes, my right hand covering my eyes, legs stretched out in front of me. No cars drove by; no people passed. Everything was closed. It was just me, a phone booth, a sleepy town closed on Sunday, and my tears.

That last time I'd cried so helplessly was a few years before. I had come home from Charlottesville for the Fourth of July celebration, and for some reason, I was not in a good mood. This usually meant that my mother and I would get into it. I was on the couch and said something snarky, probably after she asked me if I wanted something. She tends to push her love on me through food and gifts, and I just wanted to relax and be.

She said, "I am always trying to be nice to you, and all you do is act like you do not like me." Her voice echoed down the hallway as she went from the kitchen to her bedroom and closed the door with a bang.

As I lay on the beige sectional, her words hovered over me. *Was that true?* I thought, *Maybe I don't like her*. But I didn't *want* to not like my mother. What was this knot in my chest I always felt, this anger, this not wanting to receive her love? Maybe her love seemed too much, like trying to make up for something that wasn't necessary, and that annoyed me and pushed me away. My mother is extravagant, and I am a minimalist. This comes out in most things: I'd be home in New York for two days over Thanksgiving, and she would get me three different kinds of fruit, special milk, special vegetables, etc. I didn't need all of that and resented it.

It was playing out again. Arghhhh! I was mad at myself for being difficult to love at times and annoyed with my mom for trying too hard. Tears began to roll down my face. *Yes, there is something about my mother I don't like—deeper than her being too much. I don't know what it is or why.* I cried silently for a while, wetting the beige couch pillow. I was happy to be alone with my tears, even if half-exposed in the living room. Something was ready to be released, and her words had opened the latch on a door that had long been locked shut.

Unable to rest or get out of my head, I got up and put on my workout clothes, black from head to toe. I closed the back door gingerly on my way out. It was a hot summer day. As I ran down Hempstead Turnpike in Uniondale, NY, a main four-lane road past banks, Hofstra University, Nassau Coliseum, McDonald's, and Starbucks, tears streamed down my face, mixing with sweat so that I could hardly see. Running only seemed to make the crying worse. I pumped my arms harder and lifted my legs up higher and faster. A well deep within had risen up, maybe tears from years. I felt the need to talk and apologize. I had been trying to pay my mother back all of these years with a cold shoulder by rejecting her love—pay her back for leaving us at our grandmother's, for the lack that we had to endure at times, for not being what I wanted her to be—whatever or whoever that was. Someone I could look up to, maybe.

I was almost home, and the tears hadn't slowed. I ran up our long asphalt driveway, and when I got to the bottom of the stairs at the back door, I bent over and grabbed my knees to catch my breath. I ran into the house and went straight into my mother's room. I burst into the room and stood in the doorway, heaving and crying again.

"What happened?" my mother asked. "Danielle! Danielle!" She always called my older sister's name in times of crisis.

"Why did you leave me?" I said, wiping my tears. "You left me."

"What? I'm right here." She patted the spot next to her bed, motioning for me to come and sit.

My sister Danielle came to the door to see if everything was okay, looking between my mother and me.

"Everything is fine," my mother said. "Close that door."

I went to sit on the end of her bed, tears still streaming, shoulders and upper body heaving, sweat dripping. I felt like a wet blanket.

"Go ahead and get it out."

"Why did we have to live like that—no lights, heat, or water? I was embarrassed," I said as I wiped my nose and looked straight ahead at the flat-screen TV on my mother's dresser. A black-and-white movie was on the TCM channel. My mother loved old movies. It was our time to replay the past.

"And why did you have to leave us?" I went on. "I was a mess for months. And then our house on Baldwin Road was a mess too. I didn't want to live there either. Welfare, food stamps, and all. I just wanted parents to be proud of, a life I could be proud of."

"And you have done that for yourself," she said, looking me in the eye. "I'm sorry I couldn't be what you wanted me to be. I tried my best, but I was growing up as you guys were growing up. I had three kids and no high school diploma."

She rubbed my back as I looked down at the tears dropping into my lap.

"I made a lot of mistakes. I would have done a lot differently. I would have gone to school and tried to give us a better life. It took me a while, but I am finally okay with myself, with my mistakes. God has forgiven me. I have forgiven myself."

She was silent for a few moments and then wiped the tears from my cheeks. "Now it's time for you to forgive me. Not for me, but for yourself. It will weigh you down if you hold on to it, and I want you to be free."

I nodded. "Me too."

She took me in her arms, my head on her chest. I felt eight again.

"I'm sorry. I came in here to say I am sorry."

"For what, Ebony?"

"For holding all of that against you for so long. I haven't been very nice to you, and you try so hard. I'm sorry for being so hard for so long."

"Yeah, well, that mouth of yours has given me gray hairs." We both laughed. "But you have made me so proud too," she said.

"Our lives could have gone differently. But in the end, we have a nice home. You have a good job. It turned out well. We cleaned up real nice," I said, winking at her.

She grabbed my shoulder and held me at arm's length, looking me in the eye. I could see her love for me in her eyes. "Speaking of cleaning up, you smell terrible, and you're getting my bed wet with sweat and tears. I just changed my sheets," she said affectionately.

I stood up and then bent down to sneak another hug.

"You will be okay. Go clean yourself up."

"I love you, Mom," I said on my way to the door.

"I love you too, Eb."

I walked out her bedroom door and closed it gently behind me. As the knob clicked, I heard my mother's voice through the door: "And make sure you hang those workout clothes outside when you take them off. Don't go smelling up my house!"

I laughed and walked straight across the hall into the bathroom. It was time to remove these wet clothes, this old blanket of resentment. I looked at my face in the mirror. Two streams of drying tears were there. I hadn't cried that much in all of my adulthood. I needed it though—the tears, the conversation, the surrender, the release. I felt better. I shed something good that day.

I felt the same release when the tears came to an end as I sat in England, stranded at the phone booth. Relief washed over me; it was out there. I was tired of backpacking, tired of being strong. I needed help. I unclipped from my backpack, got back in the red phone box, and picked up the phone. Having run out of change from all the previous calls, I dialed zero for the operator.

"Hello, how may I help you?" a cheery voice said on the line.

"Excuse me, ma'am, I am from the US. I'm visiting Greatham for a week. I just got off the train. The place I am staying is not picking up, the cab company is also not picking up, but I do not have any more money to make another call. It's not far, but my backpack is too heavy for me to walk. Please help me. I've been trying for about twenty minutes."

There was a moment of silence, but before she could respond, I said, "Please, please help me, I'm tired and just want to get there. Here is the number to the place I'm trying to reach."

We called and it rang continuously. By this time, my head was ringing too. The operator stated the obvious apologetically: "No one is picking up."

"Can we try this cab company again? Maybe they will pick up this time."

On the fifth ring, I heard a voice. The operator said, "You are connected. I'm going to hang up now."

"Hello, I'd like a cab," I said.

A gruff and booming male voice said, "Sorry, we are closed for the day."

I felt the tears welling up again. I gave him the exact same plea I had just given the operator. My voice began cracking, eyes getting moist.

"I just want . . . I just want to get there."

"We are not taking any calls today, ma'am. We are closed," he said again.

"I have no other way to get there. I'm too tired to walk a few miles with fifty pounds on my back." I looked at my backpack.

There was a long pause, as if he were considering.

I added, "Please, this is my only hope. I don't have any more change to call anyone else."

"Okay, okay," he said. "I'll be there in fifteen minutes."

"Thank you so much. You are an angel." I took a deep breath and sat back on the ground, feeling a lot lighter and more hopeful.

When the gray-haired, heavyset cab driver arrived, my smile was so big, you would have thought he was Santa Claus. I wanted to give him a hug, but settled for a hearty, "Thank you, thank you, thank you so much."

He drove me straight to the retreat center. When the cab rounded the curve of the entrance, I saw the stone sign saying the Manor House, then the large brick house, which was probably at least one hundred years old. The house was surrounded by a large green lawn, with a small chapel tucked in the corner at the edge of a sunken green courtyard. The landscape was beautiful.

I knew that backpacking was not going to be enough for me, that sightseeing and meeting fellow travelers would wear me out. I wanted to interact on a deeper level. I also knew that after five weeks of traipsing around Europe on the train, and before my upcoming six weeks of volunteering in Kenya and South Africa, I would need a break to reflect on what I had seen and learned and what God was saying to me.

I'd heard about L'Abri, the French term for *shelter*, from a pastor friend of mine who'd worked there some time ago. Developed by a famous Christian named Francis Schaeffer, it was a community people went to for retreats, but even more so for deep questioning about life, faith, and vocation. Visitors could stay for a few days or a semester and would work their questions out while they lived together in community, working alongside one another, worshipping and sharing meals.

I got out and went up to the door that read WELCOME TO L'ABRI FELLOWSHIP on a plaque. I entered the foyer and quietly said, "Hello," looking for any sign of people. The foyer had heavy wood furniture, a long staircase, and large rugs on the wood floors. It felt warm and cozy.

A slim young brown-haired woman appeared. We introduced ourselves, and she began showing me around. She had an American accent and said her name was Laura. She noted that cell phones and computers could be used only once a week.

I nodded. I was happy to detach.

I followed her up the long flight of stairs to a long hall with many doors.

I had the camp feeling again, but I was used to that by now. In the last room, down a long hallway, were five twin beds—one along each wall and a fifth parallel to one of them. Laura told me that I would be sharing a room with Lebo, Ming, Camilla, and Marta.

I walked over to the only bed clear of stuff. It was set under two windows. *Good light*, I thought as the sun streamed through. I glimpsed the backyard with its large green lawn and the chapel on the far end. I smiled to myself. *Some light and green will be just fine.*

Laura proceeded to tell me the rules: Breakfast at 8:00 a.m., then work or study time. Teatime at 11:00 a.m., lunch at 1:00 p.m., work/study until our 4:30 p.m. teatime, and dinner at 6:30 p.m. Our work assignments for the week were listed on a chart. I had gotten used to schedules while volunteering; six days of routine would be nice. I asked if it was okay if I rested for a while.

"Absolutely," Laura said. "Can't wait to hear more about you later." She nodded and departed, softly closing the door.

I sat my backpack on the floor at the edge of the bed and immediately took off my shoes without unlacing them. I lay down with all of my clothes on, turned toward the light of the window, and closed my eyes.

I slept through dinner that night but was alert the next morning. The dining room held two long wooden tables that could fit us all. An air of warmth, openness, and curiosity blew over my skin. I breathed it in and entered. Breakfast was a sea of unknown faces and introductions, but already the place felt familiar and familial. Everyone was up—lively and chattering. I was in the company of thirty fellow travelers. We were from all over, but they, too, were on a soul journey.

I spent the morning learning names, finding out where everyone was from, how long they had been at L'Abri, and what questions had brought them there. There were a few Americans, folks from the UK like Scottish Camilla, and a Black South African woman, Lebo. Six or seven long-term staff members lived in separate houses on the grounds. A few young interns were there to work for the semester, and the rest of us were there to ask our own questions.

At breakfast, we made small talk and discussed our varying cultural contexts. Though everyone spoke English, talking was like translating to a different language, and the differences in food were often the center of conversation.

At one point I mentioned granola.

My table became quiet, faces held blank stares or furrowed brows. Someone asked, "What is granola?"

I laughed out loud, but then I realized they were serious. "Well, you take raw oats, mix with butter or honey, and bake so it's crunchy, add stuff like nuts and raisins, and put it on fruit and yogurt. It's usually eaten for breakfast."

"Ohhhh." Nods followed.

I tasted some sweet Norwegian cheese and was confused when I put it in my mouth. It was like nothing I had eaten before. "And you guys eat this with breakfast?" I asked.

"We eat whale skin in Greenland," said Ruth. I realized that even though I wasn't leaving the complex, I was having a lot of cross-cultural experiences. Under one roof there were people from Asia, Africa, and Europe.

After breakfast we had either work or study time. I would be gardening in the morning with Camilla from Scotland and Ruth from Greenland and looked forward to getting to know them a bit. Both were in transition: Camilla trying to figure out if seminary was next. Ruth taking a break from ministry.

I gave my usual spiel.

After weeding, I had the solo task of picking raspberries from a bush near the sunken garden on the other side of the property. It felt good to be alone in nature, doing something helpful. I picked these berries for us to eat. They would be added to a salad. I held the wooden bowl against my side and touched the berries gently, like they were precious, marveling at their feel, looking at their contours and trying my best to see them, to pay attention. I popped one into my mouth and pressed it against the roof, savoring the bittersweet flavor.

At teatime, I walked across the green grass to a group congregating around a tray of PG Tips British tea. I added a lump of sugar to my cup and stood watching the others, who were beginning to play soccer.

"You don't want to come and play?" one of the guys said, walking backward.

"Absolutely not. I'm going to sit here and enjoy my tea." And I sat on the wooden bench and watched.

I savored every sip as I watched the game, the soccer ball moving, feet maneuvering. I had nowhere to go and nothing to do but be here. I came to love these times—a break twice a day to congregate and have a little fun. I felt like they honored our humanity, acknowledging that we were tired, that we needed a drink and some human interaction.

Lunches were another communal practice, hosted in the cottage-like homes where residents lived. Someone would pose a question to spark conversation. One day, as we enjoyed potato soup, someone asked, "What is humanity's appropriate relationship to food and our social responsibility in buying it?" The discussion flowed freely, touching on food's cultural, utilitarian, and ethical dimensions. We agreed, disagreed, laughed, and learned from one another. It was a simple yet profound exchange that made each meal feel like a conversational adventure.

My study time was in the afternoon. I wandered downstairs to the library and tape room. There were old sermons and lectures in addition to volumes of books—Christian classics alongside books by contemporary theologians and social activists. I brushed my hands over a shelf of books, not looking for anything in particular.

What do I want to know? I thought. *What is my question?* Mostly, I wanted to rest. I picked up Desmond Tutu's book *No Future Without Forgiveness* and thumbed through it. I started toward my room, thinking of getting in bed with this book until teatime.

Lebo was in the room, reading. I went over to my bed and sat down. Not ready to read, I asked, "Lebo, what is your question? What brings you here?"

"My question is about reconciliation. Is it possible? Can we make an equal and just South Africa after apartheid? What does Christianity have to say about racial reconciliation?"

"Big questions. You may be trying to answer those for the rest of your life." I grinned, then added, "Tell me about South Africa. I am going there. What is the climate, sixteen years after apartheid?" I lay on my bed, putting my feet up and propping my head with a pillow.

Lebo put down her book. "People look to us as a model of reconciliation, but it's been hard. There's still a lot of anger, hurt, and disparity, and we have a long way to go."

"Well, in the US, we are forty-five years after civil rights, and we still have a long way to go. Similar struggle, different dynamics."

I was interested in her story and thought of doing a "Where I'm From" poem. "Lebo, would you do me a favor?" I explained the poem idea and asked if she would consider doing it sometime before I left.

"Of course," she said.

My week went by fast in this rhythm of work, study, rest, and community. I loved getting people's stories while working alongside them—the deep conversations, the lectures on faith, the laughter at every meal, the meals prepared by the collective work of the group, the film-watching, praying, and worshipping in the sunken courtyard while sitting on hay bales. This cocoon was what I needed to go on with a sense of joy. I felt like a guest, and that made all the difference.

One afternoon, I sat on my bed, peering out the windows as I reflected on my time traveling so far. "Where had I seen God?" was my question. I had seen God mostly in the people I'd met—beautiful people, struggling people, people who wanted to make a difference, people who'd been kind or hospitable and those I'd just brushed up against for a short time as they shared their stories. Their stories of love, triumph, and tragedy were beautiful. The people and all of the natural places I'd been—waterfalls, volcanoes, mountains, forests—were breathtaking. I had been brought closer to the Creator through people and places. God was also showing me that this journey wasn't just about seeing the world; it was about letting myself be seen, even by myself. I looked down on the little chapel behind the house and said, "Thank you," and, "Amen."

The day before I left L'Abri, I had four people lined up to do a "Where I'm From" poem: Lebo from South Africa, Camilla from Scotland, Ruth from Greenland, and Ming from South Korea. This time, there was less of a conversation prior to filming and more of them filling out the poem sheet. After Lebo completed her poem sheet, I got the camera rolling. We were in one of the sitting rooms of the Manor House, decorated with antique-looking wood furniture. I held the Flip camera out in front of me. Lebo stood against the wall, her poem sheet at her waist, and began to read.

She spoke of growing up in Pretoria, of "maize and poverty," of her parents' divorce, and of learning to heal through both family and country. She mentioned the "rainbow nation," the beauty of her nephew's birth and the end of apartheid—how it reshaped her sense of possibility. She closed with what brought her joy: soul music and malva pudding.

"Two questions, Lebo?" I said when she finished. "What is malva pudding, and what does 'rainbow nation' refer to?"

She laughed. "It's a South African dessert, a spongy, sweet, cake-like dish you serve with ice cream or custard. My favorite. You should try it when you go to South Africa." She continued, "South Africa is known as a rainbow nation because of its diversity. We have so many languages, races, and ethnic groups."

It was one of the places I was most excited about visiting. I'd be going to Kenya for three weeks next and South Africa for a month after that.

We filmed the poems by Camilla, Ruth, and Ming, and the next day, I got ready to go. Though I was excited, I felt sad. I wasn't ready to leave the comfort of L'Abri and my new friends, but it was time to move on. Balancing rest and movement was an ongoing challenge that I was learning to navigate better.

After many hugs, I picked up my backpack once again. It felt lighter, and so did I.

AFRICA

10

KENYA: GOLD MINES

THE ORPHANS WHO CAME AND NEVER LEFT

I arrived in Nairobi, Kenya, at the end of September, and on the drive from the airport, I relished the sight of giraffes roaming the land. But soon after, reality intruded with an unexpected change. Instead of going directly to my volunteer placement and homestay for three weeks, I stayed for a week in between two different volunteer houses, both without running water. During this waiting period, I got to know the other seven or eight volunteers, mostly from the UK, Canada, and Australia. We toured the crowded and boisterous streets of Nairobi, which felt like any other city with tall buildings and boulevards, except everyone was Black. English is one of their official languages, so language was not a barrier. We shopped at outdoor markets where we bargained for goods and art to take home. I bought a set of silver earrings in the shape of the African continent. We spent our days dropping in on various volunteer locations throughout the city and beyond.

On Saturday morning, we boarded a van to visit children's homes and drop off sanitary napkins to girls in the area, participating in what our volunteer coordinating organization called "women's empowerment." Eight volunteers, two coordinators, and two teachers made up our group.

At our first stop, two little boys were playing with a deflated soccer ball in an earthy front yard. Our group trailed into the house, passing a red, black, and white sign saying HOPE CHILDREN'S HOME set on a wooden chair on the front porch.

Mary Makena, the founder, waved us in warmly, saying, "Welcome, so glad you've come to visit Hope." A bright, toothy smile spread across her face. She was about five foot five with a small, round face, a dark brown complexion, and tiny braids pulled back into a ponytail. From the moment we stepped on her property in a residential area on the outskirts of Nairobi, I felt a positive vibe. We quickly filled up the two couches and three chairs in the front room.

"I'll get you something to eat," she said and then disappeared into the kitchen to prepare a snack. None of us were hungry, having just eaten breakfast before setting out.

As we waited, we introduced ourselves to the four girls living there, aged nine to sixteen. They wore blue uniforms with white collars and had hair cropped close to their scalps, like many Kenyan girls. Just as the introductions ended, Mary returned with a few small children carrying bright cups of pinkish porridge. She nodded at us to drink. I hesitated but lifted the cup to my lips. It tasted like unsweetened Cream of Wheat—not my favorite.

While we sipped, Mary began to share her story. She proudly pulled out a newspaper clipping and showed it to us. The headline read THE ORPHANS WHO NEVER LEFT and was accompanied by a photo of her beaming. "My name is Mary Makena," she said. "I am from Northern Kenya. When my husband died, as is our custom, I was to marry his brother. Instead, I ran away with my three children." Her tone was both practiced and genuine.

Her smile faded as she recounted coming to Nairobi, seeking work, and ending up in Kibera, a sprawling informal settlement, which people in Nairobi often called a slum. "I had to do terrible things," she admitted, her face turning solemn. "The conditions there are very poor," she added, shaking her head.

The home began when children, orphaned by disease, knocked on her door for food. "I had nothing, barely enough for my own children, but God told me to keep taking them in, to be their mother," she said. With nine children, she eventually found a bigger house through the help of friends. "Now, we have sixteen children here." She gestured around the room.

Mary explained how they lived day-to-day, relying on the generosity of others. "Our food, clothing, and rent are provided by friends like you," she said, locking eyes with each of us. She mentioned needing sewing machines so the girls could learn to mend clothes and perhaps start a trade. It was clearly a practiced appeal, yet her passion and sincerity came through.

A teenaged girl entered the room, carrying a baby boy with chestnut skin and a white onesie. Mary took him, cradling his head as she spoke. "This is George. He's HIV positive and came to us recently." She kissed his cheek and added, "He teaches me not to worry."

Mary shared a moment when George's cries reminded her to trust. "I was making his bottle in the kitchen one day, but he was wailing in the next room. Similarly, God said, 'You do not have to cry, Mary, I have something I am preparing for you.' God is providing," she said, placing her hand over her heart.

Her words hung in the air, filled with conviction. The room fell silent, reverent in the face of her faith. She seemed certain that her life—and the lives of these children—would be cared for. We opened our pockets to align with her faith.

After finishing the porridge, we followed Mary to the backyard, where a terraced garden stretched up a small hill. A few girls stirred a large pot of stew over a firepit. I wandered into the lush garden, running my fingers over kale leaves.

Mary noticed me and approached. "We grow our own kale," she said, smiling warmly. She took my hand, holding it against hers, and examined our similar skin tones. "Are you sure you are not Kenyan, daughter?"

I laughed. "No, I'm from the United States."

She pressed further. "But where is your family from?"

I hesitated, the weight of history pressing on me. "The US, as far back as I know." The pause stretched, and I took a deep breath—equal parts ache and resolve. "Our connection to Africa was severed by enslavement. Black Americans were cut off from our languages, our ethnic roots. Still, we know from history that our people were from West Africa."

She looked at me tenderly and said, "You are a daughter of Kenya now; welcome home." She put her arm next to mine and smiled. "See, we look alike."

We laughed. As she embraced me, I felt touched by the warmth of her spirit. I hoped that some of the faith, warmth, and conviction she held had rubbed off on me.

As the only Black volunteer, I seemed to garner interest from Kenyans wherever I went. At a day school we'd visited a few days before, I was assigned to a small classroom of eight to ten boys and girls between the ages of eight and ten. It was a small building, about the size of an office, with not much natural light and two to three rows of pew-like benches with desks. I stood up front. The students were intrigued by my presence. Instead of letting me help them with their homework, they quizzed me.

"Where are you from, teacher?" one bold young man asked.

"The United States," I replied. I had stopped saying America after having been to South America, because that was America too.

"Ohhh," they said, almost in unison.

A boy about ten years old slipped from behind his desk and came to stand next to me, putting his arm around my waist in a side hug.

"Are you related to Barack Obama?" he said with his eyebrows raised expectantly.

I threw my head back and laughed out loud. "No, but that is funny. His father is Kenyan, so he is more likely to be related to you."

"To Nadine?" a young girl in the back of the room asked. They were all mesmerized by the idea of the Obamas and seemed to want some relation or tie to them. I shook my head.

The questioning went on.

"Do you know you are Black like us?" said the boy who had come up and hugged me. He was now standing by the door, the light pouring in behind him.

"Of course. I've been Black my entire life, and I've always known it." This was quite an amusing line of interrogation. I laughed and played along while they tried to stump me, or perhaps just tried to wrap their minds around a Black volunteer from the United States.

In Kenya, my skin color was an asset—"Black privilege" in full effect. Kenyans warmed up to me faster and cut me more slack at markets. On the street, I blended in, assumed to be Kenyan or from elsewhere in Africa. In volunteer spaces, though, people were curious—maybe surprised to see a Black person coming to help, something often associated with white visitors, I guessed. Unlike other countries where I stood out, here they were endeared that I was Black and seemed delighted by my presence.

At the second children's center, our van rolled through tall gates into a school-like compound—green-and-white buildings, kids everywhere. About thirty girls welcomed us with song and dance for nearly half an hour. The outpouring of hospitality brought tears to my eyes. When we introduced ourselves, I said I was from the US, and the girls gave me a full standing ovation. It felt incredible to be celebrated for being Black, not penalized for it.

Blending in racially felt natural in Kenya, but being a woman came with challenges. Our visit—part of a "women's empowerment" effort—focused on providing sanitary pads so girls could stay in school during their periods. But my understanding of the "empowerment" deepened as two Kenyan women taught openly about hygiene, womanhood, and escaping sexual violence.

"Wear stockings. They buy you time to fight, scream, and maybe escape," said the woman instructor in the brown suit. "Yank on their man parts—pull or hit as hard as you can," she added, gesturing forcefully.

Her colleague in gray encouraged, "Run and tell a trusted adult. It's not your fault." Their instructions were stark, practical, and hauntingly necessary.

The room was silent as the young girls absorbed the lesson as though it were any other subject. I swallowed hard, struck by how matter-of-fact this conversation was. Studying how to defend against sexual assault was an essential learning. The burden of being a woman felt heavier than ever, a reality I carried everywhere I traveled, hyperaware of my surroundings, dress, and the constant threat of being seen as prey. My heart ached for them, and for every woman who must learn such lessons for her survival.

Later, during lunch prep, I had a revealing conversation about womanhood from one of our male guides. "So what brings you to Kenya?" he asked as we sliced tomatoes for our sandwiches.

"I'm traveling the world, volunteering, and sightseeing," I replied.

"Alone?" His voice rose with surprise.

"Yes, alone," I confirmed as I put cheese slices on the bread and sliced tomatoes.

"Are you married?" he continued. "Any children?"

"Nope, not married, no children," I said, noting his growing disbelief.

"How old are you?" he pressed.

"Twenty-nine. I'll be thirty soon—this trip is my gift to myself," I said with pride.

He looked at me like I had three heads. "You're still just a girl."

Heat rushed to my face. I paused, meeting his gaze. "Where I'm from, being over eighteen and taking care of yourself makes you an adult," I explained, my voice firm. "I have a career, pay my own bills, and can travel alone. I'm definitely a woman."

He shook his head dismissively. "Here, you're a girl until you're married with kids."

I turned back to the sandwiches, ending the conversation. His worldview was different, shaped by his culture, so there was no point in arguing. But I knew my value wasn't tied to marriage or motherhood.

MERCY ACADEMY

A few days later, I arrived in Naivasha, in the Riff Valley of Kenya, about ninety minutes from Nairobi where the landscape shimmered with rust-colored soil; the air carried a warm, earthen haze; and the streets pulsed with people and activity.

The downtown area was full of one-story buildings with advertisements for the cell phone companies Safari and Zain painted on them, roaming dogs, vendors selling fruit and vegetables, trash drifting, children playing, and adults walking. It was not uncommon to see a woman getting a ride on the back of a bicycle with her legs hanging sidesaddle.

The dusty roads danced with chickens, cows, stray dogs, and children playing. As I walked around Naivasha with a fellow volunteer from Australia, named Renee, kids shouted, "*Mzungu!*"—another name for a white traveler or foreigner—or, "Hello, how are you?" When I was alone, I never got called mzungu.

We lived with Wesley and his family. This included his wife, Lydia, and three daughters: Violet, nineteen; Eunice, fifteen; and Beatrice, thirteen. Eunice was away at boarding school, Violet was going to college for business administration (she walked us around and made our breakfast), and Beatrice was in secondary school. Lydia worked at the nearby school, and Wesley drove private transportation and thus spent most weekdays in Nairobi. I shared living space with Renee, an enthusiastic, brown-haired young journalist from Newcastle, Australia. We had a two-room area with a separate entrance from the main house. There was a toilet but no running water in our apartment. In the ground in front of our apartment, a huge square door housed water, which was used for cooking or for a bucket "shower." Renee was chatty and always excited about an adventure.

Wesley's oldest daughter, Violet, was our guide, who answered our questions and took us to places we didn't know how to get to. The youngest, Beatrice, was bubbly and curious, asking about our lives in Australia and the US. We had tea at about seven every night around their dining room table, chatted for a bit, and even watched some Kenyan TV. It was delightful seeing Black people on every channel and an all-Black news crew.

Mercy Academy had been started by Wesley's father and was named after his mother, Mercy. It was a day school for about sixty children ages six to twelve whose families couldn't afford public school fees. Wesley's family had decided to do something by starting to feed the children. Then they started to teach them, and thus Mercy Academy was born.

Renee and I arrived at Mercy around 9:00 a.m., after a twenty-five-minute walk from Wesley's house. A six-foot-high wooden fence surrounded the complex, with a MERCY ACADEMY sign in front. We entered the gate through big blue double doors that led onto an earthen courtyard with a few corrugated metal buildings painted red. The longest was a rectangular school building that held five classrooms, with openings for windows and doors. A small building used for cooking housed a large firepit of a stove.

The children were already present when we arrived, five to ten of them per classroom. They sat quietly or spoke in low murmurs behind desks that read DONATED BY K.C.B. in block letters. Usually, one of them was teaching the others or they were reading books. When I entered each classroom, all of the children stood up and said, "Good morning, teacher," and remained standing until I told them to sit down. Students with faces touched by the day's dust, close-cut hair, and tattered blue-and-burgundy uniforms peered back at me, eager to learn. I had never seen this level of respect from children of any age. They engaged with a sense of humility and gratitude. There seemed to be no entitlement.

My two favorite classes were levels two and three. These kids were a bit older, and their English was good. In class three, Samson was my favorite. About twelve years old, he was lanky and wore a blue sweater even though it was nearly seventy degrees each day. He helped lead the classes in assignments and was always the first to raise his hand. Class two was made up of seven eight-year-olds that knew less English. When I spoke, they looked at me bewildered for a minute and talked among themselves in Swahili, trying to figure out what I had said. Then one brave soul would answer.

I had four classes a day of about forty-five minutes each, mostly taught from textbooks they were working through: math, reading, science, and social studies on various levels. The children's ages in my classes ranged from six to twelve years old.

About a week into my volunteering, I had to teach child rights as part of a social studies lesson. One of the older students came up and showed me where they had previously left off. There, in a social studies book, in a day school for children who could not afford school fees, was a social studies lesson on "child rights." I swallowed the lump in my throat before I began.

"Does anyone know what a right is?"

They stared back in confusion.

"A right is something you are born with, that you deserve to be given as a human being, or a way you should be treated."

I got a few nods.

"Anyone know what your rights are as children?"

And so, we went down the list and through the pages that showed Black cartoon characters displaying the rights that little children were given by the government and their parents. Each "right" got more awkward as we went along.

"Okay, your first rights are food, clothing, and shelter. Your parents are required to provide these for you as their child."

I reflected for a minute, knowing that this lesson would get harder for me. Many of them came to this free day school to eat, which might be their only meal of the day because their parents couldn't afford to feed them. They had rights that were being violated—not on purpose, but by the circumstances of their lives, by inequity.

Clothing? I looked around the room. They wore old uniforms that were tattered, mostly red shirts and blue pants or burgundy dresses.

Shelter. "A safe and protected place to live and sleep." I knew that some of them slept with their entire families in small dwellings.

"Child rights" rang in my ears every time I said it. My voice began to quiver. My eyes became glassy.

"Can anyone think of other rights you may have?" I asked

"Clean water," said Samson, my prize student, standing up. He said it triumphantly, like he had got it for the first time.

"Yes, clean water. Anything else?" There was only silence.

With that I moved on. "Other rights are an education, freedom from abuse, good medical care—"

I stopped. I didn't want to teach this lesson anymore. I did not want to tell these children that they had basic rights that were not being met. It felt unjust, like a mean trick. "You should have all of these things, but you do not!" I wanted to scream. *Whose fault was it? Who was to blame? God? The government?* I thought to myself, spiraling inside but trying to keep calm.

They, on the other hand, sat listening intensely with anticipation. I went through the lesson as quickly as I could, trying to explain the concepts, feeling like I needed to give them an apology for not having enough. Still, they were excited to learn. I have no doubt that they knew their lack all too well, but they also knew joy and were bright, and that was the sense that they carried with them in abundance.

I was happy when the breakfast bell rang. A breakfast of porridge was served at about 10:00 a.m. each day. I went to the front of the line to help. Several of us served the fifty children lining up quietly to wait: Cathy and Mary, my host dad's sisters and our chefs; Simon, tall, nineteen, and bronze skinned, a former student who worked at Mercy; and one of the teachers. I poured porridge into small, brightly colored plastic bowls of pink, yellow, and blue. Each child looked me in the eye, said, "Thank you," and went to sit down at the table with their bowls in front of them to wait. I was shocked when I saw this. No horseplay, no sneaking a taste—they just sat quietly on their benches and waited until everyone got their food and we said prayers.

This was even more impressive given that some of them may not have eaten since the day before. I could learn from their patience. If I had not eaten in the last eighteen hours, I would probably have rushed wildly to the front of the line. Even when I am not that hungry, I am always trying to get to the front of the line and usually be done before everyone sits down. What did they know that I did not? That there was no rush? That everyone would get served? That eating together was better than being finished fast and first? How could they operate in this paradigm when their reality was full of lack? I was not sure if my faith would stand up against what they had to deal with daily. Their circumstances were obviously not ideal or to be glorified, but they carried a dignity I admired.

Whatever quietness the children experienced in the morning when I arrived, or during breakfast porridge and lunch of kale and *ugali* (a stiff, grits-like food), was expended during recess. Then laughing, running, games, and glee abounded. They ran relay races and played tag and duck, duck, goose. Renee and I either played along with them or helped the ladies and Simon cook lunch by chopping up kale in the courtyard next to the stove house. It felt more like shooting the breeze in the town square. They asked me questions about the US, and I asked them questions about Kenyan culture, their lives, or the kids at the school. Simon was always smiling at me and offering to help me. I assumed he had a crush on me; I saw him watching me starry-eyed. He taught at Mercy but had bigger dreams. He wanted to continue in school. He was kind, gentle, and patient with the kids, sometimes looking through the open window into my classroom. I decided I wanted to know more about Simon and asked him to do a "Where I'm From" poem with me.

A few days later, I gave him the sheet and explained the poems. He filled it out while I was teaching one of my classes. Once I was done, we sat down in an empty classroom, and I asked questions about things I was curious about. Simon didn't talk much, so I had to pry what little I could out of him.

Simon told me that he was an orphan, that his parents had died when he was younger, and he had been a student at Mercy. One of his tragedies was that he had to drop out of college because he couldn't afford it. He was looking at the floor when he told me this. My heart went out to him. He did, however, love teaching the kids at Mercy.

Some of the things on Simon's sheet were unfamiliar. I asked him what Jamhuri Day was.

"Jamhuri means republic," he explained. "It's Kenya's Independence Day from Britain. There are parades, feasts, and speakers. It's the most important day to us."

Everybody wants to be free, I thought. Something else on his form sparked my interest. "I know what ugali is, but what are *mukimo* and Mugithi?"

He tilted his head. "Mukimo is mash, a dish. You take a bunch of things—maize, vegetables like peas and potatoes—and mash it together, and you have mukimo."

"Ohhh," I said. I hadn't come across it. "And Mugithi?"

He told me it was a type of music, usually a single singer with a guitar playing at weddings or maybe nightclubs. He got up and started to sing a song in another language and fake-strum a guitar. I clapped when he was done. He was blushing. I smiled, because my entire time in Kenya had been full of singing. How apropos his mini performance was.

When he read his poem aloud, he spoke of things I hadn't asked about—child-naming ceremonies and the gratitude of having folks that took care of him before finishing softly, "That's where I'm from."

I was struck by how much he carried—grief and hope, loss and love—spoken with a quiet strength that made me admire him all the more.

On my last day of teaching, the children sang for Renee and me for about two hours straight. I had come to serve, and they gave me a much greater gift. I was almost in tears, so moved by their performance. They had taught me so much about hospitality, generosity, and joy that ran deeper than circumstance. Though they lacked financial means, their souls were expansive, open, and alive.

Renee and I had bought books to give out that day, and when the kids saw them, they jumped out of their seats and immediately started reading. For the rest of that day, I could hear the children from another class rereading one of the books. I left thinking about how I might approach life more as a child—as open, curious, eager, grateful, and playful as the children of Mercy Academy had been our entire time there.

MAASAI MARA

After two weeks of volunteering at Mercy Academy, I was set to go on a weekend safari in Maasai Mara, a vast national reserve in southwestern Kenya along the Tanzanian border. I was excited to see lions, elephants, zebras, and giraffes, and to visit the villages of Maasai people, an ethnic group that inhabits parts of Kenya and Tanzania.

Wesley dropped me off at the bustling bus station, where old but colorful buses idled amid a steady stream of people. Struggling to navigate the bustle, I anxiously awaited the arrival of my safari tour leader and the other volunteers from the agency who had also booked a safari tour. I scanned the crowd for familiar faces. Finally, a white van appeared, and Joe, our tour guide, greeted me with a warm smile. His reassuring presence offered a sense of comfort amidst the unfamiliarity of my surroundings. I also noticed the familiar faces of other volunteers from my first week in Nairobi.

As we embarked on our journey, Joe told us tales of past safaris, his words painting vivid pictures of the beauty as well as the dangers, like elephants that trampled people. This was exactly what I didn't need to hear right before we were going to camp in an area with wild animals. I tuned him out and focused my attention outside the window.

Passing through the breathtaking landscapes of the Rift Valley, I couldn't help but feel a sense of awe and wonder at the vastness of the land stretching out before us.

We arrived at the reserve right at dusk and were greeted by three Maasai men, their tall, lean figures shrouded in traditional red cloth and their feet in handmade sandals. Silently, they led us to our accommodations for the night—a cluster of round dwellings nestled amidst the wilderness.

Stepping inside my dwelling, I was struck by the contrast between its rustic exterior of tarp and the amenities inside, including two twin beds, a toilet, and a shower. I was excited. I hadn't taken a shower with running water in weeks. As I settled in for the night, the sounds of the wild echoed in the distance: roars and the laughter of hyenas. There was no fence or gate around the reserve. I feared being eaten, my mind playing out the worst possible scenarios. That night, I dreamed that my head was in the mouth of a lion. I popped awake just as the lion was closing its mouth on my head, awoken by the flashlight and footsteps of the Maasai man who was on security duty and walked the camp all night.

The following morning, we set out in our van, eager to begin our safari adventure. Passing through the sprawling savanna, we marveled at a family of elephants bathing in a nearby watering hole, their majestic forms silhouetted against the golden light of dawn. One flapped his ears and stood on his back legs, agitated. My mouth hung open as we sped away in our white truck.

As we ventured deeper into the reserve, our anticipation grew with each passing moment. Suddenly, Joe brought the van to a halt. Following his gaze, we were greeted by the sight of a pride of four lions, lounging in the shade of an acacia tree. It felt like a scene from *The Lion King*. We drove slowly toward them to get a closer look. With bated breath, we watched in awe as the lions roamed freely, their powerful presence commanding respect and admiration. As if on cue, a lioness approached our van, her amber eyes sparkling as she surveyed us with a mixture of curiosity and caution.

Despite the thrill of the moment, a sense of unease lingered in the air, a reminder of the danger lurking amidst the beauty. Yet, amidst the uncertainty, there was a profound sense of connection to the natural world. It made me want to reach out and touch her, but I knew better.

Later that day, we had the opportunity to visit a Maasai village, where we were welcomed by the local community. I witnessed traditional Maasai dance, the men jumping high with staff in hand. I went into the dark, windowless dwelling of a community member and was offered goat's milk, which I declined, scared of getting sick. I also bought some bracelets from the local women, posed for pictures with the village men, and even bought a wooden elephant for my mother. The Maasai men, though traditionally dressed in the red fabric wrapped around their bodies, secured an elephant by calling someone on a cell phone. The elephant arrived minutes later by vehicle. The juxtaposition of modernity and the rustic landscape was striking. What felt wild then, I now know was only my narrow view. I also never paused to ask if my presence sustained or exploited the community. I just marveled.

As the sun began to set on our safari adventure, I reflected with gratitude on the profound experiences of the day, the interconnectedness of the landscape, animals, and people. I felt deeply connected and alone at the same time. I'd had this amazing experience with folks I would never see again. I'd have no one to remember it with. My heart was full, but there was also a sinking sadness at the center; I was learning to hold both. I remembered the lone older lion I'd seen on our way back from the safari that first day and wondered if that would be me.

GOLD MINES

Before heading to South Africa, I spent two days back in Nairobi, staying at the volunteer house and meeting up with Katie, a fellow artist from the US. We'd connected before I left, and she had been in Kenya for a few months working with local art organizations.

She set up a poetry workshop for me at a youth space in the Mathare neighborhood.

We met at Junction Mall, a shopping center within walking distance of the volunteer house, the only place I could confidently navigate to. The roads there always felt like a construction site, with lots of dust bordered by cement buildings that looked incomplete. There were few street signs, and the pavement was full of dips. There were no signs for bus stops, and I had absolutely no idea where the *matatus* (white vans that were the public transportation system) were headed.

Katie—tall, blonde, American—felt familiar in an unfamiliar place.

We hugged.

"I'm following you. What's on the itinerary?" I asked.

"We'll stop by Kibera first. I'd like you to meet some friends there and then we can go to Mathare and grab lunch before your workshop."

I was excited. She flagged a matatu down, and when she asked the fare to Kibera, the man replied, pointing at me, "Ten for her," then at Katie, "Thirty for you."

Looking stunned, Katie jerked her head back in surprise and said, "What? Are you serious?"

I thought, *Black privilege!* When he didn't relent, she paid and we climbed into the cramped van. Personal space wasn't a thing, and we had to sit almost in people's laps.

Kibera—the largest informal settlement in Africa, the size of New York's Central Park but with population estimates upward of one million residents—was exactly as I'd read: small metal homes, without running water or sewage systems, clustered along muddy alleys. But it buzzed with energy. Poverty and trash were said to be rampant, but I knew from my past volunteer and life experiences that there is always some beauty growing amidst hardship. We didn't go in deep; Katie stood out too much, and it wasn't safe.

We arrived at an arts foundation, an apartment-turned-art-space with murals, a bead-making workshop, and a small music studio. Carole, one of the staff, dark skinned and robust, greeted us with warmth and a firm handshake.

"I love the mural," I said. "Tell me about it?" I asked as we moved inside. The black-and-gold *Goldmines* mural emanated from the back wall. Gold was bursting out of black dirt.

"People think we have terrible lives," she said as she gave us a tour. "But if you dig, you find gold. These kids have talent—music, art, poetry. You just have to get past the surface. There's treasure here."

After the tour, I looked out at a sea of rusted corrugated metal roofs and activity from the balcony—kids playing, vendors selling, life pulsing. The air was thick with spice and waste. I rested my chin on my arms and tried to see it as Carole did—not just struggle, but potential.

I watched the hustle and bustle until it was time to go, and then I took a few pictures. The metal rooftops had their own artistic voice. They spoke of the duality that lay beneath the roofs, gold beneath rust and soot.

We boarded another matatu and spent the rest of the day in the Mathare neighborhood at a community center that provides a gathering space for youth, sponsors school fees for students, and engages the youth in the arts. Mathare is a smaller informal settlement but residents suffer from the same extreme poverty. The community organization hoped to shine rays of light into the community.

We met the director at the front of the building, a cinder-block building with a metal door painted blue. A colorful mural on the building's exterior depicted what looked like a big community party. The walls were painted orange and decorated with children's paintings. I had been communicating with Aaron for months and was excited to do my first official workshop—to have an audience again.

Before the poetry workshop started, Aaron, dark brown and kind, took me on a walk through the heart of Mathare. "Leave your camera and things here at the Center. Taking pictures will draw attention. I don't want anything to happen or anything valuable of yours to get stolen," he said, looking me straight in the eyes. I walked behind him silently, staring at his white T-shirt against his dark skin and the gray background of the neighborhood.

Our walk into Mathare took us across a makeshift bridge of rocks over a river. The pungent smell filled the air as I carefully leapt from boulder to boulder, focusing on my footing. The water was dark brown, littered with white, black, and green plastic bags. Aaron reached back to steady me with his hand, guiding me across the uneven terrain. The path was swerving and narrow, pocked with dips and holes. On the other side of the river, men stood by rusted barrels with fires roaring beneath them, the heat shimmering in the air.

I paused, gesturing toward the barrels. "Is that where they make . . . ?" I searched for the word.

"*Chang'aa*." Aaron nodded. "Yes."

We watched as the men rotated the barrels of brewed spirit. "Is it really poisonous?" I asked.

"I don't drink it," he said, his voice heavy. "But many do. It eases the pain—desperation, hopelessness. Especially for the men." His face tightened as he spoke.

We continued along a muddy path bordered by small homes. Aaron stopped and knocked on a door. A man with a broad smile opened it, welcoming us inside a dimly lit room with a small couch.

"This is Ebony. She's visiting us," Aaron introduced me.

The man beamed. "Very good to meet you! Welcome, welcome." He reached for a bottle on a side table and poured a pinkish brew into a cup. "Would you like some chang'aa? It's homemade."

I shook my head. "No, thank you."

"It won't hurt you. We drink it all the time here," he said, nudging the cup toward me.

"I'm good," I replied, glancing around the sparse room. But I wasn't good. The weight of the poverty I'd seen settled heavily on my chest. I could write poetry with children, but it wouldn't change their reality. The stench of poverty would still overpower their community. I stared at Aaron's friend, unable to focus on his words.

Soon after Aaron and I returned from our walk, the children had started arriving and congregating at the door of the building. They were mostly teenage boys and a few elementary school aged children. By the time we started, about twenty children and youth were sitting on the floor and benches or standing—joking, laughing, and playing.

Aaron got up and said a few words about having a special guest. He gestured toward me with an open hand. I stood up from my place on a bench in the front row and introduced myself.

"We are going to do two poems today," I said. "You are going to create your own 'I Am' poem and a color poem. Let's start with the easier of the two, the color poem. It's really just the warm-up. The 'I Am' poem is the main event." I paced back and forth in front of the room as I spoke.

I asked them to introduce themselves, and they went around the room quickly, each person popping up from their seat to say their name. There were names like Lawrence, Kevin, Stephen, David, and John.

I began pacing again, making eye contact as I walked slowly. "I want you to think of a color, your favorite color. Then I want you to describe it using your five senses."

I explained simile and metaphor while they threw out some examples as practice.

"She is a shining star," said a girl named Ruth who was wearing flowered leggings, followed by "she is a giraffe" and "he is a lion."

"I am as powerful as Barack Obama," a blue-shirted boy yelled.

I wrote an example on the board using the color red:

Red is the color of anger.
It feels like fire,
Tastes spicy,
Looks like a flame,
Sounds like a blaring fire engine.
Red will prick your fingers like thorns on a rose bush.

"Nice!" Ruth with the flowered leggings said. "I like that."

I gave them ten minutes to write a poem and warned them that I'd like a few people to read theirs. As soon as I finished speaking and began handing out writing papers, the room was silent. A few boys watched through the small windows in the door, their bodies blocking the light streaming into the dim room. Behind them were a group of boys jumping on an old mattress.

I knew about this. I remember an open lot in my neighborhood in Queens, right across the street from my house. It was often full of trash and mattresses that young boys flipped on, incessantly bouncing up and down and doing somersaults, as if they were training for something. I am sure some of those same boys didn't live out their full potential; a few likely did not make it to adulthood, due to drugs and violence. I wondered what would become of these Kenyan boys.

I imagined that the boys at the door weren't completely insiders, and they weren't outsiders. Growing up in the "ghetto" and going to elite white institutions, I knew a bit about being on the threshold of two worlds.

I was pulled back into the room by an increasing level of chatter. I turned my head toward the class and said, "Time's up, poets! It's time to perform. Do I have volunteers?"

Lawrence stepped up and swaggered to the front. I knew his name because he had stuck his nametag on his forehead. I gave a few pointers about reading poems out loud.

He shifted his body and started, reading dramatically, with pauses and inflections.

Black is the color of Africa.
It feels round and cold,
It's sweeter than honey,
It looks like an angel coming down from heaven to earth.
It sounds like a whisper in the dark,
It smells as fresh as the roses in the garden.

Others shared their poems, but the first stayed with me—how Lawrence was able to see the world differently than it appeared. How in that black—where others saw darkness, danger, dirt, or grime—he saw angels, roses, and honey. He saw beauty alongside the inequity. Though we were in "the slums," the room was alive with energy—full of creativity, laughter, and vision.

Next, we did "I Am" poems, and they compared themselves to lions, Barack Obama, and musical instruments. There was pride and confidence.

Ruth, the girl with the flowered pants, asked, with her hand on her hip, "Do you know Sionne? She did poetry with us too. Really similar."

I explained that Sione had given me the "Where I'm From" poem template. I figured they might have done that already, which was why I didn't incorporate it.

At the end of our time together, there were photographs, of course, me smiling in the center. I was sad that I got to spend only a few hours with the children there. I gave them cards with my name, email address, and website on them. They were eager to become my friend on Facebook. There wasn't running water, but they had internet cafés and cell phones. This trip kept challenging and widening my perspective.

I had scheduled three weeks in Kenya and a month in South Africa, thinking that Kenya, because of its poverty, would be the harder of the two. Though confronting the lack was difficult, the spirit of the people was priceless. Kenya taught me to live in the both/and—hospitality beside hardship, dignity and beauty beside poverty. In classrooms, I met patience, curiosity, and play. In women's rooms, I met courage. In markets and neighborhoods, I met my own privilege and the limits of my "service." In poetry, I saw how we can craft our own stories beyond our circumstances. Kenya invited me to see it, not save it; to be a witness to the good already happening, to learn, and to become more human. I left humbled, with eyes attuned to the gold beneath the rust as I turned toward South Africa.

11

SOUTH AFRICA: CROSSING COLOR LINES

A MESS IN MUIZENBERG

I knew from the moment I walked in the door of the shared apartment that my volunteer experience in Muizenberg, South Africa, was going to be a hot mess. Muizenberg is a suburb about forty minutes outside Cape Town, where I would be living and volunteering. Instead of a host family, volunteers were housed in a three-bedroom apartment on the third floor of a residential building a few blocks from the beach. Our volunteer director was Jenny, a white South African in her thirties.

When we arrived, the apartment door was open and there was a bunch of commotion. Three guys in their twenties were on their way out the door. I thought, *This is about to be like a reality TV show,* The Real World *Muizenberg.*

Pizza boxes and empty soda bottles littered the dining table, the couches, and the floor. It looked like a frat house. Jenny showed me to my room. It was small, with two bunk beds. I put my backpack beside an empty bed, on the top bunk near the window. Twelve of us were living in this apartment, four people in each room. There was a room for the guys and two for the women, a small bathroom for us all, and a small kitchen. I shared a room with Charlotte from England, Naomi from Australia, and Stacey from the US. Naomi was close to my age and perhaps the only one of my housemates that I could relate to; the others felt like reckless college students. She wasn't consumed with drama, drinking, or partying.

Jenny pointed to the bottles with a stern face and said, "You guys need to clean this place up," then quickly left. She had started this volunteer organization out of her effort to teach surfing to township children in Muizenberg. Townships were the places in South Africa where Black people and Coloured people lived. My one-day orientation included visiting a Coloured township, which was not too different from the informal settlements in Kenya, with homes made of corrugated metal sheets. There were a few schools and childcare centers where volunteers worked.

Coloured people are a South African community of mixed African, European, and South or Southeast Asian ancestry. They are generally light brown, but range in complexion. Under apartheid, Coloureds were one of four major groups that included white South Africans, Black South Africans, and Indians. These groups were segregated under that system, and from what I could see, still remained fairly separate.

I was reminded of the racial hierarchy at home—white folks with access to wealth and so many people of color scrambling at the bottom, separate and unequal. It made me sad and angry.

The fact that the one-day orientation was the extent of my preparation also felt alarming, but I resolved to go with it, to stick with it as best I could.

Kuda and Rudo, both immigrants from Zimbabwe, provided the volunteers with daily support. Kuda ran one of the volunteer programs. His skin was a smooth, dark brown color and his hair was in short, spiky locs that stuck straight up. He was always smiling, with a wetsuit halfway on in preparation for surfing, exposing his muscular chest. Rudo was a medium brown woman who always wore a knit winter hat. She was in charge of cooking and cleaning. She was always pleasant, but talkative only to the Australian volunteer, Naomi.

Though our volunteer house was in a constant state of disarray, it was located about two blocks from one of the most stunning landscapes of my trip. The beach was chilly and windy, with sparkling but rough bluish-green water, great for surfing. The long, sandy beach was lined with small cottages of red, yellow, and blue. I supposed they were meant to hold people's surfing equipment. Muizenberg also had a river running through it—bluish-green, usually reflecting the adjacent mountain. Like the river that bifurcated Muizenberg, South Africa had immense beauty on one side and poverty and racial tension on the other.

On top of these tensions, there was no volunteer center, building, or headquarters. Jenny, the director, just showed up at the apartment, gave orders, and left. Those orders usually came in the form of group meetings where, instead of talking through issues, she reiterated the rules.

Jenny held two house meetings my first week. We crammed into the small living room as she paced the floor, pointing out what was going wrong.

"This is a faith-based organization, and we care deeply about displaying Christian values. You guys may not be Christian, but please respect this organization and the rules if you want to continue to volunteer here. You are to be a role model for young children." She stopped, looked over at us all, and put her hands on her waist. "Please do not smoke or drink in this volunteer apartment. And you also need to take responsibility for keeping things clean."

People rolled their eyes. She was doing more pleading than leading. We all knew she was in over her head.

She ended with, "If you have any problems, you can come and talk to me," and left quickly, as if talking was the last thing she wanted to do with any of us. I saw Jenny two times after that, and that was to take us to a worship service put on by her church.

People laughed and grumbled after she left, mocking her speech, and resumed normal activity.

Ryan and Ross, two white guys, one with a beard and the other recently clean-shaven and smooth faced, were *Mister, Mister*, our evening store service. You would yell, "Mister, mister," if you wanted some food, alcohol, or snacks while they were going to the store. I always got a chocolate bar that came in a purple wrapper. I ate chocolate every evening and took long walks in the morning to cope with the disarray. Our meals, which Rudo made, were less than stellar but sometimes consisted of South African cuisine like sausages (*boerewors*), eggs and beans, *pap* (like grits but sturdier, and you eat it with your hands), *biltong* (similar to jerky), or *sosatie* (a kabob on a stick). I was sad to not have many chances to interact with adult South Africans. Rudo, who was Zimbabwean, was kind but didn't seem particularly open to extended conversation, and I was frankly too exhausted by the dysfunction of the volunteer house to be my normal curious self.

During my first week, I asked Rudo enthusiastically, "So when is the orientation for the art program?" because that was why I had chosen this volunteer placement.

She shook her head and said, "Sorry, there is no art program. You can teach in a school, help at a daycare center, or teach surfing or soccer."

I looked past her shoulders through the window facing the mountain. I knew nothing of the latter two, and I didn't want to watch kids at a daycare center. Disappointed, I shrugged and said, "I guess I'll teach then."

"Sorry, it's a bit of a mess around here," Rudo said.

"Yes, I've noticed." I plopped down on one of the chairs in the living room and stared at the bare walls. I had spent months imagining myself guiding creative expression through art, and now, that vision was gone. The joy I had from Kenya dimmed, and I resolved to just get through my time in South Africa as best I could.

Going from Nairobi to the beach was an adjustment. But going from a home with a family to a house of volunteers was even more difficult. The transition from racial homogeneity to racial stratification and tension was also both startling and stifling. I was whirling inside but tried to stay grounded. The constant partying and drinking around the volunteer house made that hard. After a week at the Muizenberg apartment, I was beginning to feel more down than up.

On the first morning of my teaching assignment at a local school, the teacher was out, and the substitute dipped in and out of the room, leaving me alone with over forty fourth graders. The class was completely unruly—kids yelling, pushing, fighting. I tried to get their attention, but my voice was swallowed by the noise. It was exhausting. I thought back to Guatemala and Kenya and missed those kids deeply. The classrooms had been smaller, the children curious, affectionate, easier to engage. Those experiences felt meaningful. This one just felt hard.

The children here were a tough crowd. The classroom experience made me feel deeply uncomfortable, inadequate, and a bit powerless. As I walked back to the volunteer house at the end of my first week, I looked down at my dust-covered hiking shoes and muttered under my breath, "I'm tired of these badass kids," and laughed, because if I didn't, I might cry. I went to the beach to clear my head. The wind slapped my face. I knew I couldn't keep teaching in that setting. I turned around, stared at the mountain of Muizenberg, and declared to it, "I think I might do soccer. I don't know how to play, but maybe it's time I learned."

I had the mornings off, and I spent them walking on the beach trying to find serenity, but it wasn't particularly pleasant. It was their fall, cool and very windy, but I was happy to get out of the house and away from being with eleven people all of the time. I often stopped in the same internet café across from the beach to check my email, Skype with friends, and write a blog, which I published every two to three days. When my mom asked how I was doing on our weekly call, I said, "Okay," but she saw right through me and said, "You sound tired."

Weary, I said, "I am."

She said, "Just keep putting one foot in front of the other."

That is what I tried to do. In the afternoons, Ryan, Ross, the three other volunteers on soccer duty, and I followed a routine: making peanut butter and jelly sandwiches, packing them into the plastic bags the bread came in, and slicing oranges. Then, we walked about a mile and a half to the edge of the nearby township, to an empty field of sand with patches of grass, to play soccer.

I watched, learned, and cheered while the other volunteers and the elementary school boys played soccer for an hour or so until it was time to eat sandwiches and oranges. We then gathered the boys—mostly between the ages of eight and thirteen—in a circle, their blue-and-white uniforms, legs, and faces dusty with sand. I couldn't remember most of their names well, but I remembered faces—little, dark brown faces. My favorites were Lucas and Kuumba, mostly because they were good players and they interacted with me. They'd eat up the sliced oranges like lightning, tucking the rind under their lips and smiling orange. They ate the sandwiches by holding them like they were a piece of toast.

I learned to love the rhythm of those two and a half hours of activity each day, even though the rest of my time felt empty. My growing awareness of the racial hierarchy in South Africa made me feel increasingly depressed. I had a heaviness in my heart, grieving this reality both at home and abroad. This reality added to my weariness.

At the volunteer house, once the clock struck 9:00 a.m., someone was always yelling. Guys kept coming into the women's room when one of us was trying to get dressed, and a few people had their money stolen within days of each other. It was a constant game of Clue to figure out who the thief was. Some thought it was Rudo, our house manager; more thought it was my roommate Charlotte, the woman from England. I kept my money on me and my valuables locked up.

Almost every week, someone would come home without a wallet or cell phone and say, "I got robbed," and again put us on caution. A group of them went to Cape Town, and a random guy in a pickup offered to give them a lift back. About five miles from Muizenberg, he stopped on the highway, his friend pulled up in a car behind them, and they took everyone's wallets and made them walk home. I didn't like traveling in groups of reckless young white people. There would always be pressure to do something unwise, so I rarely went out in the larger group.

Naomi from Australia became my friend. In her late twenties like me, heavyset, with pale skin and dark eyes and hair, she was calm and kind. I mingled with others, but I talked with Naomi. She knew about Frank, the guy I had met in Cape Town while on an overnight trip to get away from the craziness of the volunteer house.

"So, what about that guy you met? Do you like him? Are you going to give him a chance?" She was standing, looking eye to eye with me lying on the top bunk.

I rolled my eyes. "Oh, Frank." I sighed and sat up on my elbows. "He's a needed reprieve from all this confusion, but I don't know. He's a bit over the top in his syrupy sweet texts. I am not sure if he is just one of those too-much-too-soon guys or sees dollar signs or a green card. Either way, he's cool, but I am not that into him."

"Give him a chance," she urged. "You never know."

"I'm leaving in a week and a half."

I rolled onto my back and looked up at the ceiling, fingering the painful stye that had come to rest upon my right eyelid. I had been hit in the face by a soccer ball the day before.

"I'm going with him to see the penguins at the end of the week," I said. Without waiting for Naomi's response, I put on my eye mask and inserted ear plugs. It was only 8:00 p.m.

FRANK

I'd met Frank the week before at Camps Bay Beach when I was exploring some of Cape Town's touristy spots on a Hop-on-Hop-off tour. There was a poetry open mic that evening that I planned to attend and stay in the city overnight.

I hopped off the red double-decker bus at Camps Bay. In front of me stretched a beach of white sand bounded by large boulders and turquoise water. Behind me were views of the Table Mountain. Posh restaurants, cafés, and cocktail bars with patios overlooked the promenade. The weather was chilly, and the wind blew my hair straight back as I walked along the beach. When the wind became too much, I began heading toward the Hop-on-Hop-off station. Then, I heard a voice.

"How long have you been growing your dreads?"

I jerked my head around, startled. I'd thought I was alone. A few feet away from me stood a thin man with a round, dark face. He was smiling and wore a brown fedora.

After a pause to get my bearings, I replied, "It will be two years in December."

"They are very nice." He came closer. "I'm Frank." He asked questions about me and my hair, which hooked me in for a few minutes. "Can I take you out for a drink this afternoon?" he asked as I was walking away.

I turned back. "No, I have plans tonight, and I am only going to be in town for another few weeks, so I am not interested." I resumed walking.

He walked alongside me, matching the increasing speed of my stride. I was relieved to see my bus coming a ways off. I kept trying to dismiss him, when he finally said, "Wouldn't you do the same thing if you were me? You are beautiful, and I want to get to know you. If you were me, wouldn't you be persistent? Wouldn't you try your hardest to get you to go out?"

That one got me. He had a point, and I could tell he was not going to be easily dismissed. To get him away from me, I said, "Okay. I'll be in town at this poetry event if you want to buy me a drink. I'll be there tonight at eight thirty."

"Where is it?" he asked.

"At a place in Greenmarket Square—I can't recall the name. If you want to see me, you will find it."

My bus was approaching, and I was glad to have an excuse to walk away. As soon as I hopped on the bus and was headed for the next stop, Frank slipped out of my mind completely. I did not think of him again until he walked into the restaurant later that night dressed in black slacks, a bright red shirt, and a black fedora. He sat next to me, and I just smiled and let him buy me two Amarula drinks. A cream liqueur made from the fruit of a South African marula tree. It was my favorite. I thought of it as the Baileys of South Africa.

We watched poet after poet get up into the spotlight of the dimly lit room and share their story. One light-skinned woman got up and performed a poem about being Coloured and the implications and identity crisis that comes along with being in between. In the US, her light skin and kinky hair would have made her Black. Race and skin color were even more complicated here than in the US. The stratification was more pronounced.

The show was over around 11:00 p.m., and Frank and I looked at each other, wide-eyed, not knowing what to do next. He'd endeared himself to me by showing up. Since we did not get a chance to talk during the performances, I suggested we walk to the strip on Long Street to find a place to chat. We found a café and grabbed two seats at the counter.

"So, tell me about yourself, Mr. Frank," I said. "How is it that you came to the beaches of Cape Town?"

"God brought me here and gave me the idea to do art, and my faith sustains me." He looked me in the eye intently. I could tell that this was not a cliché for him, that he really meant it. His passion was cute. I leaned in, wide-eyed and interested.

Frank was from Zimbabwe, or "Zim," as he called it. He had come to South Africa a few years earlier because of the political and economic turmoil his country was experiencing. His entire family, except his brother, were still there, and Frank went back every few months to renew his visa. He began making street art when he got to Cape Town to sustain himself. He talked about his profound experience with church and God, how his life had been turned around. Now he attended church, and the people there acted as his family.

His faith was so real and raw that it took me a minute to speak when he asked me about my relationship with God. Most of the time, I was the one asking questions and getting the details of people's lives. But here was a chance to reveal mine, so I told him my story.

I didn't grow up in church, though faith showed up in grace before meals and my praying maternal grandmother, Anne. I became a Christian in college. After attending a bunch of Sunday services to watch my friends sing in Georgetown University's gospel choir, I started studying the Bible and praying with them.

I took a breath and sipped my decaffeinated coffee.

During my senior year, my faith became my own. I started working out and reading scripture daily—shaping my inner and outer life in preparation for adulthood. The following year, full of the joy of a more personal connection to God, I even considered seminary. I signed up for a year-long Christian leadership program in Charlottesville to discern my next steps in ministry and discovered community development. That led me to graduate school in urban planning at the University of Virginia, then to work in the city's planning department. Homes, churches, and friendships seemed to appear just when I needed them. I've always seen that as God—nudging me forward, making a way.

Frank was a good listener, which made me even more drawn to him in that moment. "This is how The Poetic Justice World Tour came to be," I went on. "An opportunity presented itself in the form of an idea, and I ran with it."

Frank looked at me mesmerized, like he was falling for me. I liked the way he looked at me and thought he was attractive, but was growing tired. I took the last sip of decaf and placed it on the counter with a thump.

"Okay, Frank, it's getting late and way past my bedtime. How about we call it a night."

To get a break from the volunteer house, I was staying in Cape Town for one night at a hostel a few blocks away from Long Street. We walked slowly in silence. When we arrived at my hostel door, we stood facing one another.

"Where do you live? The train has stopped running—how will you get home?" I said.

"About thirty minutes away. I will call a cab or have a friend come and get me."

"Really, can you afford that?" I assumed he was a starving artist.

"Don't worry about it. I—"

He was mid-sentence when I realized I wanted to kiss him. I said, "Stop talking," and pulled him toward me. We fell right in sync. A few guys walked by, eyeing us, but I really didn't care what they thought.

Frank pulled back. “Can I come up?”

I looked up at the window above us. I had the room to myself, but I wasn’t ready to throw caution to the wind. I thought of all the bad ways this could end. Reality set in. I thought about the high prevalence of HIV/AIDS in South Africa. Here I was, out with a guy I’d just met.

“No, I can’t have guests at my hostel, and I don’t think that is a good idea.”

His shoulders sank.

I gave him a peck on the lips. He asked me what I was doing each day that week.

“I work until five, and the last train out of Muizenberg to here is at four. If I left then, I wouldn’t be able to get back,” I said, slightly irritated. I hated being pressured.

Instead, I suggested he come with me the following Sunday to see the penguins near Simon’s Town, a popular tourist attraction I had yet to visit. I put his number into the new, prepaid cell phone I’d bought when I got to South Africa and went upstairs to my room.

I peeked out the window and saw Frank looking up in anticipation. His bright eyes lit the dark street, along with that red shirt he had on. We waved. He sent me a good night text message as soon as I moved away from the window. I shook my head. He had that look in his eye, the one that said he was enamored. *Oh gosh*, I thought. It seemed that guys kept falling for me, but I didn’t feel the same. I was happy to have a romantic rendezvous abroad, brief and beautiful, but that was the extent of my hopes. Maybe I was too practical to think things could ever go beyond that.

After a week of getting sentimental texts from Frank, we decided to go to Simon’s Town on Sunday afternoon to see the penguins. I was excited. I had not known that penguins lived anywhere other than places that were really cold. I loved traveling for that very reason. What you think you know is challenged, and a new world of possibilities and realities become present to you. I wanted to experience the penguins with someone, and my fellow volunteers were loud, boisterous, and full of drama. Although I welcomed any opportunity to connect with someone who wasn't a Westerner, I was a bit unnerved by Frank's profession of love. I just wanted to hang.

I met Frank at the Muizenberg train station at 1:00 p.m. He hopped off with a bit of a leap as soon as he saw me. He wore a bright white smile, sunglasses, and another one of his signature fedora hats—this one brown. He gave me a hug and tried to give me a kiss, but I turned my head away so that his lips landed on my cheek. My excitement from the other night had worn off. Frank seemed unfazed, and we waited for the next train and then got on a bus to the penguin stop.

Having been to the market earlier that morning, I mentioned that here and in Kenya, the merchants inflated their prices for white customers, and I got vastly different prices than my white counterparts. I wondered what his practice was. "Frank, do you charge white people more than your Black customers?"

"Oh yes!" he said proudly. "It is payback for colonialism, for them taking so much from Africa. If they come here to be tourists, they have money, they can pay."

"I figured you would say something like that." I understood his reasoning. If whites failed to bargain and could pay, why not? Even inflated prices were nothing to them and could mean so much to somebody like Frank.

"It seems unfair, but I guess life isn't fair," I said, "and the pillage of African countries has certainly not been fair."

"Yes, life in Africa is not so fair. I'm giving white people the opportunity to share in the unfairness."

We chuckled and then fell silent, looking out of the bus

window, watching the scenery go by. Frank put his arm around me and moved in a little closer. He was staring at me, and I didn't want to make eye contact and see that starry look in his eyes. I liked him okay, but didn't feel the same intensity he did. So I just looked out the window.

When we reached our stop, we had to walk quite a distance to see the penguins. Frank kept trying to hold my hand or put his arm around me, but I sidestepped each attempt, feeling smothered. He talked endlessly about "us," about him moving to the US, and how I was the answer to his prayers. The walk stretched long, following signs marked PENGUINS AHEAD. At one point, we rested on a bench near some rocks. I could feel his gaze, then he said, "Kiss me, please." He removed his glasses, repeating, "Please."

I kissed him—not out of desire, but to shut him up. Rising quickly, I said, "Now let's go see some penguins," and walked on.

When we reached the penguins, my mood shifted. About thirty black-and-white birds waddled atop enormous rocks along the turquoise ocean. The scene felt like a private sanctuary. We took pictures, and I crouched to get closer to a penguin, noticing how tight my pants had gotten during my four months of travel—thanks, in part, to the chocolate bars I'd been indulging in during my chaotic South African volunteer placement. This moment with the penguins felt like an oasis in the midst of the noise and disorder.

On the walk to the station, Frank started talking about us building a future together. I couldn't believe all this after only two dates. "How many children do you want?" he asked eagerly, as if marriage was inevitable.

Annoyed, I finally said, "Frank, there's not going to be a relationship after this. We can be Facebook friends, but that's it. I've enjoyed my time with you, but I'm leaving soon for a solo trip along the Garden Route and then on to Johannesburg."

"I'll come with you," he offered.

"No, I'm going alone. This ends here."

When the train stopped at Muizenberg, I stood. "Let's say goodbye here," I said. We shared a short hug before he squeezed me tightly and said, "I love you."

I replied, "Thank you," and walked away without looking back at his sad face.

As I strolled along the beach, kicking sand and listening to the waves, I felt conflicted. Frank's intensity had hijacked our day, but part of me wished I liked him more. A romance could have been nice, but it all felt too much, too fast.

During the lovely nine-day solo tour of the Garden Route that followed, I couldn't help but wonder if spending my thirtieth birthday in Cape Town with Frank would have been better. He would have celebrated with me. But then again, maybe his intensity would have driven me crazy. I'll never know. In the end, I chose to explore South Africa's beautiful landscape alone—to be true to myself in solitude rather than accept the comfort of company that didn't quite fit.

COLOR LINES

I'd planned to celebrate my thirtieth birthday the entire month of November with treats and small splurges. At the start of the month, I went wine tasting with Silvana, a Swiss volunteer who lived in another volunteer house. She was close to my age, wore glasses, and had shoulder-length wavy brown hair. We had planned our trip a few days before, and a white van picked us up early in the morning.

I was happy to be out of the dusty clothes I wore daily to put on something nice, the same red shirt I had worn wine tasting in Tuscany. I was quiet and mostly looked out the window as we rode through the Stellenbosch and Franschhoek wine regions—mountains rising above pastoral valleys against a bright blue sky. In Stellenbosch, the town's oak-shaded streets were lined with cafés, boutiques, and art galleries. For a moment, one could forget about the townships; this was another world of fine wines, stunning views, and luxury. Everyone on this side of the landscape was white. White families were out for a day of leisure. I thoroughly enjoyed the day, but I couldn't shake the reality that I was one of the only Black people I saw enjoying this—the reality that a world existed that was the opposite of this world. Unfortunately, both at home and abroad, I knew too well how it felt to go back and forth across the color line and feel caught between worlds that were still separate and unequal.

In the second grade, I was bused from my Black neighborhood in Jamaica, Queens, to a predominantly white elementary school in Woodhaven. Even then, somehow the connotation was that white was "better." Not that I thought that; it seemed to be apparent in the differences. I knew I was an outsider. I saw it when I got my class picture that year, and I was the only Black child there. Everyone was smiling but me.

Years later, I took the Greyhound bus from my majority Black and Latino, working-class community in Hempstead, Long Island, to the wealthy white area of Georgetown in Washington, DC, and the well-regarded majority white institution of Georgetown University. Georgetown was welcoming to Black students, and I existed happily in my all-Black enclave of friends. Overall, I had an outstanding experience. Yet in this supportive environment, during my junior year the president of the Black Student Alliance received hate mail, and a good friend found *nigger* written on his door. Even welcoming and inclusive places couldn't shield us entirely from the realities of the world around us.

Since college, I'd had one foot in a world that was all Black and another in a world that was all white. I volunteered in an all-Black and disinvested area in southeast DC, tutoring Black children who looked like me. I returned to learn in a largely white environment, taught mostly by white professors from books written mostly by white authors (except in my African-American Studies or English classes). I learned to go back and forth between these two dichotomies, to be comfortable with being uncomfortable. My old world was predominately Black and working class, trying to make ends meet; my new world was educated, upper middle class, and white, with generations of wealth, power, and education.

Charlottesville, Virginia, was the whitest place I had ever lived—nearly 70 percent white. In 2003, I'd gone to a fairly white Presbyterian church there, both politically and religiously conservative, as part of a one-year leadership program I participated in. I was the only Black person. I lived with a host family in a gated community. I was out of my element, coming from a Black Baptist background, a Democrat from a single-parent household. I felt off, out of it, a grain of pepper in a saltshaker. My host mom, while loving and kind, thought racism was a thing of the past. It was also an election year, and everything felt more polarized. I could feel the tension whenever John Kerry came on television. *How did I get here?* I wondered.

During that fellowship year, we volunteered in a lower-wealth, majority African-American side of town and tutored children in a low-income housing community. Again, I was one of few Black people volunteering to serve Black kids. Growing up, my life had been much like these kids' lives, and I identified more with them than my fellow volunteers. It was an uncomfortable year. I almost left.

I stayed because I believed it must be possible for people on the other side of race, economics, and politics to build relationships, to get along. Our faith brought us together, even though I believed rather differently than the white parishioners did. I felt stifled at a church that did not respond to the preacher with amens, didn't stand and clap and sing with enthusiasm and emotion. However, I began to love people who were different from me, and I even found our commonalities.

I left that church and went to a Black church for a while, one that was more prosperity preaching. But I didn't feel connected with them either, even though everyone was Black. Right before I left for my around-the-world trip, I found a majority white church that was accessible and freeing. I could be myself and didn't have all of these hoops to jump through to be welcomed. In some ways, that felt like home, but being the one Black person in the midst of an all-white environment was always unsettling.

In the US, I lived in Black and white. South Africa reminded me of my in-betweenness and my separate worlds. Though it was beautiful, South Africa itself didn't really sit right with me. It reminded me too much of home, and there, too, I struggled to find my place.

The same day I met Frank at the beach, I had gone to the District Six Museum, which highlighted an area in downtown Cape Town that had been multiethnic in the early to mid-1900s. After the many apartheid laws were enacted, sixty thousand people were forced out of their homes and into townships on the outskirts. It reminded me of the same story in the US— urban renewal razed Black neighborhoods, with many families ending up in public housing. Similar story, different country: Black people displaced to "ghettos" and townships.

The dichotomy of race and privilege in South Africa was wearing on me, especially because I didn't really fit into either place. My skin color placed me on one side, but my access to money and middle-class status, my privilege, placed me on another. I felt constantly caught between worlds—between wealth and struggle, between Black and white.

Other than Naomi and Frank, the only other solid connection I made was Wanda, an American who had lived in South Africa for several years. She was a friend of one of my church elders. Wanda was an older Black woman with deep brown skin, her hair short but always curled. She wore solid-colored pantsuits.

One day, I made my way to Wanda's house by train; she lived in Fish Hoek, not far from Muizenberg. She picked me up from the station. It was good to see someone from the US, someone Black. She sat me down in her living room and made me a cup of tea.

"So how are you liking South Africa?"

"Love the scenery, love Cape Town. It's beautiful. I live by the beach, which is amazing. The racial segregation is too much for me, though. Too close to home."

She leaned back, took a sip of her own tea, then placed it on a side table. "Yes, that is something I will never get used to."

Wanda invited me to her church the next day. It was right around the corner from the volunteer house. It may have been the only multicultural space I experienced in South Africa, maybe in most of the world. It was truly mixed. Finding a place where the color line wasn't so pronounced was refreshing. There was not a clear majority or minority. It was a breath of fresh air not to have to stand on one side or the other for a few hours.

I left the volunteer house in early November, a week early, so I could celebrate my thirtieth birthday in peace. I traipsed along the Garden Route and spent a few days in the Johannesburg area. The entire time, I kept tripping and falling over the color line.

The Garden Route in South Africa is a string of beaches and vacation areas along the coast north of Cape Town. I was in Mossel Bay for my birthday, where I ate ostrich and treated myself to a massage and a chocolate body wrap. I was the only Black person taking part in these services. At dinner, I conversed with the Black server for company.

"You are not from here," he said.

I wasn't sure how he knew. Perhaps a Black woman eating alone wasn't commonplace. Everywhere I'd gone so far, I was the only Black traveler doing touristy stuff amidst white vacationers. All the other Black people were service workers.

After Mossel Bay, I went to the Knysna Heads, the meeting place of two land bodies. In between them was some pretty rough water. I enjoyed the nice waterfront and took a sunset cruise around the lagoon. It was exquisite, but again, all white.

Earlier that morning, I visited a township less than a mile from the town of Knysna. One mile up the hill, tucked away from the vacationers, was a completely different world. The township was home to Black South Africans, many living in substandard housing and struggling with poverty. A small boy took my hand while I was walking. He wore a yellow shirt streaked with dirt. He had no shoes. He led me past a spigot in the center of the township, where women waited with blue, green, and yellow pails for water.

My head was spinning with the dichotomies of that day. Though I tried to be present for it all, the beauty and all the touristy things, I was, however, getting a bit numb from the reality of all of the juxtapositions. I moved daily between awe, excitement, weariness, and being overwhelmed.

W. E. B. Du Bois said that the problem of the twentieth century was that of the color line, and it was splitting me in two each day. Being in South Africa and reflecting on the issues at home made it more clear how much change is still needed. The color line persists in the twenty-first century, not just in the US, but internationally.

During my stay in Johannesburg, I visited Constitution Hill, the Apartheid Museum, and Soweto, the country's largest and most well-known township, home to 1.3 million residents at the time. Constitution Hill was my favorite—a redemptive space where South Africa's Constitutional Court now sits. Cases of constitutionality and human rights are heard there, on the same grounds where a notorious jail once held Mandela, Gandhi, and countless others under appalling conditions. The site that once embodied violation now safeguards dignity. Learning this history reminded me that even the most painful places can be transformed into spaces of justice, healing, and hope. It was a salve for my racial wounds, a flicker of hope in the heaviness.

In Soweto, I was given a personal tour by Mimi and Sipho, friends of a friend. Their company was a welcome reprieve from traveling alone, a chance to touch and taste the vibrancy of local life and cuisine. We shared plates of *chakalaka*—a spicy vegetable dish of onions, tomatoes, peppers, carrots, and beans—alongside pap, the grits-like staple of South Africa. After lunch, we stood outside the modest homes of Nelson Mandela and Desmond Tutu, neighbors in legacy, before walking through the sobering Hector Pieterson Museum. Hector was the first child killed in the 1976 student uprising, when thousands of youth poured into the streets to resist apartheid and were met with gunfire. It was a difficult history to take in, and I was grateful to have local guides to walk me through it. Though only a day, my time with them gave me the cultural connection I had been craving. They filled my belly and my soul.

Later that week, I stayed with another friend of a friend, Martin, his wife, and their children outside Pretoria. They were white South Africans. Over poetry, wine, and long conversations, I met other white South Africans who seemed genuinely hopeful for their country's progress, yet unsure of their place in it. They welcomed me warmly, yet the fences—brick, barbed wired, and often electrified—that towered around their neighborhood and homes told another story: the unhealed wounds of inequality, the deep divisions still etched into the landscape. Even in hospitality, I felt the haunting weight of history, of inequity. The fall of Apartheid still fresh, reconciliation still unfolding.

The movement between poverty and privilege, between Black, Coloured, and white communities, was dizzying. South Africa's natural beauty is undeniable, but its racial complexity pressed heavily on my spirit. The day before I was scheduled to leave, I lamented that I was too weary and overwhelmed to cowrite a "Where I'm From" poem with anyone there. But, when I pulled out my marble journal with SPOKEN SOUL glued to the front, I remembered Lebo, the South African woman I wrote a poem with at English L'Abri. I smiled. God had provided. Though gratitude lightened my load, I wished she was there to process with. Our conversation felt unfinished. My emotions toward my experience, conflicting.

South Africa left me with this: Race is heavy. In the midst of reckoning, there can be beauty, redemption, even hospitality, but I didn't expect resolution. All I could do was move through the heaviness, set it down when I could, and keep living. There was nowhere on earth to completely escape racism, colonialism, or white supremacy. Later, I would make racial equity the centerpiece of my professional life and learn that reckoning with racism is lifelong work. In that moment, though, I simply held on to hope, gathered what South Africa had taught me, and prepared myself for whatever India would bring.

ASIA

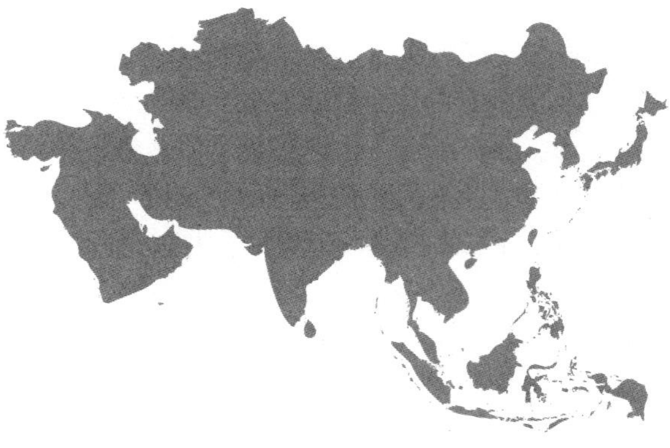

12

INDIA: INCREDIBLE INDIA!?!

Indira Gandhi International Airport lacked clear directional signs, so I clung to the directions I'd been sent by email from the volunteer placement agency like a lifeline. At the pickup area, no one was waiting for me—just a few faux leather chairs and payphones by the sliding doors. All I had was a name—Arun, the India volunteer program contact—and a number. I called the number, but the phone rang endlessly, my hope draining with each unanswered call. *Not this again.* I thought back to that phone booth in England and began to panic. After several attempts, a voice finally answered. I told him who I was and asked when he would be there to get me.

"Oh, you're arriving today?" Arun said, surprised. "I wasn't expecting you until tomorrow." Relief washed over me. I was not going to have to navigate Delhi alone. I didn't even have a guidebook. "I'll be there in twenty minutes," he added.

An hour later, Arun appeared, out of breath. He was short, with a full head of black hair parted down the middle. "Sorry I forgot, and sorry for being late. I got pulled over for speeding and had to bribe the police," he said, shaking his head. I raised an eyebrow but said nothing. That was a reason for being late I hadn't heard before.

We sped through Delhi's busy streets in his small white car, weaving through traffic and honking constantly. INCREDIBLE INDIA signs flashed by, but I wasn't convinced—yet. We pulled up to a stone-colored high-rise, and he led me to an apartment with bare tan walls, three bedrooms, and a sparse living room that opened into the kitchen. The window overlooked a gritty mix of buildings under construction and new concrete high-rises.

Two young white women, Jess and Amy, were already there. Jess was a Canadian volunteer, short with brown hair, and Amy was a dark-haired American. We had paid extra for an orientation week of Hindi lessons, Delhi tours, and a trip to the Taj Mahal. A thin young Indian girl served us meals. Her hot pink sari, gold earrings, and long braid were the same every day. She worked silently, placing food in front of us on a silver plate and sat off to the side, sheepish and detached. Her presence made me deeply uncomfortable. She felt like a servant. *Is this child labor*? I wondered.

That first day, and every day thereafter, our food was laid out on a sheet in the middle of the living area, and we had a lunch of chapati and curried cauliflower. After lunch, we jumped right into our orientation to India (history, customs, religion, food) and then learned some Hindi greetings. Arun paced and said words in English and Hindi, and we repeated them in Hindi.

"Hello is namaste," he said as he paced. "See you later is *phir milenge*. How are you is *aap kaise hain*."

This is going to be a long week, I thought. But I kept repeating after him.

On the second day, during a break, I ventured out with the two other women to explore central Delhi. Walking through the crowded streets—me, a Black woman, and two white women—felt disorienting amidst the sea of Indian men. A young girl, no older than seven, appeared, her frail frame draped in a frayed, pale-pink dress. Dirt smudged her face and her hair was disheveled.

"Please, please," she pleaded, her hands mimicking eating. Her persistence intensified as we tried to escape her. Arun had warned against giving money to begging children, but guilt tugged at me.

The clanging of her "please, please" followed us incessantly for over five blocks.

Finally, I stopped, turned to her, and placed a few rupees in her hand. She looked at the coins, then back at me with drooping eyes and held out her hand again. I added more rupees and walked away, conflicted. My thoughts lingered on the girl and my uneasy role in her world. Was I enabling exploitation, or was ignoring her denying her humanity?

As she departed, the cacophony of Delhi surged—honking horns, a mix of buses, rickshaws, cows, and colorful saris weaving through traffic. It took nearly ten minutes to cross the four-lane road to the train station as we navigated a carousel of vehicles and pedestrians.

The loud whirlwind of activity outside contrasted sharply with the quiet, sleek interior of the new train station. Jess guided us as we reviewed a system-wide map. When the train arrived, the first car was nearly empty, while the last seven were crammed with men. Women in uniforms patrolled with sticks, shoving men back as they tried to board. We entered the women-only car, settling among a few women and children.

"Whoa," we said in unison, struck by the stark contrast. Seeing the crowded men's car, I exhaled, relieved to avoid any potential groping or staring. I presumed that was the reason behind the women's-only car after seeing so many men and few women on the streets. After five months of feeling the fragility of being a woman, this car felt like a triumph—an acknowledgment of women's needs and a rare moment of safety, freedom, and escape from the vigilance required of a woman traveling alone.

Back outside the station, we navigated a bustling roundabout lined with shops. A nice purse vendor directed us north when we asked about a mall. Moments later, a teenage boy approached, eager to help. "Come, come! You can buy what you need this way," he said, leading us to a red building and down into a basement of small shops. Definitely not a mall. Thankfully, it was just a ploy to lead us to some vendors, not anything more sinister.

"This could have been so much worse," I said, rolling my eyes.

For the next three days we did our lessons in the morning, had lunch, and went on adventures throughout the city with our hired taxi driver. Everywhere we went, we were stared at and followed. When we visited the Red Fort, a historic fort and palace in Old Delhi, a group of eight uniformed boys, with backpacks and blue-and-white checkered shirts, ran up to us as we were sitting in the grass. They giggled as they snapped pictures of us with their phones and even sat next to us and put their arms around us without permission. We left, and they ran behind us until I turned around with my hand stretched out in front of me and yelled, "Stop! Leave us alone." They turned around and left.

At Gandhi's Eternal Flame site, three Indian men asked if they could take a picture with me. I obliged, but being a spectacle was exhausting. I was glad to have the shelter of the apartment at the end of those days. India was a sensory explosion, and I was desperate for an escape. Everything was so alive, so fragrant—the food spicy and aromatic, with curries and other colorful sauces; the streets crowded by a diversity of sounds and people; the markets full of colorful bags, fabrics, toys, and trinkets; women in saris of every color of the rainbow, bright and flowing.

Books were a way to endure this endless bombardment. In the evenings, I clung to the second novel in Stieg Larsson's series, *The Girl Who Played with Fire*. When we arrived back at the apartment, I went straight to my room and curled up with my book under the buzz of the dim yellow light.

For our weekend trip to the Taj Mahal, I expected an official tour guide. Who we actually got was a short, balding driver with a potbelly who swooped Amy and I up at four in the morning and drove us to Agra on a frenzied, four-hour racecar drive. On the way, we saw a couple of smashed cars in the night, reminding us of our possible destiny. I sat hunched in the back seat with my hand over my eyes, bracing myself for the extended roller coaster ride.

When we arrived, the first thing I saw was an elephant strolling down the road and a monkey wearing a tutu and lipstick. We stood before the entrance and the iconic cream marble domes of the Taj Mahal came into view under a cloudless sky. Crowds swarmed ahead, women's vibrant saris contrasting with the tan tunics of the men.

Inside, an empty reflecting pool stretched toward the mausoleum while lines of visitors snaked around the platform. We took turns snapping pictures near the pool. I wore a T-shirt with my late brother-in-law's face on it, a way of taking him to the world's wonders he never got to see. Meanwhile, others snapped pictures of me, phones lowered awkwardly to their waists in futile attempts at stealth. I'd catch their eyes, give a tight-lipped smile, and move on.

The Taj Mahal looked like the postcards, but up close, the intricate details in the marble—the inlaid vines and jeweled flowers—were mesmerizing. Built over twenty-two years, it houses the remains of Mumtaz Mahal, who died in childbirth, and later her husband, Emperor Shah Jahan. It was a monument to love and death, two of life's deepest experiences. I wondered if anyone still loved with such intensity, enough to create something so enduring and extravagant. Would I ever love someone with that kind of abandon? I wasn't sure, but I hoped that I might—though, given my past, I wasn't convinced.

The faces of the men I had dated through the years flashed across my mind. First was my high school boyfriend's. I remembered our last conversation the summer after my senior year of college. I paced my mother's basement, a gray cordless phone in hand. The conversation got more and more heated with each step.

He wanted us to be together, to have more than random hookups when I came home from college. I wasn't interested. He asked, "Why won't you let me get close to you?" I knew he was right in holding my feet to the fire, but after being pressed to answer, the truth flew out before I could catch it. "I don't really like you like that," I said, harsher than he deserved. I stopped pacing. It was out there, and I couldn't take it back. That was the truest thing I could say then. I wasn't ready to give my heart to anyone, or maybe just not to him. We never spoke again.

I had a few crushes in college, but the people I liked never liked me, and the people who liked me, I never liked. One crush on a friend ended with a kiss but ruined our friendship. He didn't feel the same way and was coupled soon after. We stopped being friends. Each time we passed each other on campus, my heart sank, heartbroken that our friendship was over.

In my junior year, I met a guy on a dating site who lived in the DC area. He was tall, light brown, and heavyset. My friends affectionately called him Internet Guy. We went on wonderful dates all around the metro area—dinner, long drives, walks in the parks, the works. I liked him a lot but wasn't attracted to him beyond friendship. After over a year of trying to court me, he moved on and dated someone else. I didn't blame him.

After college, I dated another guy who wanted to get serious too soon. I was twenty-five and didn't want to be serious after dating for a few weeks, so I broke it off. He had made me pie, recited poetry, and taken me on long walks. He had done the same things with several of my friends, I would later learn.

My instincts always led me the right way, and I didn't regret these endings, but they chipped away at any confidence that I would find love. This was coupled with the fact that, more than love or marriage, I always wanted to be my own, not to belong to another person or be an accessory to someone else's future and dreams. I was too wrapped up in my life. Being free to pursue my purpose, my first love, was my priority; relationships with men were secondary. Also, having very few (if any) models of good relationships growing up didn't give me much confidence that being in a relationship would improve my life. Singleness felt inevitable and indefinite.

I blinked back tears at the Taj Mahal, not at its beauty, but at being faced with the depth of my uncertainty about finding love.

I hadn't found lasting romantic love, but love was always present in my life. My mother's love for me felt like a double portion. She always told us she loved us, always hugged and kissed us whenever she got a chance. Maybe she was making up for my father, or maybe she just wanted us to know we were loved. Although she had disappointed me in some areas, I believed she tried to do her best.

"You can do whatever you want," she'd say. "Don't be like me. Get your education. Boys and babies will be there when you finish."

I took that advice to heart. My mother's love and the care and provision of my extended family (a maternal grandmother who prayed for us, a paternal grandmother, aunts and grandfather who stepped in for my father) were my solid places, my support for gaining success. They held me up, helping me to believe in myself and feel confident in my ability to carry out my dreams. The mistakes I didn't want to make propelled me forward to try to build a better life for myself.

An intrusive camera flash awakened me from my daydream, and I moved up a few steps in the long line that mirrored the maze-like lines at amusement parks. Looking at all of the families, I wished that I could have come here with my loved ones. This trip had a cost: I had to do it alone. As Amy and I inched closer to the entrance, the details of the building got clearer, and suddenly, instead of wishing for something that was not going to be, I was simply grateful for what was: I was about to enter the Taj Mahal. This was just one of many thresholds I would cross alone, and I did so with love, in honor of the emperor who had built it out of great love.

Later that week, Jess and I moved to Dr. Bhanu's house, a one-story women's dormitory near the university, joining Allison, a tall, heavyset Canadian with dirty-blonde hair. We shared a small, creaky room with twin metal-frame beds and a tiny bathroom off to the side. At night, I zipped myself into my sleeping bag to keep out the mice that scurried around our beds. One evening, while Skyping with my mom in the backyard, I saw what I thought was a small being scaling the fence. My mother was commenting on how much better my voice sounded since I'd left South Africa—lighter, happier. Before I could respond, the person came closer, and I realized it was a monkey. I said, "Mom, let me call you back. There is a monkey coming toward me." I bolted inside and told the others. Allison, unfazed, shrugged and said, "This is India!" before returning to her book.

India continued to surprise me. After a week of exploring, I felt ready to dive into my volunteer placement: a children's home on the outskirts of Delhi.

BE LIKE LITTLE CHILDREN

Sahil swept briskly—harshly, even—at the dusty cement floor in the center of the courtyard. The spot he swept was surrounded by a few rooms for sleeping, two workrooms for sewing, a small kitchen, a squat toilet room, and a spigot. I sat outside the kitchen, watching him, listening to the honking and zooming car sounds coming from outside the white cement wall surrounding the children's home. The wall was lined with round brown cow-dung patties the size of large pancakes. I waited at a small wooden table next to the kitchen while Amir, the ever-smiling cook who always wore a pink hoodie, was making chai by boiling some brown bits of seasoning with milk that came from a bag. The rest of the children were at school.

This four-year-old boy was sweeping intensely, mimicking the movements of the women who had done the same in his presence at the Anmol Children's Home in an area about an hour outside Delhi. He was only a few feet tall, with a curved scar from his hairline to his eyebrow. His brows were furrowed as he swept. He'd been abandoned at the Delhi train station by his mother; no one at the home was sure when. No one was sure how he got the scar, if it was an accident or if someone had intentionally hurt him. The founder of the children's home, Ravi, had found Sahil eating out of the trash. Now he lived at the home that housed about ten boys and two girls. The older boys learned how to make bags from scraps of clothing to help support the home. I supposed Sahil's violent sweeping was indicative of his being stuck in survival mode. He was harsher and harder than the other children. During the few weeks that I volunteered there, I watched daily as he hit and snatched.

He saw me watching him sweep, dropped the broom, and came toward me, yelling, "Didi, Didi!" This was what everyone called me—"Didi, as in sister," they told me. They yelled Didi as if it were my name, and I responded to this little term of endearment with joy.

Sahil ran over to me like a roadrunner and joined his hands in a prayerlike fashion, fingers pointing toward my chest. "Didi, Didi!" he yelled. He spoke little English, but he knew this game, and he knew how to get my attention. I met his fingertips with mine and moved them as he tried to slap mine. I moved quickly, as he hit hard. After several rounds of catching his small hands as he tried to outmaneuver me, I allowed him to catch mine. It was a hard "clap." It didn't hurt; it was just a bit rough. Life had roughened him a little too much by four. I allowed him to catch my hands again, another "clap," and this time there was a little sting. I sat him on my lap despite his resistance and began to softly rub his face, murmuring, "Nice, nice. Nice, nice." I reached for his hand to let him rub my face, but he beat me to it and landed more of a smack. "No," I said softly and took his hand, saying, "Nice, nice," guiding him to rub my face with the same measure. He got it. He began to gently rub my face and say, "Nice, nice."

Amir came out of the kitchen and put a cup of chai on the table next to me. I settled Sahil on my right leg and threw his legs across my lap. He put his head on my shoulder, and we sat for a minute. We went back and forth, rubbing each other's faces gently. I prayed he wouldn't haul off and slap me or jump up and knock over my chai. Once he got settled into my arms, dozing, I took a sip and looked around at the stack of cow-dung patties near the wall, at the dusty floor in the center, and at the spigot we pumped to receive water. "Didi," Sahil whispered. He shook his head slowly, as if trying to fight off the impending sleep. I sipped more chai and peered up at the buildings being constructed in the distance, listening to the rickshaws zooming by. Sahil was falling asleep, and I was falling in love with this rush of life swirling around me. The warmth of his body in my lap matched that of my heart, and I thought for the first time in my life, *I could be a mother*.

I had never really thought about children while in my twenties. So many people I knew growing up were single mothers and were strong, wonderful women, but I did not want to be a single mom. Marriage was never on my mind much either. I hadn't really seen a marriage that worked well, and long-term relationships—a prerequisite to marriage—apparently weren't my thing. I had never found anyone I liked enough. On top of that, I wasn't really the kid-loving type. They were cute, but I loved giving them back to their parents, and I loved my independence. The image of myself as a nurturer and a caretaker wasn't solidified in my imagination or in the future vision of myself. I saw myself as strong, but holding Sahil in my arms let me know that it was also okay to be soft.

My mornings were slow. I would take a "shower" in the dark, closet-sized room with a spigot next to our volunteer apartment. I'd walk a few blocks on dirt roads, where I would often run into cows, to get my morning samosas from a food stand. The price changed daily and ranged from one to three rupees. Sometimes I would haggle with the attendant, a young guy who was nineteen at best. Other days I would chalk the price change up to TII—This Is India—meaning anything could happen. Then it was off to the Internet café next door to the food stand, where I would check my email and post almost-daily updates and photos on my blog. At 9:00 a.m., the rickshaw would arrive to take us to the children's home.

Before 2:00 p.m., when the kids arrived from school, the center was quiet. Between 10:00 a.m. and 1:00 p.m., the volunteers walked three-quarters of a mile down an unpaved road full of lumps and bumps and potholes to Kamala's house to help her make handbags out of old newspaper. This was her business—the business of quite a few women in this area. They earned a few cents from each bag they crafted out of newspaper, and the bags were then sold overseas. I remember sitting on the cement floor one day and seeing President Obama's face on one of the newspapers. He had visited recently. "Obama!" Kamala said with a smile. Obama was a hit globally.

Kamala was in her mid-thirties. She always wore a pink sari and a gold nose ring. She lived in a square cement apartment off an alley. While I and the other volunteers, Claire and Denali, hammered out bags on the floor of her living room, she made us tea, and we ate cookies. One day, around morning teatime, a crowd of five girls gathered in the doorway, giggling and pointing. All of us were anomalies: two white women and a Black woman in the middle of a fairly exurban area. One of the girls came up to me, her nose almost touching mine. She looked intently at my face and hair. When I said, "Hello," she just kept staring, and after a minute too long, I moved away. I got used to the stares, but I always felt more comfortable behind the walls of the children's home, which felt like being at home with family. No one there seemed to really notice or mention too often that I was Black. Everyone was intrigued by my hair though.

Thin and short, with a loose black ponytail, Sanya looked more like eight than twelve. She was smart, and she was my favorite, probably because she spoke English better than any of the other kids there. She was the oldest of only two little girls at the home, which primarily housed boys. Sanya and her little sister Dali and baby brother Raj were not orphans. They were the children of Maya and Ravi, who'd helped start the center and still helped run it. Though they often stayed at the children's home, the family's house was next to the two-room volunteer quarters a few miles away. Each day, five volunteers took a rickshaw to the children's home, where most of us spent our time as caretakers and entertainers. In my case, the young ones were entertained by my hair.

"Is it real?" Sanya said to me one day.

I looked at her strangely. We were sitting on a bench in the courtyard not too long after she had arrived from school.

"Is it real, your hair? Is it real?" she repeated.

I chuckled. "Yes, it is real."

"How do you get it like that, Didi?"

I took one of my longest locs and rolled it through the palms of both my hands, showing her how I twisted them.

She breathed out an airy, "Ohhhhhh," her mouth open.

"Can I touch it?" she asked, coming closer. Under normal circumstances I might have been offended or annoyed, but their curiosity was innocent. This fascination with touching my hair was pervasive both at home and abroad. I always thought, *What am I, a petting zoo?* But Sanya was twelve, sweet, and my absolute favorite.

"Sure, Sanya."

"It's soft," she said, as if surprised. "I like it. Can you do my hair like that?"

"You could, but your hair is a lot straighter than mine. It wouldn't look the same," I replied.

"Hmm," she said and did what I thought of as the Indian nod—moving her head from side to side in a wobble, like a bobble head.

"Do you want to watch me jump rope, Didi?" she said abruptly, apparently done with the matter of our hair.

"Of course I do."

And so, we moved into our daily routine of Sanya jumping rope and me counting the turns until she messed up. I counted, and she sang a song she was learning at school: "Roundabout and roundabout and roundabout we go. Around the merry roundabout we are riding high and low. Our prancing horses leap and bound and gallop high above the ground and roundabout and roundabout and roundabout we go."

"Sixty-seven," I said as she tripped on the rope. I'd heard the song over twenty times by then, but we started all over again—jumping, singing, and counting. We both had fun. Sanya, vibrant and talkative; me, attentive and amused. It was here that I learned what presence and play were all about. I was not sure what I really had to offer this home but my presence. The children just wanted my attention. Yes, I helped cook and clean, I helped them with their homework and English, but mainly we laughed, sang, and danced. I realized, as I watched and counted, that a piece of me—in all of my busyness, ambition, and diligence—had forgotten how to play. I had forgotten how it felt to be carefree and just have fun.

One afternoon, right in the middle of homework time, what must have been a hit song came on the radio. All of the children from four to sixteen got up, leaving their pens, paper, and the sewing machines, and began to dance. There was a lot of hip and shoulder shaking.

I moved to the back of the room and watched, but they would have none of it.

"Dance, Didi, dance!" a few of them said.

"Come on," Sanya said. "Dance with us, Didi Ebony, please!" She tugged on my arm.

"Okay, I'll follow you."

They showed me their dance moves, and I followed. We forgot about schoolwork for a good twenty minutes and just danced. I threw my head back and laughed. I was supposed to be teaching English to young people in India, and they were teaching me how to dance and be present.

This was true of every school, children's home, or after-school center I visited. I was learning and being changed much more than I was teaching and changing lives.

During those two weeks of volunteering, my days moved slowly in the mornings while we lingered in the village with Kamala, and quickly when the children came home from school. The day before I was supposed to leave, I remembered that I needed to find someone with good enough English to do the "Where I'm From" poem. Sanya spoke the best English and was the most outgoing of the youth.

As soon as she came in from school, I asked if she would help me out. "Sanya, I need a favor for a project I am doing," I said, before she could grab her jump rope.

"Yes, Didi." She laid her book bag beside me.

I explained the project to her and described what I wanted us to do.

She nodded. "Okay, Didi. Afterward, will you count while I jump?"

"Of course."

This was a much-needed break for me from our singing and

rope-jumping routine. It is fascinating how much of a rhythm and relationship you can develop in just over two weeks. It felt like we were old friends.

I grabbed my marble notebook and pen to record her answers. "Sanya, what is your favorite food?"

"Rice and *daal*," she said resolutely with a nod. I was leaning on the cement wall, and she was standing across from me, leaning against the building's white wall. It was the only place we could get a little quiet and privacy.

"What is your favorite festival or celebration that you all do here in India?" I asked.

"Diwali, the Festival of Lights, and Holi, the Festival of Colors. Very fun—lights and fireworks and playing with colors."

I wrote her words in my marble notebook. "Tell me one of the happiest times in your life."

"We had a wonderful exhibition at school, and I was so happy they put my work up. I was so proud," she said with her chest thrust out.

She answered all of what might seem to her like random questions, but they did give me a flavor and diversity of names, celebrations, monuments, and favorite foods to work with. Once we'd practiced her answers a bit, I got my camera. She stood up straight against the white wall with its streaks of dirt.

"Now, just read from the paper," I said. "Begin with 'I am from,' and end with 'that's where I'm from.'"

She must have thought I said speed read, because although we'd just written it together, with her speed and accent, I could barely understand what she was saying. The noise of the street also became more apparent—the trucks zooming past and the incessant honking, our background music.

After many takes and attempts to get her to talk more slowly, we finally got it right.

In her reading, she spoke the names of her family members:

Maya, Raj, Vansh, Ichacha, and Dali. She talked about the time she got in trouble at school and how excited she felt when her work was displayed in an exhibition. She mentioned badminton and jump rope as her joys, the national treasures of the Taj Mahal and India Gate and how proud she was to be Indian, before ending firmly: "That's where I'm from."

"Cut! Thank you, you did great," I said. We were both exhausted but ready to resume our jump rope routine.

"I'm going to make it up to a hundred turns today, Didi," Sanya said as we were walking toward the courtyard.

I nodded, but then I switched to the bobble head nod I'd seen so many Indian people do. We both laughed.

On my last day at the home, I walked through the complex with the awareness of how attached I had become to the children and the place after only two weeks. The kids loved to have their picture taken, so I had a photo shoot with all ten of them. We went on the red rooftop one floor up, where we were surrounded by tall buildings being constructed in the distance. Next door, a beautiful older woman was squatting and making patties out of a greenish-brown mound of cow dung with her bare hands. She had about twenty almost perfect circles of patties lined up in four rows. I looked down from the roof into her backyard.

"Can I take your picture?" I said, holding up my camera toward her.

She nodded, which I took as a yes. Her head was wrapped in a green scarf, her lips red, her eyes bright, and she wore a gold-colored nose ring.

"Picture, Didi, picture, take my picture," one of the older boys asked as I turned back to them.

Everyone wanted a solo picture near the ledge of the roof

overlooking a square green field, with the sun setting in the background. This landscape was stark; there were the open fields of a more rural landscape and then tall concrete buildings being constructed right next to one another.

"Where are you going next, Didi?" asked Sanya as she sat on the roof ledge next to me.

"To Thailand," I said and pulled out the deflated globe from my backpack. I blew it up and showed them India and Thailand.

"I want to go to Thailand one day," one of the older boys said, tall and lanky.

"You can, if you keep making those beautiful bags."

Then I remembered the reason we were up there and yelled, "Next!" Only half of the kids had taken pictures.

Each child created a distinct pose, everything from waving to kneeling to sitting on the red wall that surrounded the roof. A few of them wanted to take pictures with my marble notebook. They held it up in front of them, showing the words SPOKEN SOUL on the front. The notebook held notes, poems, my daily budget tracking costs, journal entries, and the names of the many friends I had made in the previous six months.

Each of the children wrote their name and a note in my marble notebook. They had waited eagerly in a line to do so. Even four-year-old Sahil scribbled something.

After homework and dinner, it was time to go. My heart was heavy. The rickshaw that came nightly to take the volunteers the few miles to our apartment pulled up with a slew of beeps and a bright light.

I gave all of the kids hugs, one by one. I looked around for Sahil, but he was sleeping in one of the bedrooms. I gently shook him to say goodbye. He opened his eyes halfway to say, "Bye, Didi," as I kissed him on the scar on his head. Sanya was the last to give me a hug. It was long and tight, and then she proceeded to walk me out to the street. Halfway to the entrance she gave me another long hug and then we were at the entrance, rickshaw in front of us, the four other volunteers waiting. I picked Sanya up with one arm, swung her around, and gave her three bunches of kisses on the forehead.

"Bye, Didi Ebony," she said sadly.

"Bye, Sanya. You are my favorite."

The finality of this goodbye felt weighty, and my eyes were getting moist.

I climbed in the rear of the rickshaw and watched as Sanya stood at the door, jumping up and down, blowing kisses and waving goodbye as we drove away. I blew kisses back. I would miss my chai teatime and my daily breakfast samosas. I would miss eating curry dishes with my hands, on the floor, surrounded by kids. Most of all, I'd miss watching Sanya jump rope. I marveled at how easy it was to fall in love with people and a place. The children loved easily and were easy to love. I learned to play and just be. What a gift!

IN SEARCH OF A TIGER

For my last weekend in India, I debated between staying in Faridabad, heading to Jaipur alone, or joining my fellow volunteers for a group trip. Claire paced our dimly lit two-room apartment, flipping through her *Lonely Planet India* guidebook. The apartment was gray and dank, with little light and no real windows—the perfect setting for indecision.

"Oh, how about this?" she said, stopping mid-stride. "Corbett National Park, Tiger and Wildlife Reserve."

I liked Claire; she was spunky and easygoing, and her suggestion was tempting. "I haven't seen a tiger my entire trip. Maybe it's time. Read more."

While I wanted to go to Jaipur, I wasn't up for navigating the trip alone. India, with all its color and intensity, felt too overwhelming to navigate alone as a woman. The tiger reserve, though, seemed manageable—and I'd have company. *People are better than no people.*

The next day, Jess, Allison, Claire, and I set off from the Delhi bus station for the seven-hour journey to Ramnagar. The station was a maze of gray buses parked every which way. All the buses were marked only in Hindi. We stood bewildered at the entrance, trying to figure out which one would take us to Ramnagar. "Ramnagar? Ramnagar?" we repeated to anyone who seemed official. We were directed to one bus after another, only to be met with shaking heads.

Before tackling the mystery again, we opted for a bathroom break and walked toward the pungent smell of urine. A man blocked the entrance, demanding five rupees. "It's not free?" Allison asked, incredulous.

"Five rupees, five rupees," he insisted, holding out his hand. At that moment, a police officer with a stick nudged him aside, waving us in. The tricksters were daunting.

The smell inside was overwhelming and the optics were even worse—squat toilets, with feces smeared on the floor and walls—but we braved it. India had a way of testing my limits at every turn.

Finally, after we'd asked at least five people, a potbellied bus driver gave the side-to-side wobble head nod that could mean: yes, no, maybe, acknowledgment, or agreement. We decided to gamble and got on the bus. Herding past the stares of middle-aged men in sweaters and women in brightly colored saris, the four of us squeezed into three seats, with Jess balancing precariously on the edge of the aisle seat.

The nine-hour ride (two hours longer than expected) was an endurance test. Honking filled the air, a woman near us spat out the window every few minutes, and someone's handheld radio blared music. A child vomited in the aisle and the yellow chunky mess slid slowly toward the back of the bus, leaving a sour stench. Vendors shoved snacks and trinkets into my face despite repeated refusals, one even poking a trinket under my nose until I turned my head to the window in frustration.

By the end, I was stir-crazy, soothing myself with nineties R&B on my iPod. "What a day," I whispered to myself as we pulled into Ramnagar around 10:00 p.m.

The streets of Ramnagar were dimly lit, lined with flickering bulbs and pink-hued buildings advertising cell phones and skin-lightening creams. Claire led us through the maze of streets, guidebook in hand, searching for a recommended hostel. After touring several overpriced, grimy rooms, we stopped for a snack at a street cart lit by a single bulb.

The vendor fried Amritsari fish, red and crispy, pulling raw pieces from a paper bag with his bare hands. "You guys are missing out," Claire declared, her lips red and greasy from the fish nuggets. "I just hope I'm not shitting myself tomorrow while we're driving through the reserve." We laughed.

"Let's go find us a shitty hotel!" Claire said, rallying us onward.

We finally found a place that was decent enough and booked two rooms. The air in our room was damp and the faint smell of mildew lingered, but it was better than the alternatives. I double-checked the locks, slipped on my eye mask and earplugs, and fell asleep replaying the day's events.

Morning arrived with an onslaught of noise—honking horns, blaring music, and voices shouting in Hindi. My earplugs were no match. "Good morning, sunshine," I said to Claire as she lay staring at the ceiling.

"It's a lively morning," she replied dryly.

After a breakfast of samosas, we decided to start the day with an elephant ride before heading to the tiger reserve. The elephant, its trunk painted with pink blush, looked tired. Four of us climbed onto a metal harness seat, swaying unsteadily as the elephant plodded forward. Trash lined the forest floor, and we had to duck below branches. The guide prodded the elephant on the head and side with a pointed stick until I finally snapped.

"Stop! Leave him alone," I shouted, motioning no. I felt guilty for having participated in what felt like animal cruelty and couldn't take it anymore.

He relented, but I still felt sorry for the animal, who was clearly miserable.

When we reached a riverbank, the stillness was a welcome relief. The elephant stood on the rocky shore as the sun glistened on the water. Despite my discomfort with the animal's captivity, the moment had its own beauty—one I tried to savor as I rested against my friends.

On the way back, the guide performed a trick—having the elephant retrieve a ₹100 bill from the ground. Claire volunteered to have the elephant do a trick with her ₹500 bill, but the guide pocketed her money and refused to return it. Frustrated and disillusioned, we were glad to dismount.

Back at the hotel, I settled in for a nap, but my rest was interrupted by banging on the door next to ours, where the two other girls were staying. A man shouted, "Sex yes! Sex yes!"

Too scared to open the door, Claire and I waited in tense silence until the commotion stopped. Once it was quiet, we rushed next door to check on Jess and Allison. Jess sat on the bed, wide-eyed, knees pulled to her chest.

She recounted how a man in the market had followed her, grabbing her before she escaped and ran home to lock herself in the room. He had followed her, repeatedly saying, "Sex yes."

"I'm shocked, but I think I'm fine," she said. "None of us should go anywhere alone."

We nodded in agreement, the weight of our vulnerability as women sinking in more and more every day. It was a burden that I had to carry everywhere, guarding myself at all times. I was glad

I had not gone to Jaipur alone. There was at least some safety in numbers.

The tiger reserve, much like the rest of the weekend, was a letdown. We drove around all day in a white truck and saw deer, elephants, and lizards, but no tigers—just paw prints. As if on cue, right before leaving, a passing jeep stopped to take pictures of us. "I guess we're the main attraction now," I muttered.

The bus ride back to Delhi was equally eventful. At one point, we found ourselves stranded on the highway in the middle of a sea of people, standing outside their vehicles and yelling in Hindi. There was some kind of roadblock ahead. Instead of waiting, cars and buses started to drive over the median and go the wrong way down the highway, all while honking incessantly. I shook my head in disbelief as I stood in the middle of the highway, snapping photos to capture the moment. I was glad my fellow travelers were there with me, equally confused and frustrated. Our common misadventures bonded us, and that was more important than seeing more sights.

What I thought would be a simple excursion had turned into one of the most eventful, yet disappointing, weekends of my trip. I thought back to the Incredible India signs. Yes, incredible—intense, vibrant, and unpredictable. During my few weeks there, I learned to live with uncertainty and let go of the need for order. Life would not be what I wanted or expected—maybe even the exact opposite—but every day amidst the horns blaring, streets buzzing, colors colliding, I tried to find beauty and even play in the storm that always seemed to be swirling around. It was then that the turbulence actually became incredible.

13

THAILAND: PRESENT MOMENT, WONDERFUL MOMENT

WEEKEND IN BANGKOK

I arrived in Bangkok on Thursday, December 2, 2010, at 7:30 p.m. I planned to tour the city for the weekend and then fly north to Chiang Rai to begin my two-week volunteer placement. Now on the latter half of my trip, I'd decided to splurge a bit more in every country, and although I'd have to return early because of it, I enjoyed every mini adventure.

No one was at the airport with my name on a piece of paper when I arrived. I had emailed a few hosts from the international hospitality organization, Servas, a few days earlier to ask for a place to stay—I had let go of overplanning in advance—but got no leads. However, a Servas member, Nan, though she couldn't host me, had agreed to meet me for a late dinner and then escort me to my hostel. The train had TV monitors showing advertisements, so I knew that as soon as I stepped out of the airport that I was stepping into a different rhythm of urban life. I was also stepping into humidity—the air was thick and heavy and over eighty degrees. Discarding my jacket, I sported the South African World Cup T-shirt that I'd bought as a souvenir.

Nan, a young Thai woman in her mid-twenties, wore a huge smile and a wing-tipped bob. She took me to a small take-out place, where we had delicious pad thai, and she gave me a primer on Thailand. Lesson one was how to *wai*, a greeting of putting palms together in a prayerlike fashion, bowing your head, and saying *sa wat dee-kha/krup* (female/male). Depending on the age and status of the person you are greeting, you may wai high (near your forehead) or wai low (center of your chest). "Monks get a high wai," Nan instructed me. She also told me that heads are sacred and not to be touched, and feet are dirty. "You must take your shoes off when entering a house. Don't point your feet at people, and don't touch people with your feet."

With her help, I was a little more ready to enter a new culture. A guidebook and a local friend go a long way.

I got to my hostel around 10:30 p.m. and had my first real shower with hot water in three weeks. In India it had been basically cold water, a spigot in a dark room. Much had changed in that four-hour plane ride.

Thailand is twelve hours ahead of the US, so I Skyped my mom, as I did once a week or whenever I arrived in new countries. "I made it to Thailand. Only three more countries to go!" I said, pumping my fists. I was happy to be on the other side of the world and more than halfway home. I updated her on my plans to visit the megamalls, markets, and temples I had heard about from Nan and my guidebook. Mom ended like she always did, with "God be with you," and "Be aware of your surroundings!" *Yes, prayer and presence have indeed gotten me this far*, I thought.

For the next two days, I was in a state of play and discovery. The warm smiles of Thai people made me feel freer and more uninhibited than I had felt in a while.

I started my adventure at a few of the megamalls near my hostel. One had eight levels—the largest mall in Southeast Asia. I was in awe as I watched the escalator go up and up. An entire floor was dedicated to food.

Next, I perused day markets and night markets, tasting things

I had never seen or heard of, like papaya salad (unripe papaya mixed with vegetables) and little gummy things that looked like eyeballs. I ate fried bugs from street vendors and smelled flowers of every color and variety at the twenty-four-hour open-air flower market. I visited golden temples and saw many statues of Buddha, one gold and reclining that took up the entire room. It was the king's birthday, so festivities on the streets abounded with parades, dances, and music. Monks were all over, with shaved heads and their bodies wrapped in orange cloth. I saw a monk on the train using his iPhone and snickered. *Tradition meets modernity.* That image seemed to sum up my experience in Bangkok—striking and Eastern. I loved every minute of it.

CHIANG RAI

I began my two weeks of volunteering by riding in the back of a blue pickup truck with eight other volunteers. We rode from the airport to the campus through a lush green landscape, surrounded by large banana leaves. I volunteered at a nonprofit foundation in Chiang Rai, a city in northern Thailand, that supports the Indigenous peoples of the high mountainous regions—often referred to as Hill Tribes. These groups include the Karen, Hmong, and Lahu, who face challenges such as lack of citizenship, drug abuse, cultural erosion, and the trafficking of women and children.

Although us volunteers rotated teaching English at six schools in the area, I spent a good portion of my days lounging around the ponds with Jared, a curly-haired Australian, and Andrew, a Korean-Canadian. The other volunteers were from the US, Australia, and Canada. We were under the care of P'May, a Thai woman who worked there. P'May coordinated tours for volunteers and tourists, arranging the logistics for our trekking, sightseeing, and stays with families from Indigenous communities in northern Thailand.

Volunteers followed a rhythm of mealtimes interspersed with volunteering and relaxing. On weekends we took trips into town or went on tours. P'May would come in and out as her work permitted, or sit with us by the pond and chat while we were lounging.

One day, I was sitting in the *sala*, a gazebo next to the pond, when P'May came over to sit with me. She was thin, wore a ponytail, and appeared to be in her late thirties. She spoke very good English. She was curious about my hair. I took a few strands and looked at it myself. It had gotten longer since I started my journey and was now almost chin-length. Though it felt like the hundredth time, I explained my hair to P'May like it was the first time I'd been asked. I took a loc and rolled it in my hands to explain palm rolling. P'May was one of few Thai people who really spent time with the volunteers on campus. I knew she would be the person I'd do my "Where I'm From" poem with.

Posted around the volunteer campus were two distinct signs indicative of my life as a volunteer, with its daily trials of living with the bare minimum and learning how to use the toilet. The two signs were The Life of a Volunteer and How to Use the Toilet. Someone with artistic skills and a sense of humor had made these comic-book-like signs, laminated them, and put them in the common area, a building in the middle of the campus.

The Life of a Volunteer summed things up in four terms, with corresponding drawings:

"Itchy"—I was bitten by at least ten mosquitoes a day. Between 7:00 p.m. and 8:00 p.m. in the volunteer office, mosquitoes came out in full force. All of the volunteers' legs were red and blotchy.

"Stretchy"—There was a decent amount of downtime, and to take a break from eating rice meals, we ate junk food. I was getting wider and wider. Seaweed-flavored chips were my favorite.

"Beds are hard as a rock"—We basically slept on bunk beds with a board and a mattress maybe one-and-a-half inches thick, which felt like compressed cardboard. In my room there were spiders and three-inch geckos on the walls. I often heard strange noises. The bathroom housed a large gecko about a foot long. I never actually saw it but heard the sound randomly, as if someone was yelling "gecko!" out of nowhere. I could hear it through my earplugs. There were also rumors of a family of mice that jumped into beds. If that wasn't enough, the keyboard to my computer was overtaken by ants. I killed six of them one day when I was blogging.

"Rice for breakfast, lunch, and dinner"—To be fair, the rice was usually paired with something really good and lots of veggies, but we ate rice, rice, and more rice. The captions on the sign with the cartoon read:

"Oh, I am really hungry. What is for breakfast?"

"Rice."

"Not that hungry." (Head on table in bewilderment.)

Those were the four hallmarks of life as a volunteer in Chiang Rai.

In the bathroom, which was similar to a communal restroom with stalls, there was the sign, How to Use the Toilet. I was glad the sign was there, because I would have been utterly lost about what to do. Each stall held an almost-empty toilet bowl, a hose, a bucket, a trashcan, and a roll of tissue.

The sign said, "For number one—go, wipe dry, and put the tissue in the trash."

"For number two—go, wash with the hose, blot dry, put the tissue in the trash, and then fill the bucket with water and pour down the bowl."

The second seemed like a lot of steps to go through when your pants were at your ankles. Figuring out how to go to the bathrooms was my least-favorite part of traveling. At least it wasn't a squat toilet, but I just wanted to push a handle and flush.

These inconveniences were frustrating but not terrible. They reminded me that life was hard for most people around the world.

Washing clothes was interesting too. You couldn't get too preoccupied with other things, because a few steps required your attention, involving turning the water on and off at intervals and being vigilant about taking your clothes out as soon as they were done.

Depending on how humid it was—and it was pretty humid—it could take a few days for your clothes to dry. If you got distracted and forgot to remove them soon enough, your clothes mildewed. Mine were all thin or quick-drying, so they took only half a day. I tried to look on the bright side. *It's a lot better than washing by hand.*

Growing up with limited resources and having to deal with things being broken and imperfect had prepared me for these inconveniences. Knowing how to improvise made life as a volunteer easier for me than for some of the others. I'd washed my underclothes by hand a time or two. I'd borrowed water from neighbors and ran extension cords through windows to share electricity. I'd been waiting and excited about the food stamps that came in at the beginning of each month. I'd slept on creaky bunk beds and had my bed propped up on crates. I survived that; sure enough, I could survive this. My life was about improvising when there wasn't enough or when what you had wasn't sufficient or comfortable. I didn't love it, but it wasn't unfamiliar.

There were more interesting things to encounter besides my daily discomforts, like a horse that would chase you if you looked it in the eye. That was a bit random and crazy, but the more engaging elements were the Indigenous women of northern Thailand—particularly among the Akha and Lahu—who chewed betel nut, a practice that stained their mouths a deep red so that, at first glance, it looked as though they were bleeding. Monks were everywhere, a reminder that for many young boys in Thailand, entering the monastery was a path to education. Boys with close-cropped hair were wrapped in orange cloth, observing the discipline of novice monks. They could not touch, or be touched by, women. Moments like these made my days as a volunteer feel textured. Life held a richness.

During the day, I did some lesson planning and taught elementary students English, but it was the end of the year and not much was happening in the schools that a new volunteer could jump into. Alternatively, we worked on a drainage project at the complex so that the pond in its center would not overflow. That required a lot of shoveling dirt. I kind of appreciated that manual labor.

This rural area of Thailand felt and looked like the photos I had seen of Vietnam—lush, green, leafy, and relaxing. Being away from the hustle and bustle of a place like India, and even Bangkok, was a needed reprieve. I almost forgot that I was volunteering. The quiet was soul nourishing. Everything spoke volumes, but not much was said. A smile, a nod, a breeze; it was enough.

One day, I saw P'May sitting in the sala and decided it was time to do a "Where I'm From" poem. I had explained it to her earlier in the week, so she was ready to go. I ran down the little dirt path to my building and grabbed my notebook. When I returned, she was smiling as usual. It was the thing I associated with Thai people: Everyone always seemed to be smiling.

P'May said she had time for the poem, and I began to ask her questions. The first thing she said was that although most volunteers called her P'May, her name was Nalinee. She also told me her parents' names, which I couldn't pronounce or spell, so I gave her the notebook to write them in: Pibook (father), Nipaporn (mom), and Chompoonuch (older sister).

"P'May, tell me what you love about Thailand. Are there any festivals, foods, places, or aspects of your culture you love?"

"Very relaxed lifestyle," she said. "You are relaxed here, right?"

I nodded, and we both laughed. It was hard not to.

She continued, "Thai people are always smiling. That is good. My people are friendly."

She told me that Thai New Year's was in April and was celebrated by firecrackers to repel bad luck. On the day after New Year's, people prepared food and brought offerings to the monks at the temples. People had to go to temple to make merit (goodwill) and bathe Buddha's statue, after which they poured water on the hands of elders and asked for their blessings. During Loy Krathong, or Full Moon, in November, people made decorated baskets, which were then floated on a river. It was a symbol of letting go of the past.

"These New Year's and Full Moon festivals are very Buddhist, like most Thai people, but I am a Christian." She seemed proud. I asked her how that happened. She'd been converted by Christian missionaries, which there were pockets of in the north. "Knowing God brings me so much joy," she said, touching her heart. She also liked working at the foundation, which gave her the ability to own her own land and home.

"Anything pumpkin!" she said loudly and enthusiastically when we talked about her favorite foods. I was surprised. I didn't know pumpkin was a thing in Thailand.

One of the volunteers needed her, so we had to wrap up quickly. Though she wrote down responses to all of the poem prompts, I didn't get as many details of her life as I wanted. She alluded to being away from home while young, but we didn't have time to go into why.

When she read her poem aloud, she also referenced: the sadness of losing her puppy and the small pleasures of ice cream, sushi, Caesar salad, and, of course, her beloved pumpkin. And true to most of my interactions with Thai people, she smiled through it all—even the hard parts. As always, I smiled back, grateful.

Our crew of volunteers often ventured into Chiang Rai to go out to eat, drink, and dance as well as to visit cultural attractions. One day, we all rode into town together but split up to visit different things. I was looking for the Black Temple of Chiang Rai with Jared, the dark-haired Aussie, and Andrew, the Korean-Canadian, who I thought was a smartass. I didn't like Andrew; he was abrasive, annoying, and always talking about what he knew. When he spoke, I always wanted to scream, "Shut up!" People don't usually annoy me much, but for some reason his voice was like nails on a chalkboard.

We took a *songthaew* into town. These are shared taxis made from a pickup truck with a covered bed in the back and two benches along the sides. We then took a bus and got off at the spot noted in our guidebook, onto what seemed like a random spot on the side of the road. We saw few buildings, no people, and no sight of the Black Temple we had come to see. We walked east for a while to no avail, and then west, and then back to the place where we'd initially been dropped off. At that point, we saw the tip of the Black Temple in the distance, but we weren't sure how to get to it.

"Okay, guys, we need a different game plan," I said. "We have been walking for about twenty minutes and do not seem to be any closer to the Black Temple."

Andrew suggested that we walk down the road and see if there was anybody we could ask.

"We've tried that already," I said. "We do not know the Thai name, and saying Black Temple in English has not worked so far." I threw up my hands and sighed.

Andrew turned to me, his head cocked to the side. I knew the smartass was about to rear its ugly head. "Ebony, are you afraid to ask for help?"

"No. We have followed your suggestions for the past half-hour, and it got us nowhere. I am just tired of you, to be honest."

I was mad at both his statement and all of the times I'd wanted to tell him to shut the fuck up in the past week.

Jared jumped in the middle of us. "Hey, calm down, guys. We are on the same team. Let's just try this way"—he pointed down the nearest side street—"and follow it to see if it leads anywhere. If not, we can just take the bus back."

"Fine," we both said in unison, our eyes on Jared.

We walked on in silence, but Andrew's comment reverberated in my head. *Am I afraid to ask for help?* Was I always trying to do something myself first and only asking for help when I was at my wits' end? I had asked for help on my around-the-world trip, which was a grand gesture, but I couldn't remember doing it often in my day-to-day life. I chewed on the question and flipped it over in my mind. Andrew was an ass, but he may have been on to something. I rarely thought I needed any help, so it never occurred to me to ask. I'd have to pay more attention to see if he was right.

From a young age, I'd liked to do things my way and have my own money. I was always trying to earn money so I wouldn't have to ask anyone for small things. I could buy them myself. Before I was twelve, I'd run a few businesses. I had started a pedicure business and did pedicures for people in my family for ten dollars. It was going well, but a few weeks into it, I made an appointment to do my father's feet. He was recently home from jail and staying at my grandmother's house while Danielle and I lived there.

He sat in the big black patent-leather chair in the den and took off his socks. At the foot of the chair, I had set up a yellow pan prepped with warm water, clippers, and a pumice stone. I kneeled down and looked at his feet, which were white with crust, his overgrown toenails long and black. I began to gag, jumped up, ran to the bathroom, and dry heaved.

"It's okay. You don't have to finish," he said gently from the other room. The kindness in his voice was softer than I usually heard, and it remains one of the few tender memories I hold of my father from childhood. Either way, I clearly didn't have the stomach for pedicures. That was the end of my pedicure business.

I got Eunice, Suzette, and my grandmother to pay me for odd jobs around the house: cleaning, gardening, or raking the backyard. I wanted pocket money to buy my own stuff—school supplies or candy or clothes or sneakers I liked.

Later, I had a business ironing clothes for family members, namely my Aunt Suzette, my father's sister, who paid me twenty dollars to iron all of her family's clothes for the week. The summer before high school, I also had a job taking my cousin Cyancé, Suzette's son, to preschool. Sometimes I walked him to his school, which was a little less than a mile away, but most of the time I rode him on my bike's handlebars. This seems so hazardous now, but to my middle-school brain, it made sense. He was three and probably scared, so he remained still and silent. I had no trouble until I ran into a pothole going at top speed, and we both flipped over the handlebars and landed hard in the middle of the street. I think we were both too shocked to feel our hurt. I gathered him up and put him back on the handlebars and dropped him at school. He never mentioned it, and neither did I.

I was happy at fourteen when I was able to have a summer job. This would provide me with ample money for school clothes and sneakers, and I could buy a few luxury grocery items. I was used to hearing my mother say about money, "I don't have it," and often the same from my father. Having my own money meant a bit of freedom to buy brand-name clothes and not play the part of poverty.

College was my ticket to freedom from the "I don't have it." I had to figure out college admissions myself. I went to the library and researched schools, filled out every application, went on every college tour, wrote every essay, and applied for every scholarship myself. I learned to sign my mother's signature and filled out most of my financial aid forms myself. I even got a letter from my guidance counselor so that I could be approved for application fee waivers. My family was always supportive and loving, and that helped—it provided the confidence that I could succeed—but I was self-motivated. I would not have to wait for others, for a welfare check, for a man, or for anybody, for that matter. I would do it myself. And I did. It had worked for most of my life, but there, on the side of the road in Thailand, I realized that although I had mastered self-sufficiency, maybe I needed more practice in asking for help in ordinary ways—in daily interdependence.

PRESENT MOMENT, WONDERFUL MOMENT

As my last weekend approached, I was looking forward to going on a three-day trek and homestay, something the foundation set up for volunteers. We were supposed to stay with a family from one of the Indigenous communities of northern Thailand and do a teaching or construction project. Instead, we ended up volunteering at a substance abuse rehabilitation center. I was disappointed at first because I'd been looking forward to the cultural experience, but it ended up being just what I needed.

The rehabilitation center was a new, plush complex located about thirty minutes outside of Chiang Rai, in Wiang Chai district. It sat nestled among mountains and rice fields. There was a swimming pool; two long one-story beige buildings that housed our guest rooms, each with a nice bed and bathroom; and a beautiful lake nearby. There were five of us volunteers and seven residents in addition to the two keepers: one a former German monk, the other more of a mindfulness guru. We did yoga and meditation every morning in a multiuse building with a wood floor. We ate in a dining room at a long table surrounded by glass doors that got incredible light. While eating dishes like curried eggplant over rice, I pondered the sign that read PRESENT MOMENT, WONDERFUL MOMENT as a daily practice.

The center provided a serene space for people struggling with addiction, focusing on mindfulness as a path to healing. Mindfulness, I learned, meant being fully present—embracing both the good and bad moments without distraction. For those in recovery, they emphasized, this was critical as addiction thrives on escapism. Meditation was central to their practice, a way to stay grounded.

I had always struggled with being present. My mind constantly raced toward the future, planning every step. Traveling forced me to slow down, to taste, see, and hear the world around me. This also helped me adequately retell my adventures on my blog. However, with my trip winding down, my focus shifted back to planning for home. The reminder to live in the moment was timely. I thought of a friend who once said, "We're always chasing the perfect day or week, but I want to start relishing the perfect moments."

That Saturday, I decided to savor perfect moments wherever I could.

The dining table was long, covered in a white cloth and set with bamboo placemats. Twelve of us surrounded it—Thai people and visitors, those in recovery and volunteers. At least one meal a day was eaten in silence. I looked down at my plate of chicken and coconut curry eggplant, took a bite, and chewed slowly. The sweet and spicy flavors danced on my tongue, and the quiet around me felt sacred. Perfect moment.

Later, Andrew and I were tasked with painting the entrance gate a bright orange. I dreaded working with him, but we had to get it done. Armed with a roller and brushes, I proposed that we take separate sides of the gate. He agreed, and we worked in silence until I needed the ladder stabilized. I hated asking him, but I needed to practice asking for help.

"Andrew, can you steady this for me?" I asked, rolling my eyes.

He obliged without a word.

Eric, a towering Dutch monk who ran the center, came by to check on us. With his bald head and kind demeanor, he radiated warmth. He picked up a paintbrush and joined us, easily reaching areas we couldn't.

Curious about his story, I asked questions about what monastery life was like.

He had been a monk at a monastery that helped people struggling with addiction through the chemical-dependency phase of kicking the habit. They made some kind of medicine that helped. He'd stopped being a monk to help people transition into the next phase of their recovery. "We ate only once a day," he said, "and at first, I'd stuff my face. But I learned that slowing down helped sustain me longer." Faster was not always better.

We finished painting the gates in an hour, and as I looked at our bright-orange finished product, I felt a sense of pride. The conversation while we'd worked on it together was great. Even the aversion I felt toward Andrew was toned down. He wasn't that bad; I just preferred him silent. Perfect moment.

The next day brought more unexpected joys. We played basketball, and though I was terrible, I managed to score a point. The satisfying swoosh of the ball through the net had me jumping up and down as my team cheered. Wonderful moment.

Later that day, I borrowed a bike and rode down to a nearby lake. The narrow dirt paths were flanked by lush green fields, and the breeze brushed my face as I stood up on the pedals. The forest was alive with quiet beauty, the lake still and serene. Not a soul in sight, just me and nature. Perfect moment.

On my way back, I passed a small house where two older Thai women sat on the porch. One wore a pink shirt, the other navy blue. They waved me over, with warm smiles. I parked my bike and walked over. The woman in pink gestured at my hair with curiosity, and I rolled it in my palm, mimicking how it got that way. The woman in the navy blue shirt pantomimed eating, but I shook my head, smiling, as I didn't want to ruin my dinner. They nodded in understanding.

Pulling out my camera, I asked to take a picture with them. Arms draped around one another like old friends, we snapped a selfie. As I rode away, they waved goodbye, their spirit of welcome lingering. How easy it was to connect without words. Wonderful moment!

That evening, our last at the center, we gathered around a fire. Residents and volunteers shared stories, the night air thick with smoke and memory. Two Thai teenagers recovering from *yaba*, a highly addictive drug, spoke bravely.

"I started at eleven," Nang said softly. "Almost everyone does." We sat in silence, the weight of her words pressing against the crackle of the fire. Then she lifted her gaze.

"I'm glad I found this place. It's peaceful here. I feel free."

Her words pierced me. I realized I, too, was addicted—not to drugs, but to busyness and self-sufficiency. Like Nang, I had found peace in practicing presence. Thailand reminded me that presence is power, that peace is not a destination but a practice. I would carry that lesson with me into the next stretch of my journey, and hopefully, back home.

14

CHINA: HALF OF HEAVEN

HALF OF HEAVEN

I planned to spend two weeks traversing China at the end of December, basing myself mostly in Shanghai and Beijing and taking day trips to smaller cities. China, I loved for the tastes and sights that were so different from the West. The buildings with their eaves pointed upward, red lanterns, Chinese characters, street food that looked nothing like I had seen before (spiky round things, a lot of pork, meat on a stick or hanging from a string, fried food, sweets) and milk tea, which I drank every day.

Shanghai was hustling and bustling like any other major city, bursting with people and filled with Christmas decorations. I thought I might escape the consumerism of Christmas, but MERRY CHRISTMAS signs were everywhere. Trees and lights decorated the buildings, and Mariah Carey's "All I Want for Christmas Is You" blared from mall speakers. My days there were full of markets, malls, and museums amidst the freezing weather. I had to pull out the green-and-white North Face jacket that had been sitting at the bottom of my backpack since the beginning of the trip. I was bundled up with a gray hat, scarf, and gloves that I had bought from a street vendor, but that didn't stop me from seeking and searching for experience, for adventure.

While walking through the city, I heard the constant sound of people spitting, walked through the gray haze that lingered in the air, and saw groups of Chinese people in their fifties and sixties doing tai chi in the park. In the markets, tiny Chinese women in aprons approached me hundreds of times, saying, "Hello. Hi, lady, would you like to buy . . ." and even pulling on my arm to get me to look at their merchandise. Other than the earrings from Nairobi, I hadn't bought much on the trip except postcards to send, food to taste, or refrigerator magnets for my mother. In China, I bought four red carved bracelets. They were compact and wouldn't load down my bag, and when people asked about them back home, I'd have the pleasure of saying, "I got them in China." I had traveled nearly thirty thousand miles and wanted a little something to show for it.

Getting around the city was fairly easy because the metro system was bilingual. I would have been completely lost trying to decipher Chinese characters. Riding the train and bus in Shanghai gave me a real whiff of the reality that the Chinese numbered more than one-sixth of the world's population at the time. There were just masses and masses of people, all bunched together in crowded train cars. I had to elbow my way out at my stop. Oddly enough, though I was in a sea of Chinese people, no one gave me a second look. It was like being in New York. Most people were so busy going about their business that they didn't really see one another.

I didn't make any connections in Shanghai. I was too tired of introducing myself to make friends at the hostel and didn't feel like reaching out to a Servas host. I read in my guidebook that you had to watch out for English-speaking Chinese students who would come up to you, act friendly, and want to talk. They were known to target tourists, become fast friends, go to tea or dinner, and stick you with the bill.

David, a young Chinese man, sat next to me on a bench in the Shanghai Museum and sparked up a conversation. I had to wonder: Was he was just a nice person who'd sat down for a rest and decided to be nice to a stranger while practicing his English, or was he a preying con artist? Who can ever tell these things? We had a nice conversation then I left him there and proceeded to finish my museum tour. I think traveling made me realize that people around the world are much nicer than you would think, but I also had to keep my guard up. It was kind of unfortunate that sometimes I had to ask myself, "Why is this person being so nice?"

I spent Christmas day at a very packed and glamorous Chinese acrobatic show. At one point, six people were riding motorcycles around in this giant ball cage, women Hula-Hooping with twenty rings so that it looked like they were inside a slinky, and all kinds of other spectacles. It was the oddest Christmas I'd had, lonely but very entertaining.

For my last two days in Shanghai, I had hoped to visit the cities of Suzhou and Hangzhou. I had read in my guidebook of these two supposedly heavenly cities full of gardens, temples, canals, and lakes. I decided to go on a bus tour of both cities instead of going by myself and roaming around for the day. The cheapest option was to take a one-day bus trip from the Shanghai tour bus station. Simple enough, but this bus station was for Chinese tourists, so everything at the station was in Chinese characters. The tour would be in Mandarin as well. That was fine with me. At that point I'd rather go on a tour with ten people in a language I didn't understand than roam around in the cold by myself. I just wanted to be immersed in Chinese culture and have someone take me to the important places. I was ready to be led.

At the tour's booth in the bus station, the attendant did not speak English. I tried to really enunciate when I said, "Suzhou," and "Hangzhou." I mouthed it slowly, several times. She nodded. Perhaps both of our tongues and ears betrayed us that day—I learned the next day that my ticket was to somewhere else. When we got off the bus to what I thought was Suzhou, a Chinese American woman in her forties, who was there with her family of four, looked at my ticket and said, "That says Xitang." I shook my head, defeated.

Xitang was a pretty cool place though. It is a seven-hundred-year-old water town with canals, kind of like Venice. People get around by boat and via stone bridges over the waterways. Gray one- and two-story buildings were clustered up against the narrow walkways next to the canals. I roamed alone around its shops, bridges, and canals. I had some of the best fried dumplings and potatoes of my trip from a street vendor and some good milk tea. Some Chinese-American people on my tour helped me out a little, letting me know what time to be back on the bus.

Wherever I was—lost or confused, in the right situation or, in this case, on the wrong bus—someone or something would step in and take care of me. More than halfway around the world, I was learning to trust that the universe would respond to my needs, if I let it.

I saw the helpful Chinese-American woman and her family throughout the four hours we were in Xitang; we'd pass each other on the narrow paths and nod or wave. I saw them through the window eating at a restaurant as I passed, the four of them—her husband and a son and daughter in their teens. I wished at that moment that I had my family here or a family of my own. I ate lunch by myself while walking.

I sat down on the edge of one of the bridges over the canals. A man on a tiny boat rowed down the waterway. Passersby stared over my shoulders as I wrote a postcard. I was unsure whether they were intrigued by my writing in English or being a Black person. Out of nowhere, a person sat very close to me and wrapped her arm tightly around my shoulders. In front of us was her friend, pointing a camera in my face. I looked up and there was a flash, and before I could say anything, they were gone. At least in India they asked or took photos surreptitiously. Here someone just appeared next to me and started taking pictures. I felt violated, my personal space and privacy invaded. I actually would have said yes, if asked.

It was jarring, but what else could I do but smile and laugh? Thailand had taught me to smile more; it just makes life more pleasant. I probably smiled more there than I had in half my life in the US. You can only smile back when people are smiling at you. So I smiled at the Chinese people who grabbed me and stole my picture. Smile, you're in China!

The next day made up for the previous day's mishaps. Blessing number one—I did indeed get on the right bus. Number two—A few people spoke English, so I knew where we were going. I also made two lady friends, Thali and Kris, who became my two Asian mothers for the day.

Thali, a Chinese woman in her fifties, with bangs that covered her forehead and black chin-length hair, stopped near me in the bus aisle. She waved and asked if I was alone by pointing to the seat next to me. I nodded and said, "Yes, it's just me." She sat down next to me.

Then she gestured that it was cold outside by rubbing her biceps. She looked at my jacket, felt the fabric, and looked up at me, frowning, as if to say, "This is all you have? Not warm enough." I unzipped my jacket and showed her that under my green-and-white North Face shell were a fleece, cardigan, and shirt. I wore all of my warmest clothes every day I was in China, as it was below freezing. She smiled and nodded in approval, as a mother would.

Later, seeing that I was drinking tea with nothing else (I had already eaten my bread snack), she took out some of her raisin bread and offered it to me. Raisin bread was my favorite. She also offered me an orange and some candies, which I ate gratefully. When we needed to leave the bus at points during the tour, she pulled my arm or pointed, making sure I kept up. I spent the day with her and her friend Kris, who spoke good enough English and had the same haircut as Thali, but a rounder face and glasses. Thali was from Taiwan and Kris from Malaysia. Also on the bus was a portly, middle-aged Chinese man from Singapore who spoke English very well. He had worked in Oklahoma for two months and said, in a surprised manner, that Americans are hard workers. He liked the country but thought there was a lot of waste and was baffled that it seemed that many people had two cars. "Lots of buffets," he said, "for $9.99." I laughed at his takeaways from America—too many cars and buffets.

The three of them were very helpful as we went to lunch and took a cruise around beautiful West Lake at the center of Hangzhou. It felt like a large Chinese garden, serene and surrounded by trees, small mountains, numerous temples, pagodas, and artificial islands within the lake. The view made me want to sit, stare, and listen to silence.

I was happy to tag along with my new friends, to have eyes watching and people who were concerned about my well-being. It was nice to receive their hospitality. Because I took the Chinese tourist bus, I had the pleasure of spending the day with twenty-five Chinese travelers from across China, along with a few who lived or were born elsewhere. Of course, like everywhere, everyone wanted to know where I was from and asked if my hair was original and how did I make it like that. Next time I travel the world, I may cut my hair off. It drew too much attention. Or maybe I should have been happy to be seen as intriguing and mysterious. All I could do was smile.

We went to a silk-making factory and then stopped at a village and had some green tea. Thali, Kris, and I toasted to our trip, our one day of friendship. I toasted to being invited in by them, to the beauty of Hangzhou. It was overall a great day, indeed a bunch of perfect moments.

Each day had its own set of joys and challenges. Some of the joys of today made up for the woes of yesterday. Some things couldn't be recovered—I didn't make it to Suzhou or have a family to eat with, nor could I take back the photo violation. I could, however, receive the beauty of Xitang and the hospitality of strangers, and again open myself up to the good moments of my day with Thali and Kris. Who can complain about that?

I was learning, at each step of my trip, to take things in stride. I was learning that even with the best attempts at planning, life never turns out the way you want, and sometimes getting lost or meeting an unexpected turn of events, while frustrating—even saddening—may also offer a glimmer of light.

In Heaven
There is no doubt splendor all around.
On Earth
there is Suzhou and Hangzhou,
two twins of magnificence.
Who would not be eager to enter their bliss?
Yet, in this instance
I was deceived by my own tongue into visiting Xitang
in ignorance.
Upon the second day
I did reclaim my fate
to take in the great West Lake and
scenic settings of Hangzhou.
That's good enough for now.
I've seen half of heaven,
Can I ever complain of having to do without?

Not reaching Suzhou was a small reminder of a larger truth: So much of life is learning to live with what you hoped for but did not get. My life had prepared me for not getting everything I wanted and learning to be okay anyway. I had experienced both lack and abundance in my thirty years. I was blessed in so many ways, but in my twenties a serious romantic relationship and a relationship with my father still eluded me.

In 2007, a few months after I started my first job as a city planner in Charlottesville, Virginia, I got a random call from my father while I was at work. I was so surprised at seeing his number that it took me a few seconds to pick up. I knew he wanted something, because he never called me. I cut to the chase.

"So what's up?" I said, leaning back in my office chair.

"Yeah, um, my car broke down and I need some money to get it fixed. We have some money, but I'm a bit short, ya know?"

I was immediately annoyed. He never called, and now he wanted some money? Unbelievable. We didn't have a relationship.

I kept my voice neutral. "How much?"

"Six hundred?" he said as if he were wincing—it was more a question than a statement.

"I don't feel comfortable with six hundred. I can do three hundred," I said. I had more, but part of me just didn't feel like I needed to extend myself for him.

"Okay, well, whatever you can help with would be good."

I hung up, steaming, and I couldn't figure out why. My heart was beating fast. I was off-kilter and unable to focus on my work. I opened up a blank document on my computer and began to write my feelings down. In what would become a four-page, single-spaced document I wrote that:

I was upset that he had never called me for anything in my adult life and now he expected money.

It wasn't about the money. It was the lack of relationship that pissed me off. He felt like a stranger asking me for money.

How my view of him as a child was of an "asshole," which came from seeing him be an asshole to every woman in my life that I loved.

How I felt like we had to beg him for things, things a parent knew their children needed. How demoralizing it was to have to continue to ask. How that made it seem like he was more interested in wielding power than in providing for us.

I wrote down most of the memories I had of him, to solidify why he put a bad taste in my mouth.

I told him that we had no relationship. That I didn't know him and I didn't feel like he knew me. That this made me sad.

I told him that I hated how he thought he was a good dad because he'd bought us some stuff here and there—that it wasn't enough, that being a father was more than that.

I told him that he'd failed, but I could forgive him. We could move on, but we first had to stop pretending we were something we weren't. I would not pretend.

I mailed the letter to his house in North Carolina, where he and his wife and my half-brother lived. I asked him to write back.

He called me a few days later. I was sitting in the driveway of the house I shared with four roommates in Charlottesville. I stared at the steering wheel of the plum Saturn he had bought me a few years before as we spoke.

"I got your letter," he said.

I was quiet; I had said everything I needed to.

"I never wanted to be a father. I was too young. Your mother wanted marriage and all of that. I was more interested in the streets, in making money."

"Hmm." *Not an apology, but at least some honesty*, I thought.

He went on about his own childhood, how his parents weren't affectionate. About his life and story, how he got caught up in the drug game but wished he had gone to college. How he tried to give us what he had, and when we had to wait, it meant he didn't have it but was trying to get it.

I still thought he'd been an asshole unnecessarily but didn't need to press the point. My letter had said it all. I wanted to move on. "You can't change the past, but we can move forward—but it's going to require you to make an effort, to try," I said.

"I'm willing to try." He sounded sincere.

"So am I."

I felt better after that call. At least the air was clear. I had said my piece and he was able to say his, more honesty than apology, but it was something, I guessed. I was twenty-seven, and it was our first real heart-to-heart conversation; that was enough.

But after that, nothing really changed. I waited for him to step up. He never did. He struggled with sobriety, and I suppose that affected his ability to be present. Our relationship is still defined by his absence.

My mishaps and hidden blessings in China reminded me that disappointment is a part of life. But they also showed me that happiness doesn't have to depend on what or who is missing. I could choose to focus on what I did have, rather than dwell on what I did not.

After five days in Shanghai, I was excited to ring in the New Year in Beijing. By then, I had learned not to overplan. I'd just book a hostel for the first night and figure out the rest once I arrived. I chose the Downtown Hostel in the Old City, not far from Beijing's most popular attractions: the Forbidden City, once the vast palace of emperors; the Temple of Heaven, where they prayed for good harvests; and Tiananmen Square, forever marked by the 1989 massacre of pro-democracy demonstrators. While visiting these places I saw armed guards in green uniforms, a reminder that this was not a democratic state. That reminder rang true online as well, when I was blocked from sites like Facebook.

My hostel was in one of the best *hutongs* in the city. Hutongs are old alleyways lined with gray courtyard homes, red trim, and a mix of shops and residences. The streets were crowded with pedestrians and cyclists, impossible not to bump into people as

I wandered, snacking and people-watching. Walking in this area was captivating—there was so much intensity and newness.

I went to Wangfujing, a pedestrian area of malls, markets, and food vendors lit up like Times Square. Steam billowed from grills where scorpions on sticks stood in rows beside skewered beetles and starfish, enticing buyers. It was fascinating and off-putting all at once, the kind of scene that challenged my stomach even as it dazzled my eyes. I played it safe with pork buns. They were like little white clouds filled with meat.

On New Year's Eve, I booked a tour to the Great Wall. I froze my butt off as I climbed up and down the endless stone steps, the wind whipping my face and making my nose run. The wall snaked across the mountains in both directions, vast and gray. Between staircases stood ancient watchtowers, now prime picture-taking spots. I often stopped to look back, awed by the immensity and by the fact that I was here, in China, at the Great Wall. Surrounded by mostly couples and families, who had the pleasure of experiencing this together, I recalled all the people who had helped me reach this place and all those I had met along the way. I let out a deep breath that looked like a puff of smoke. I was not alone, not one bit. The sun, the moon, and the stars had kept me company all along.

That night I splurged. At a white-tablecloth restaurant I ordered Peking duck, roasted and carved at my table. Wrapped in a pancake with crisp skin, tender meat, and a sweet purple sauce, it melted in my mouth. Later I stumbled on a Chinese reggae band led by a thin man with dreadlocks down his back in a Bob Marley T-shirt, rocking out on guitar. From imperial delicacies to reggae in Beijing, the city kept surprising me.

On my last day, I took a dumpling-making class in a hutong home. Four of us stood shoulder to shoulder in a small kitchen, folding translucent dough around minced pork and vegetables. The dumplings, shaped like tiny flowers, sat in my palm like art.

Triumphant, I took a picture of them in my hand. I'd post it on my blog as soon as I was done.

Later, we gathered at the table, drinking tea and eating from blue-and-white china. This was the only Chinese home I entered. There was no "Where I'm From" poem, no friend to guide me, but the simple act of cooking and sharing food gave me a sense of ease. By the end I was full—of dumplings, of gratitude, of pleasure from my experiences in China itself.

China was one of the few places I longed to return to, knowing I had only glimpsed its vastness. Though my budget was dwindling and my body weary from tours and sightseeing, I left with more than I expected—a mix of awe, letdowns, hospitality, and surprise. The next day, I boarded a plane for Japan, grateful for what I had received and glad to get closer to home.

15

JAPAN: NEW YEAR'S CELEBRATIONS, NEW CONNECTIONS

Food was such a central part of my time in Japan—in every country, for that matter. It was a point of exploration and wonder, of connection with the people and culture, of hospitality and generosity. But sometimes, especially when I was backpacking, it was a reminder that I was alone.

On all of the seven days I was in Japan, I ate my new favorite Japanese delight, *onigiri*, and savored the fact that it was cheap, portable, and delicious. If you touch the pointer finger and thumb from both hands together to form a triangle, that is the size and shape of onigiri—rice wrapped in seaweed with some filling in the middle. I always got the type with salmon. Japan was expensive, so to preserve my backpacker's budget, I'd grab one at a convenience store. I felt a little guilty about going all the way to Japan and eating food from a convenience store, but they were such a great snack anytime of the day and only ¥105, less than a dollar.

On my last day in Japan, I scoffed an onigiri down in four bites at the base of Mount Fuji while my breath blew soft white clouds into the cold air between bites. We—ten other tourists and I—were ending our four-hour tour that had originated in Tokyo. During our few free minutes to mill around the visitor center before we headed back, I sat at the base of the mountain, chomping. I stared up at the white, snow-covered monstrosity, taking in its sheer mass. It was closed for traversing because it was January and dangerous. I took a picture to say I was there.

I'd taken the tour because at this point in my trip, I wanted to be guided and accompanied. I was ready to get home. I had taken so many photos in front of world wonders, ancient buildings, and landscapes all over the world. These were the pictures I had to take, but my sense of awe and wonder was now exhausted by the extraordinary. I'd come to prefer the ordinary people and things in each place. Toward the end of the trip, I just went through the motions, sometimes forcing myself to be present. What you see in those photographs is me smiling, looking happy to be there—and I was. What you don't see is my tiredness. It was hard to stay open and be awake—all day, every day.

I felt guilty sometimes. Here I was traveling the world, on this fun adventure, but exhausted. I learned something new daily, and something in me would never cease to snap awake, but I had taken in too much and wanted to zone out. A piece of me yearned for sameness. In my hand was a bite of Japan in a sushi triangle, but my heart felt conflicted—partially full of the beauty of the moment and partially drained. I tried to hold them both. I was learning that I could hold both, that life and being human meant allowing myself the range of experience, often at the same time.

I ate onigiri every day in Japan because they felt similar to sushi, but in a different form—familiar enough to satisfy my desperate need for comfort, yet different enough to remind me I was far from home. In that vein, I'd also eaten ramen earlier that week at a place about half a mile from my hostel in Kyoto. It was a crowded little hole in the wall about the size of a bedroom. Japanese people were bunched together at small tables with their faces hovering over large black soup bowls, coming up only when they raised the long noodles into the air to lower them into their mouths. I had once thought of ramen as nothing more than a cheap meal as a college student or an after-school snack in high school. But here, it was rich, flavorful, and deeply cultural.

I ordered, and when it came, I looked down at the contents of my black bowl. What sat before me looked much better than a ramen package, though similar: steaming yellowish broth, egg, and a piece of pork on top. Delicious. I couldn't work my chopsticks as easily as everyone else, but I was patient. I didn't have anywhere in particular to go. To eat in local restaurants with Japanese people was what I had come for. It's a very different thing, however, to eat among Japanese people than to eat with a Japanese person. The latter is where the magic of connection and cultural exchange really happens.

The connection I yearned for came in the form of Naoko, someone I'd met on a couch-surfing website. Before that, I didn't know that you could meet up with folks from the couch-surfing website and just have coffee, a meal, or they could show you around town. I thought it was just a way to get a free overnight stay. But as I learned, it was a way to forge a friendship.

After a few messages through the site to introduce ourselves and see if we could find a mutually agreeable time to meet, I met Naoko at the main train station in the center of Kyoto on my second day in Japan. She would show me around for the day. I told her to meet me on the steps; I'd be a Black woman with a green-and-white jacket and black jeans. We greeted each other with a handshake. She was about five foot five, medium sized, with her black hair pulled back in a ponytail and a black winter coat. Her face was round and open. She spoke English well. She had trouble rounding some of the letters, so it sounded a little muffled, but I understood just fine. I couldn't imagine what my Japanese would sound like.

I thanked her for meeting me and said, "I have been saving my money for a nice meal when I hopefully meet up with someone. This is my splurge."

"I think you will like it." She was taking me to a sushi place her friends visited often.

We arrived at a nice restaurant with dim lighting in the middle of the day. It had a relaxed vibe but an upscale ambiance. People were generally dressed up. I felt a bit out of place, with my T-shirt, jeans, hiking shoes, and North Face jacket. Once we sat and looked at the menu, I tightened inside. This would be a twenty-dollar meal, much more than my backpacker's budget allowed for. Then, I realized that I only had another three weeks left in my trip. I could spend a bit more than usual; I'd be home soon.

I began to bombard Naoko with questions about the menu, trying to get a better understanding of what I was seeing. She ordered a variety of sushi and sashimi for both of us, delivered in red bowls. As she picked up her chopsticks, I decided to ask the proper way to use them.

Naoko demonstrated. "Rest the bottom stick on your ring finger, use the pointer and index finger to move the top one and grab."

As she spoke, I moved into formation and grabbed a piece of sushi.

She raised her eyebrows. "Your skills are actually pretty good! We have to practice when we are kids. Picking up little beans. Nowadays a lot of the kids go to second school late at night, miss chopstick lessons, and do not use them properly."

I popped the sushi in my mouth and triumphantly pumped my fist. Naoko laughed.

"Second school?" I asked. "So that is school after you get out of day school?"

She nodded.

"So that stereotype about Japanese kids working overtime is true—pressure to overachieve, huh?" I said.

"Yes, very competitive. If you do not do well, it affects your future, and there is a lot of pressure from the parents and the culture. There is also competition among peers."

"This is off topic, but I have been wondering about something over the past few days. What is up with the Japanese people wearing these face masks?"

Since I arrived at the airport, I had seen only the eyes of many Japanese people. Their faces were covered with medical masks that a doctor would wear, either light blue or white. At the airport, they had a quarantine station at immigration where they looked at people's eyes and throat. I was concerned. Was there an epidemic that people were trying to avoid?

Naoko laughed. "The Japanese are very germ conscious and do not want to catch colds."

She cracked that question for me. I had been confused for days. About one in four people on the street were wearing masks. It was a thing!

After lunch, we walked around Kyoto and went to the market. My senses went on overload as soon as we stepped in. I loved Asian markets. It was such an experience. Unlike Thailand and China, I was excited to have someone to explain it all to me and could ask questions with abandon. I felt like a kid skipping through a candy store.

In the market, all kinds of unfamiliar foods were on display: fruit in unexpected colors, seafood, spiky things, and candy. I repeated over and over again, "What's this?" and "What does that taste like?"

Naoko was gracious enough to answer all of my questions. She seemed to like giving me a brief education.

I walked up to an orange-like fruit or vegetable hanging from a string. "What is the name of this?"

"Those are *hoshigaki*, persimmons dried for like a month. That is why they are on a string, to dry. They dry and are massaged to have a nice flavor."

I snapped pictures before we strolled on, taking in all the things that were unfamiliar to me. Pickled vegetables were everywhere. After pointing out their abundance, Naoko suggested I taste one. "Go ahead, you can try one for free."

I picked up something random and green, put it in my mouth, and immediately scrunched up my nose and shook my head from side to side. "I am not a fan!" She laughed.

We also tried a bunch of sweet black and red beans. "Good!" I said after I tasted those. Naoko handed me things with a nod, saying, "Try this," and I obliged, having total trust in my new friend. We ate these gummy green things with sweet bean paste inside. They were good, but I couldn't get past the consistency.

"It's like gummy bears meet uncooked dough," I said.

We tried loads of other things: dried fish, dried fruit, crackers, and cakes. Looks were deceiving. I picked up something that looked like an orange but tasted more like an apple. We came upon these large fish that were dried so hard they looked like pieces of wood. The fish were then shaved to make what looked like wood flakes, which were sold and used in soup.

"Wow, now that was an adventure," I said as we walked out of the market. My curiosity and stomach had been satiated for the day. It would have been so much less fun and educational if Naoko had not been there. Her company was far better than walking around alone or paying for a tour.

We stood outside the market for a second and looked around. "Where to next?" I urged.

"It's the New Year, so we will see a lot of people visiting the shrines if we walk a little way up. Interested?"

"Of course!" Having led myself so much of this trip—so much of my life—I was happy to follow, to have someone else to set the agenda. We walked a while in the same direction as droves of other people. Naoko explained, "In Shintoism, during the New Year, there are a lot of people going to the shrines and making offerings and wishes for the year."

There were masses of people everywhere, walking up to pillars, buying leafy branches with charms attached (*omamori*, small amulets for blessings or protection) that represented their prayers.

Others bought small wooden plaques called *ema*—with drawings or handwritten wishes—that they hung or tied on the pillars. Men and women in white robes stood behind counters, selling charms and branches, while others on stage waved them over altars and addressed the crowd in song and prayer. I watched, engrossed, as the crowd moved and bowed in synchronicity. Everyone had grave and determined looks on their faces. This was serious business. They were decisive in choosing their *omamori* or *ema*, sure of where to place them. I had no clue what was going on, but I understood the need for humans to make sense of the world, to create ceremonies that brought meaning and made known their hearts to the universe, or in this case *kami*, or Shinto gods.

Before this outing I knew nothing of Shintoism. I wondered what new and different things people wanted to explore in the New Year, what past pains they wanted healed, relationships repaired, or financial blessings they hoped for. During my seven months of travel, I had learned above all how to pay attention to people, to listen, to be present and curious about their experience. As I was learning to see the heart of a person, a people, I was also learning to see and pay attention to my own desires, my heart, myself. Everywhere I went there was always some kind of spiritual ceremony or celebration. A time when people returned to the center, their deity, but also to the center of themselves, back to the core of their hopes and desires.

I looked around at the masses of people who stood around us, watching and bowing with the white-robed Shinto priests, called *kannushi* on stage. I looked over at Naoko and realized that one of my core desires was connection. The days where I had someone local to show me around were the best: having sushi with a Japanese friend, going to the market, visiting a shrine and attending a festival, doing what they did, eating what they ate, and being immersed. I smiled at Naoko in gratitude as we did our last bow. She smiled back.

Her time that day meant a lot to me. It meant I was a lot less lonely and confused, that I wasn't relegated to being an observer. She helped me participate. I felt less like an outsider. I felt revived from my exhaustion.

Naoko helped me realize how much I had always been carried by friendship and faith. Living six hours away from my family in New York, I had to cultivate a community of chosen family. My friends and faith communities were my chosen family during my time in Charlottesville, which began in 2003 with a one-year leadership development program at a conservative white church. They were loving, but so far away from my reality as a young Black progressive woman from the north. I was supported, but never felt like I belonged.

After the program ended, I found a group of about ten Black Christian friends. We were connected to or had graduated from the University of Virginia. We hung out, had potlucks and Bible studies, and prayed for one another. They brought so much color to my life and were a lifeline. We laughed loudly on weekends in the red dining room of my house as we ate and played Taboo. Many of them were first-generation college graduates like me; some of them had known poverty, too, so I felt at home.

During that time, 2004–2007, I lived in an old mini mansion called the Manor House with four white women. We had moved into the neighborhood intentionally as Christians, to support a nonprofit organization that was investing in the surrounding low-income Black community. I loved my housemates, and we had fun. We went on trips, ate together, served and prayed together. This shared faith, service, and community complemented the belonging I had found with my Black friends. Life with all of them was rich.

The three Black teen girls I mentored from the Prospect Avenue neighborhood in Charlottesville also brought a sense of joy and belonging to my life. They were smart, and sassy, a little rough around the edges but witty and hilarious—kind of like me. I wanted to be for them what I hadn't had much of during my young life: a mentor and role model. I picked them up and offered them advice. Together we joked, ate a lot of ice cream, and I tried to share whatever wisdom I had to give. They called my purple two-door Saturn "the Batmobile." I'd like to think that I came to their "rescue" on a few occasions. I tried to be a solid place in their lives amidst shifting boyfriends, financial woes, and riffs with parents. I did this out of a sense of purpose and passion fueled by my faith. To whom much is given, much is required.

In 2009, I found a new church, All Souls. Though I was one of only a few Black people, I felt at home in this faith community. After my first visit, I volunteered to read scripture in service. Later, I started reading poetry. Though I looked out at a sea of white faces, I felt like I could be my full self. I could be my uncertain, questioning self there, something new for me, and that was freeing. We shared stories and scripture. It was artsy, intimate, and contemplative. They helped me see God everywhere and find the voice of the spirit for myself, within myself. This church was the perfect setup for my travels and for finding my voice through poetry.

Like many others before her, Naoko had been Godsent. Now she tapped me on the shoulder, letting me know it was almost time for us to get going. The men in white robes waved palms over the crowd, and people bowed. Following Naoko's lead, I bowed too. Her calming presence felt spiritual to me, a connection that bound us together for the day. She helped me understand a little about Kyoto in a way I would not have gotten from a tour or guidebook. Her friendship was an invitation to be led, cared for, and guided without needing to be in charge. It was a soft landing after months of exhausting, albeit enriching, travel.

We finished our evening off with some Japanese beer and a beef bowl. Since Naoko and I had spent the day together and she was likely the only Japanese person that I would have this level of comfort with, it was time for a poem.

"Naoko, I want to thank you for the day. It's been great. But I have a favor to ask." I explained the concept of the poem. All she had to do was fill in the blanks.

"Okay," she said, though she sounded a bit hesitant.

I told her that I'd videotape her at the end. She looked concerned and asked, "Where will it go?"

"Up on my website."

Her eyes became wide.

"It's fine," I reassured her. "I will lead you through it like you led me through the market today. If you don't like the video, I won't post it." She nodded.

It was late, so I hurriedly asked Naoko a few questions and wrote down her answers.

"What's one of your favorite celebrations in Japan?" I asked.

"The Gion Festival," she said. "It's in Kyoto every July. People wear *yukatas*—summer kimonos—and there are floats, food stalls, parades, so many people in the streets. It is one of the biggest festivals in Japan." I wrote it down quickly, picturing the color and pageantry.

"What's one of the happiest moments you remember?"

She thought for a moment. "Flying for the first time, when I went to the United States for a homestay. It was exciting and scary. I lived with a family and practiced my English."

I nodded, smiling at her mix of nerves and pride. "And one of the hardest?"

Her eyes fell. "My friend died in a traffic accident. It was very sudden and sad."

I let the moment rest, then asked, "What about foods you love?"

She brightened. "Sushi, sashimi, and rice," she said. "Always those."

When she read her poem aloud, starting with family names like Sateshi and Takamis, she was nervous—her eyes shifting, her hands shaking—but she made it through, ending softly, "That's where I'm from."

Even in that brief time together, I felt the richness of her story—tradition and travel, celebration and loss, all grounded in the simple comfort of food that tasted like her home.

My tour of Mount Fuji and onigiri from 7-Eleven later that week paled in comparison to my day in Kyoto with Naoko. This was evidence of how one can visit a different country, see the sights, and even eat the food without being moved by the spirit of the people and touching the heart of the place. Making a friend made a world of difference to me and closed the gap that could have kept us worlds apart.

AUSTRALIA

16

AUSTRALIA: LASTING IMPRESSIONS

When I landed in Australia on January 11, 2011, I couldn't believe I was down to the last two weeks of my trip. I was relieved to trade my North Face jacket, hat, and gloves for eighty-degree weather, and just as relieved to know I'd be home soon. By then, I had shaved off time in several places: a week in Peru, a few weeks in Kenya, two in India. At the beginning of January, I couldn't imagine meeting one more person, telling my story again, or making a new friend I'd have to leave behind. I was tired.

The day before, I'd Skyped my mom from my hostel bunk in Japan. She asked if I needed anything when I got home.

"Like what?" I said.

"I don't know," she replied. "Like underwear."

What is it with moms and underwear? I thought. *Do they ever stop wanting to buy it?*

I said, "No, what I will need is a vacation."

"A vacation?!" she shouted. "Isn't this a vacation?"

I laughed. "This is definitely *not* a vacation. It's an adventure, an experience, but not a vacation."

The truth was that it had been one of the hardest, most exhausting things I'd ever done, and also the most incredible. As I deplaned into Cairns, Australia, country number seventeen, city number seventy, continent number five—I felt weary but hopeful.

Maybe, just maybe, I could make the last two weeks of my trip feel like a vacation.

CAIRNS AND ABORIGINAL AUSTRALIANS

I booked a three-night hostel stay in Cairns, where it was eighty-six degrees, with beaches and palm trees all around. It felt tropical, like a real vacation.

That afternoon I went to the Lagoon at the Cairns Esplanade, about a mile from my hostel. Right in the heart of downtown and bordered by the ocean, it was one of the most amazing public spaces I'd seen: an aqua-blue lagoon, a boardwalk, and a plaza where you could walk straight into the water. Five silver poles topped with fish shapes marked the entrance. Under banyan trees, Australians grilled at tables while kids splashed and adults talked in groups. I sat on a bench at the water's edge, somewhere between pool and beach, and watched it all.

What struck me, though, was who wasn't there. I didn't see any Aboriginal families enjoying the space. In fact, in Cairns I'd seen only a few Aboriginal people at all. On my way to the promenade, a brown-skinned, kinky-haired man with a wide nose called out, "Teresa," thinking I was someone he knew. I wasn't Teresa, I replied, but after being the only Black person in most of the places I'd visited for the past month, it felt nice to look familiar to someone.

The next day, I visited a cultural center about the Tjapukai, an Aboriginal people from the region. It was entertaining and informative, yet felt like a theme park. Barefoot employees, their bodies painted in white, black, and yellow, greeted us at every station, dressed in loincloths and feathered headbands. I wasn't sure if it was genuine culture or commercialization. Conflicted, I recognized it offered both history and jobs, so I tried to stay open.

The cultural center's campus was lush and had a large lake at the center. Visitors were given a map showing the walking trails and attractions where they could stop and see a number of shows, talks, and demonstrations. We learned about some Aboriginal folklore, instruments, hunting tools, and home remedies.

First, we saw Aboriginal art that displayed dreamtime stories—their creation stories. The paintings featured colorful dots that came together in patterns to form large circles and animals.

At the women's hut, a table displayed native plants, seeds, and nuts ranging from the size of a coffee bean to a potato in carved wooden bowls and trays. A thin Aboriginal woman with a brown two-piece outfit lifted up each item, said the name and what it was used for, and passed it around so that we could touch it. The men's hunting station showed tools and spears that Tjapukai men used. Not too far from there was a spear-throwing station.

I was excited to throw a boomerang, an Aboriginal tool used for both hunting and play. Each person got three chances to throw a boomerang across the open green field bounded by trees. The guide, dressed in similar clothing to the others, instructed us: Grip the end, stand at a forty-five-degree angle from where the wind is blowing, step back, and throw forward—with a quick flick of the wrist upon release. We watched his boomerang fly off about thirty feet and then ducked as it came whipping back toward us. I was amazed. He made it look so easy, but when I tried it flew out a few feet and dropped. After a few tries, I had it.

I also got to play a didgeridoo, which is a long instrument made from a hollowed-out eucalyptus tree trunk. They are tubes from three to ten feet long, their smooth, polished surfaces painted with pictures and patterns. Beeswax around the top opening acts as a mouthpiece. They sound like horns, a low humming sound. The instrument I tried reached to the floor. I blew air into it, and it hummed for me.

It was an entertaining day, but what I learned about the history of Aboriginal people in Australia and their current-day situation haunted me while I went through the park and during most of my days in Australia.

Aboriginal Australians are the Indigenous peoples of Australia, including hundreds of nations, languages, and cultures that have thrived for more than 60,000 years. Before Europeans arrived in 1788, their numbers were somewhere between 250,000 and 500,000, spread across the continent, living in deep relationship with the land. Like Native Americans in the United States, they faced what seems to be a familiar pattern when Europeans show up: disease, land taken, families displaced, cultures pushed to the margins. The weight of colonization pressed hard here too. And yet, like Indigenous peoples everywhere, they continue to resist, to hold fast to culture, language, and identity.

I spent the following day with an older white Servas couple and their grandkids and asked them about Aboriginal Australians. Over lunch, the wife told me that race relations in Australia were complicated. Aboriginal people, she explained, were often pushed to the margins, losing access to traditions, language, and jobs. She felt government programs were more about words and handouts than real solutions. "Prejudice exists on both sides," she added, though it was rarely violent. What weighed most heavily on her was the reality that too many Aboriginal people were behind bars and too many families struggled with violence.

On a later museum tour in Sydney, I learned that between 50,000 and 100,000 Aboriginal children had been taken from their homes between 1910 and the 1970s. Called the Stolen Generations, they were placed in institutions or foster care as part of a policy of forced assimilation and cultural erasure. Some were taken as school-aged children, others as infants, before they could even remember where they came from.

I also learned that Aboriginal Australians were marginalized by European descendants throughout history. Many of them lived on reserves; they couldn't vote until the 1960s, and they needed special permission to do things like marry or travel. Some of these injustices continued until the 1980s and 1990s. Until recently, history books barely acknowledged that anyone inhabited Australia before it was colonized. Because so many people were killed, a lot of pre-European history was lost, despite the fact that Aboriginal culture is one of the oldest living traditions in the world.

While Aboriginal and Torres Strait Islander people make up only about 3 percent of Australia's population, unemployment and poverty are higher, and life expectancy is years shorter than for other Australians. In Cairns, I noticed that many of the people visibly struggling on the streets were Aboriginal. It was hard not to see the weight of colonization, displacement, and racism still pressing on their communities.

One thing is consistent all over the world: Indigenous people get pushed to the margins. It was sad and disturbing. Sometimes my quest to learn how marginalized communities lived put a damper on my travels, but I felt that it was important to know the truth of a place and its people, especially nondominant groups. I wanted to make an Aboriginal friend to do a poem with, but I never got the chance.

Despite my disdain for the injustices born by the Aboriginal people, I found Australia to be a beautiful country and rather easy to navigate. Since I had spent so much time volunteering with Australians all over the world, I felt at home amidst the lingo—I had already heard so much of it from my volunteer mates. I learned to translate various phrases:

How are you? = How ya going?
Friend = Mate (They really do say, "G'day, mate!")
Jacket or sweatshirt = Jumper
Thanks = Cheers
Good job, or good for you = Good on ya
Breakfast = Brekkie
Dude = Bloke

Many Australians love Vegemite, a black spread they put on toast. You basically put way too much butter on a piece of toast and add a bit of Vegemite. It's salty and, to me, did not taste good.

I also had the pleasure of snorkeling on the Great Barrier Reef, probably the best coral reef in the world. I was supposed to scuba dive, but they wouldn't let me because I was finishing up my malaria medicine. They took a group of fifteen or so of us out on a midsized motorboat. We went about ninety minutes to the coral reef, geared up, and jumped into the water, which was about three different shades of blue-green, clear, and pristine. We all wore wetsuits and goggles, with a breathing tube and a noodle. I couldn't swim, so I had to go out with a staff member and two older ladies. She dragged the three of us along holding on to a life tube. Once out, I stuck my head below the surface to see an electrifying oceanic paradise. There was a whole different world under there—fish with bright colors, stripes, and dots, some two-toned. The coral itself was full of color: electric blue, yellow, pink, purple, you name it. Amazing! I saw a turtle and a clam my size.

I watched a school of Nemo fish striped orange, yellow, and black swim through the coral, which looked like a colorful mix of broccoli and little branches, like bushes with no leaves. After I got the hang of it, I went out at the second reef with another snorkeler, without the staff member, and felt relaxed and confident.

While glancing from the oasis of turquoise water that surrounded us to the lively scenery on display beneath us, I said to myself, "Yes, this is what a vacation feels like."

Later that week, I hit the Great Ocean Road, Australia's rival to the Pacific Coast Highway in California. It's a 240-kilometer stretch of road that borders southern Victoria (the state Melbourne is in). I took a drive along it and visited some beaches, gorges, and the Twelve Apostles—a series of rock formations. This area reminded me of Cape Town and the Garden Route in South Africa, which had similar rock formations, crashing waves, and vacation appeal. South Africa also had what they called Twelve Apostles, but there were really seventeen of those, and Australia actually has only eight. Why people liked to name rock formations the Twelve Apostles, I wasn't sure.

It was during this week of touring that I saw a koala bear. It was way up in a eucalyptus tree, just sitting there, relaxing. Though they look cute and cuddly, they have sharp teeth and claws and are not actually bears but relatives of kangaroos. I saw kangaroos one day when I was walking back to the hostel—a family of them were bouncing around in an open field. I stood and watched, then the biggest one saw me and stood still. We were eye to eye for a second and then it bounced away, but not before I got a picture of it. After that, I always got a kick out of seeing KANGAROO CROSSING signs.

MARTI, A LASTING IMPRESSION

By the time I reached Sydney, my last stop, I was done. I had crossed everything off my list: the Great Barrier Reef, learning about Aboriginal people and culture, kangaroos, and koalas. I had only a few days left before my flight back home. My time in Australia had felt like a vacation. I'd been glad for the eighty-degree weather and the beaches. But I was just buying time with walking tours and tourist sites. The months of experiences that had come before Australia still had my body and brain on overload. I hardly wanted to talk with anyone.

Then Marti from Barcelona, Spain—or Catalonia, as he would probably prefer I say—tapped me on my shoulder during my first day in Sydney.

We were just beginning a free walking tour near Sydney's Town Hall, a nineteenth-century stone building with a four-story clock tower. "What did she say?" he whispered with a heavy Spanish accent.

I repeated the tour guide's sentences without turning my head. "She was talking about how we would be going from the history of Sydney as a British penal colony to the bustling metropolis it is today."

"Sorry," he whispered again. "I do not speak English very well and she talks really fast. I can only get about half of what she is saying."

"Mmmmm," I replied, still staring straight ahead, resolute in my defenses.

"I'm Marti." He held out his hand. I looked down at it for a second and then up into his dark eyes for the first time. They were kind. He had short black hair, tanned skin, and a long nose.

I faked a smile and said, "Ebony," while I shook his hand.

"Evony, very nice. I've never heard of it before." The tour guide began to move, and I walked on, leaving him there with his mouth open, about to say something.

He caught up. "Evony, where are you from?"

Here we go, I thought and rolled my eyes. Exactly what I was trying to avoid—people asking me the same questions I had answered a thousand times before in sixteen other countries. But something told me that I was not going to be able to shake Marti.

"I'm from the US. I'm traveling around the world, seventeen countries. This is my last and I have been traveling for almost eight months," I said in one breath, with a tinge of annoyance.

He took a mini step back.

"I just wanted to get all of that out, because that is what most people ask me first." I paused for a minute, softening. "I've been asked the same three questions a thousand times and this is the last week of my trip, and I am a bit tired."

"I will not ask any more. But can you do me a favor?" he said.

"Depends on what it is." We began to walk again, but now at the back of the group, whispering our conversation.

"Depends?" he asked.

"It means maybe. Just tell me what it is."

"I need help. I don't understand everything she says. Can you tell me?"

"Sure, just tap me when you need something repeated." I knew what it was like to be far from home and need help with the language.

"Thank you very much."

However, Marti and I ended up walking and talking for pretty much the entire three-hour tour. Marti was twenty-six, worked in IT, and was in Australia for a year to improve his English. I helped him with his English words and with understanding what the tour guide was saying.

The tour was great. We saw the old part of Sydney (the Rocks), and I took some pictures of the Sydney Opera House and Harbor Bridge. When Sydney was a penal colony, Britain sent many prisoners there to serve their time, and they had built much of the city.

When the tour was over, Marti and I were still chatting. I asked where he was going. He said Bondi Beach, which was exactly where I was headed. We decided to go together. We navigated through the city and found the bus to the beach. Once we arrived, I felt like I was on vacation again, lulled by the movement of the turquoise water that morphed into a deep blue. The beach was sprinkled with hard white bodies in trunks and bikinis and bordered by rock formations that housed expensive beach homes. The beautiful scenery made me feel frumpy in my travel clothes of gray hiking pants and a blue T-shirt. Over the past eight months I had worn these items out and gained a few pounds.

It was warm at about 1:30 p.m., but we were both tired after walking for three hours. We grabbed a sandwich from one of the stores fronting the beach and sat near the boardwalk. The chatting died down quickly, and we just lay there, side by side. I dozed off for at least half an hour. Marti was quiet, so I presumed he was sleeping too. I felt comfortable and safe with Marti, and that was freeing. You know you have a connection when you can just sit and sleep or be quiet with someone and that is perfectly okay. On the last days of my trip, there were few things I had the mental and emotional capacity to work hard for, and a new friendship was not one of them. To my surprise, this was easy. What I did have a hunger for was real companionship. I didn't want to shoulder the burden of figuring out what I was going to do that day and doing it alone.

We awoke at what seemed like the same time. I looked out along the curvaceous beach full of people sunbathing, wading in the ocean, chasing children, or taking a stroll. The sky was clear and blue. I looked at the rock formation, with what I assumed were million-dollar houses sitting atop them, and saw a path along the rocks.

"Do you want to walk a little?" I asked Marti.

"It looks like there is a path to go along those rocks. Let's follow it." He pointed to the path I had been eyeing.

And so, we walked and talked about our families, our lives thus far, what had brought us to traveling. The path rounded the rocks and gave us a view of another beach around its curves. Men and women jogged by us every few minutes.

"I love hip-hop," Marti said.

"What?" I teased. "What do you know about hip-hop? You're from Spain."

To prove me wrong, he launched into The Notorious B.I.G.'s verse of "Get Money" by Junior M.A.F.I.A., talking about sipping champagne on the living room floor. I jumped in after the first few words. He kept going, his Spanish accent making everything funnier, his English suddenly sharper as he rapped with hand gestures, playing like he was tough. I nearly fell over laughing.

Then I tested him with the opening lines of "Nuthin' but a 'G' Thang" by Dr. Dre and Snoop Dogg. I started by saying, "One, two," and without missing a beat, he picked it up by the time I said the number four—and carried it all the way through. By the end, we were doubled over, amazed that two strangers from opposite sides of the world could meet in Australia and bond over hip-hop.

We recited many nineties hip-hop songs and compared our favorite artists as we walked along the coast. At one point, we stopped at a rock outcropping and stood atop them rapping, as if they were a stage and we were giving a duet hip-hop performance.

I loved hip-hop; I had grown up on it, and in a sense, it had helped raise me. I knew lyrics like the back of my hand. They were my first poems, my first stories. Dr. Dre and Snoop, Tupac, Biggie and Lil' Kim, and the Queen of Hip-Hop Soul, Mary J. Blige. She had me reminiscing on love I'd never had. The hard edge, the baggy clothes, the gold earrings, and Adidas sneakers. Hip-hop always brought me home. I remember taping hip-hop songs from HOT 97, a radio station in New York. We couldn't afford all the new albums, so I had to be resourceful. I remember the first time I heard Biggie's "Juicy" on the radio. It stopped me in my tracks.

I turned up the dial and began to bop my head to the beat and then sing the chorus. I quickly learned the lyrics so I could rap along every time it came on. It was the realness, the rawness, the eloquent storytelling, the rhythm and the rhymes of hip-hop that drew me. It was the way urban Black America told our stories—and they were raw, sometimes tragic, sometimes rags to riches, sometimes bragging or beefs, sometimes socially conscious. It was all there, in hip-hop. Hip-hop had brought the mess of life and the beauty of resilience and creativity together for urban Black America. That's what I was trying to do with this trip, with poetry, with the "Where I'm From" poems, with my life. I had embarked on this solo journey to see the world's mess and magnificence, to collect stories, to create poetry with marginalized communities, to write an adventurous chapter of my own life, and to find God in it all. But that moment with Marti made me realize that my love of storytelling had begun with hip-hop and culminated in poetry, at home and abroad.

I began writing poetry in 2009, the year I started hosting the WordSmith Poetry Jam. A friend had asked me to help with marketing for a community event to honor a poet. I agreed and suggested that I be the host. The night went so well that I continued hosting the event at various venues every month. Quite a few things stood out to me that first evening: creativity, diversity, beauty, and brokenness. In the same room were professional poets and novices, professors and service workers, baby boomers and millennials, African Americans and Caucasians, performing and applauding together. The restaurant was packed, the energy was high, and the creativity was amazing. People took the messy moments of their lives, stewed them with wordplay and imagery, and served their meal to an audience of strangers.

I enjoyed the craft, but writing poetry was not part of my life until I found myself in the middle of those powerful and vulnerable acts of storytelling at WordSmith. I saw people telling their stories beautifully, so I began to do the same. A fountain of words emerged. Creating a space for a diversity of voices to be heard not only broadened my perspective but also provided space to find my own voice and a truer sense of calling. I wanted to create more space for that kind of thing to happen in Charlottesville—and to see how it happened in the rest of the world.

As a teen, I would never in a million years have imagined myself rapping my favorite hip-hop songs in Australia with a Spanish man, at the end of a world tour centered on poetry. My youthful ideas of success were about money and achievement. But this was living, and I loved every minute of it. Australia was a long way from home, but I felt closer to myself than I had felt in a long time. Hip-hop was my heart, so Marti captured it easily. He felt like home. I even recited a few of my spoken-word poems for him. My past and present converged with ease.

Talking with Marti was hilarious and familiar. He felt like an angel that had saved me from my crankiness during the last few days of my trip. Though his English was good, many things were still lost on him. Like when I pointed out all the joggers that passed us, he said, "What is jogging?" He was like a little kid, learning many new words. As we talked, he repeated all the new phrases I would throw out there in fascination.

My favorite question of his was, "What is the difference between beach and bitch?"

I replied, "Do you want to know the difference in meaning or pronunciation?"

"Pronunciation. When I try to say beach, it sounds like bitch."

Indeed, it did. We worked on that one for about ten minutes and his beach still sounded like bitch. Oh, the subtleties of language. It's funny how mispronouncing one syllable can have you saying something completely different. Marti told me a story of him talking to someone, imitating a "rapper," and saying, "Look, I am a rape-r."

"Ouch!" I said, guessing that that mistake didn't go over well. He marveled at how much he was learning from talking to me, much more than any book. He asked me about things he'd heard in rap songs, but didn't understand, like one hundred bucks, or one grand, or a *G*.

Our coastal walk ended up lasting a few hours. We took the same route we'd come by to return to the area where we arrived, talking the entire way. When we got back, it was time for dinner, and we found a pizza place with an outdoor eating area. We sat at a sidewalk table as the sun was going down. Marti had on a yellow shirt and there was an orange glow behind him as the sun was setting. I thought this would be a good time to do the "Where I'm From" poem with him. He was from Spain, and I hadn't interviewed anyone from Spain.

I pulled out my marble notebook from my daypack and asked Marti about himself, about his life. Like many people I met around the world, he loved pizza, but there was this special Spanish dish he loved and missed, *pa amb tomàquet*. I asked him to repeat the pronunciation and to tell me about it. He folded his arms on the table and leaned toward me. "It's bread, with tomato, olive oil, salt, *jamon*, and cheese." His eyes were bright. "You would like it very much." I had no doubt I would have. I just wished I had tried it while I was in Spain.

Then he told me about his friend dying in a car accident when he was twelve. I looked down at my pizza and then back up at him. I hadn't had anyone close to me die, but almost everyone I interviewed had. My heart sank. In that one moment, I felt his pain and remembered the tragedies of all of the other people I had interviewed. On the joyous side, he lit up when he talked about how proud he was of himself for coming to Australia to live for a while. I was glad to have run into him on his journey.

When he read his poem on camera, he proudly recited the names of his family—Francesco, Olga, and Laia—and spoke of

Catalonia National Day, a September celebration of Catalan identity and pride. He included a Spanish saying, "*Lo cortés no quita lo valiente*," which means something like, "Being polite doesn't take away from being brave." He spoke of his excitement about graduating with an engineering degree and of the music he loved—old-school hip-hop, drum and bass, reggae. He finished rhythmic and strong, proclaiming, "That's where I'm from," with a crooked smile.

I was again mesmerized by how easy it was to get the details of people's lives and how open people were to my curiosity. I loved how he looked up to remember, how intense he got when he told a story from his past, and how sacred a conversation about someone's life could be.

By the time we arrived at the front of my hostel, we had already made a plan to hang out again the next day. He met me at 9:00 a.m. at my hostel, and we spent the day on a hike in the Blue Mountains outside of Sydney. That day was just as splendid as the day before. We took an hour-long train ride and stopped off in a village to get a beer at 11:00 a.m. We hiked the mountains—up and down rocks, water, and passageways only one person wide. I recited a few poems of my own on our way up the mountain. He was mesmerized and thought I was really good. We sang hip-hop songs from artists like N.W.A., Fresh Prince, Run-D.M.C., and others.

When we finally got to the mountaintop, the view was breathtaking. Green mountains and grayish rock formations rose on every side, wide and expansive, up in the clouds, sturdy and self-assured. They reminded me of the Blue Ridge Mountains in Charlottesville. The Three Sisters, a rock formation of three pillars, sat to our left. We stood shoulder to shoulder and took in the view, the sun shining on our faces.

Then we continued along the path, past waterfalls and a small river. We were silent, tired from the hike but content to be together.

On our train ride back, we were staring out the window sitting opposite one another. Marti broke the silence. "I looked you up on Facebook last night. Wow, your pictures are beautiful. The black-and-white one is great."

I knew the photo. If I sang or put out a spoken-word album, this would be my album cover. It was me with short locs, fifteen pounds lighter, in front of a mic, in a brown-and-white halter dress, looking my best. Now I felt frumpy, weary, and a lot less beautiful. My hair had grown; I was in the same hiking shoes I'd worn for eight months, a turquoise tank top, and worn hiking pants. I wished I felt beautiful at that moment.

"That is what I looked like before backpacking for eight months." I knew I looked like I was at the end of my rope. "Tonight, I am going to an outdoor opera concert with a Servas friend. Do you want to join?" I said, changing the subject.

He declined and I asked him what he was doing the next day, trying to prolong our time together. He was going to some other beach. I was all beached out. We would be going our separate ways.

He walked me back to my hostel and we stood out front, knowing the end was near. We said a slow goodbye, both kind of sad, but happy we got to spend time together. We hugged.

"Take care, Marti. Enjoy your time in Australia!" I yelled as he walked away.

"Get home safe!" he shouted back with a wave.

Though I would likely never see him again, he was definitely a gift for two days, one I am glad I opened. His company reenergized me. I was happy that I did not have to see the last bit of beauty I would encounter on my trip alone. I was grateful it was easy, that I could connect with a man from Spain who was working on his English over tours, the beach, food, hiking, hip-hop, and poetry. It was worth it to open up again and again, to connect, give, receive, laugh, and love, even though it would not last. Wasn't that the point?

NORTH AMERICA

17

HOME AGAIN

At the end of the trip, I was happy to be getting home to familiarity, to the people I knew and loved, and to lay down the backpack, which had become a burden over those eight months. I had carried the weight of my entire life on my back. I realized that was how I'd been traveling through life for too long, as if I was a solo traveler. I was ready to lay that down as well.

The evening before I left Australia, I went to the small computer lab in the basement of my hostel to print out my tickets and realized that Tim, my travel agent, had sent me a booking but had not confirmed my tickets. I had not even heard from him since I'd arrived in Australia. Panic began to rise in my chest. *Oh no*, I thought. *I need to get home*. It was 10:00 p.m., and the flight I thought I was supposed to be on was set to leave at 8:20 a.m. I searched through my email to get the flight information. I tried to check in online, but no flight was found. I called the airline, and indeed, Tim had not confirmed my booking. Sydney was sixteen hours ahead of New York, so I was able to get someone from Tim's travel agency on the telephone.

Tim did not work there anymore. He had been let go a week ago. There were some shady dealings with him, apparently, and a return flight had already been booked on my account, though it was not for me.

"I need to get home!" I shouted into the computer headset. "I need to get home tomorrow!" I rubbed my head as the thought of being on the road one more day overwhelmed me.

There was nothing they could do. The woman said, "Buy a ticket home, and we will sort it out when you get back to the US."

I screamed into the phone to no avail. I hung up without a ticket. Desperate, I looked online. The same flight that Tim had supposedly booked for me was available but cost $1,400. "Fourteen hundred dollars," I said in disbelief. I needed to get home, so I gritted my teeth, took out my credit card, and spent money I did not have. I'd later learn that Tim was indeed shady and had bought someone else's ticket with my money. It took me a month of yelling and screaming and a report to the Better Business Bureau before I finally got a full refund. That night, however, I was just happy to have a flight and went to sleep dreaming of home.

I wanted to kiss the UNITED STATES OF AMERICA sign when I entered the country. After thirty hours of traveling, from Australia by way of a two-hour stop in Fiji and a ten-hour layover in Los Angeles, I arrived at LaGuardia Airport to no one waiting for me. We had gotten our wires crossed, and my mother and sister Danielle thought I was coming home the day before. No sign with my name on it, no hugs—but it was an airport I knew and a language I spoke, and I knew my way home.

I arrived at my back door, which was plastered with handmade WELCOME HOME signs from my family. I walked in and loved that I knew this place. I knew the table and the wall signs and the smells. Inside, they'd put together another hand-drawn sign on white poster board paper that read HAPPY THIRTIETH BIRTHDAY, HAPPY NEW YEAR, AND WELCOME HOME. There was a big globe in the middle. I dropped my bags, touched the globe, and closed my eyes. *I've been around this.* I took a deep breath and exhaled a wow. I looked at the side of my mom's refrigerator, and it was plastered with the postcards and magnets I'd sent her from everywhere I'd been. I read a few. I was glad to have been to all of those places, but more than anything, I was glad to be home.

I was a bit broken and battered by my travels, full of experiences but exhausted by all that I had encountered. Mostly, I felt exposed. Somewhere along the way my protective shield had cracked. By the end of the trip, the shell that I lived with for so long had completely fallen off. I felt a lot softer, more open, more flexible, and more fragile. Off-balance, even.

I walked into the living room, sat on my mother's red couch, took off my hiking shoes, and looked at the bottoms before setting them on the wood floor. *These have been on six continents now*, I thought, shaking my head. I stretched out, closed my eyes, and let images flood my mind: people and places, laughter and tears, food and smells, wind and water. What had I learned? How had I changed?

I thought of Mateo in Guatemala, Sanya in India, and Marti in Australia—each of them gifts. I had gone around the world in search of adventure but had found my own heart. I'd shed the armor of independence and self-reliance, discovering both my limitations and the beauty of companionship. I learned how easy it is to fall in love with people and places—and how hard it is to leave them. Yet love, even when it hurts, always asks us to risk again.

Though my introverted self relishes solitude, I discovered that people are better than no people. I didn't want to walk alone or do life all by myself. I needed help, comfort, encouragement, companionship, and connection. Facing those needs was humbling, but it was also a relief.

The postcards on my mother's fridge showed wonders of the world, but they paled in comparison to the people: Isabela in Guatemala, Sofia in Costa Rica, Mary Makena in Kenya. Their resilience—through abuse, loss, or poverty—shone brightest. I saw love covering hardship, redeeming brokenness.

I had witnessed the triumph of the human spirit. I met women like Ms. Ana in Guatemala and Mary Makena in Kenya who faced injustice with courage, transforming their compassion into organizations that changed lives. Their strength taught me that nurturing and softness are not weakness but power. In them I saw a maternal, healing strength that I realized also lived in me. I thought of Sahil and Sanya in India, who drew out my nurturing side, a part of myself I had not always embraced but came to love. I learned I could be both strong and soft, firm and tender.

I thought of Raj in Costa Rica, TK in London, Frank in South Africa, and Marti in Australia. Of the four men I'd encountered, the two I connected to most deeply were not physical. We had friendship and things in common, we lingered, we laughed, and we discussed what was important to us. I was reminded of what I already knew—that for me, soul attraction wins over physical attraction any day. I wanted more, and that was okay.

Traveling also revealed the paradox of beauty in brokenness. In townships, settlements, and schools, I always found light in the darkness, laughter alongside lack. I came to hold joy and sorrow together in myself, past and present braided into one story.

In Thailand, a framed sign at a drug rehabilitation center read PRESENT MOMENT, WONDERFUL MOMENT. Traveling taught me what that meant. With nowhere else to be but where I was, I learned presence. I breathed in smells, savored flavors, wrote names, captured details, knowing I'd write about them later. Being present made me more alive than I had ever been.

And when plans fell apart, I learned to let go. The times I mapped everything, I missed what mattered. By the end of my trip, I planned only the first night in a new place, then let the rest unfold—asking questions, following local advice, saying yes to surprise. It was the flow that gave me joy.

I also learned through paragliding in Switzerland with Peach and the welcoming spirit of folks like Margarita from Costa Rica, the Carvers in Compiègne, and Naoko in Japan, the freedom of leaning on and into people—into life itself. The hospitality of humanity was like a warm hug, and it felt good to finally lean in.

From Peru's National Museum to South Africa's Apartheid Museum, I learned the importance of remembering—of facing our wounds honestly. Sometimes we need a memorial, mural, or museum, and sometimes we need to take our difficult circumstances and turn them into something beautiful, like the kids in Kenya, by making art or writing poetry.

Through the "Where I'm From" poems, I learned that people are more alike than different. We all laugh, cry, mourn, and celebrate over the same universal things: births, deaths, disasters, healing, love, purpose, meaningful work, and home. I never failed to connect. Those poems helped me connect to people and their stories and ultimately find peace in my own story.

They also taught me the gift of curiosity. I connected because I asked: Where are you from? What do you love? What brought you here? I asked, and people opened up. That curiosity carried me into kitchens, temples, neighborhoods, and friendships I never could have planned. It helped me listen more deeply, and in listening, I learned to see.

And the places themselves, the natural environments—mountains, volcanoes, coral reefs, animals, rainforests—took my breath away. The pearls were in the pastures, the earth radiant with divine design, beauty interwoven with dynamism.

Before I left the US, I think I pretty much loved myself. In the end, I loved people, and I got to know myself by getting to know them.

This remembering while I rested in silence and solitude went on much of the day, until I heard the doorknob jiggle. My mom walked in the back door, saying, "Eb, are you home?"

I ran into the kitchen and met her a few steps away from the door. We embraced for a long time. My mother kissed me all over my face and started crying. "You made it back, you made it back, praise God, you made it home."

I joyously received all of the hugs, kisses, and tears she released on me.

"Yup, I'm home!"

I am Ebony Walden,
I am from Jamaica, Queens, and Hempstead, Long
 Island, in New York.
I am from Henrietta, Ricky, Theola, Anne, Buford,
 Suzette, and Eunice.
I am from "just put one foot in front of the other."
I am from fish fries on Fridays, individual sweet potato pies
 made on Thanksgiving by my grandmother, and hot
 buttered bagels from the corner store.
I am from Jamaica, Queens, near Sutphin and Linden
 Boulevards, with the McDonald's on the corner.
I am from summer backyard BBQs at 34 Allen Street
 and summer nights at Lincoln Park.
I am from a single mom; having no lights, heat, or water
 at times; and growing up on welfare.
I am from finishing high school as number four in my class,
 being the first in my family to graduate college, and
 traveling the world.
I am from New York–style pizza, beef patties on coco
 bread, and anything curried.
I am from hip-hop, R&B, and neo soul.

That's where I'm from.

EPILOGUE

As I sit down nearly fifteen years later to reflect on the journey that began with a single idea and spanned continents, cultures, and countless moments of self-discovery, I am reminded of the profound impact that travel has had on my life. My around-the-world trip was a spiritual awakening built on the foundations of letting go, being present, embracing connection and community, and relishing in the interdependence of all things. I learned that my hardships as a child molded me into the woman I am today—brave, strong, tender, curious, and determined. I learned that I do not have to leave those stories behind, but I can bring them with me. No matter where I go, I can take a sense of home with me. This trip helped me find home within.

Returning from my trip, I was myself thrust into a period of even more transformation—where I grappled with the weight of all that I had experienced and learned. I felt fragile, weak, and raw from the ways the winds of the world had blown through my protective layers. I was softer, and that was a good thing, but it was painful.

The three and a half years that followed marked a season of navigating the liminal space between my old self and the person I was becoming. Supported by my spiritual community, daily rituals, and moments of quiet reflection, I slowly began to piece together the fragments of my identity, weaving them into a tapestry of newfound wisdom and understanding.

One pivotal moment came in the form of a poetry reading for my thirty-first birthday. I wrote a series of poems about my early years and paired them with the more confident, triumphant poems of my adulthood. It was a two-part performance called *Trial and Triumph*. Again, poetry helped me bring my separate selves together. It was a liberating evening in my friend's backyard. I stood on the stage we created out of their back porch. The moonlight shimmered on the caring faces of friends, old and new, Black and white. They were the first audience for a more integrated, authentic me. My thirtieth-birthday trip inaugurated the breaking open. The thirty-first symbolized the start of the stitching back together.

A second pivotal moment was a tribute to my journey. In 2012 I curated an exhibit—*Around the World in Eighty Photos*, which visually displayed the stories, sites, and people from my travels, accompanied by a poetry reading and musical performance. It was a celebration of how I'd been shaped, a testament to the power of storytelling and creative expression to bridge the gap between cultures.

Over the years, even as I found solace in the embrace of art and community, there were moments of heartache and loss—a failed romance, a move to a new city (Richmond, Virginia), and the ongoing struggle to reconcile my past with my present. And yet, through it all, I remained steadfast in my commitment to growth, embarking on a quest to explore the corners of my own soul, my own country. From the rolling hills of Virginia to the White Mountains of New Hampshire, from the majestic landscapes of Alaska to the sun-drenched shores of Hawaii, I journeyed through all fifty states.

After about five years, I ventured back into the realm of international travel. I've visited fifty countries to date, exploring distant lands and immersing myself in unfamiliar cultures. I am always looking for and trying to hold both the beauty and brokenness that these places offer, that life holds, that exist within me.

It has taken me ten years to write this book. It started out as a gift to myself, a way to detail the specific ways I had changed and the lessons I learned. It has become much more than a recounting of my adventures—it is an homage to the transformative power of travel, a call to dream out loud and embark on the journey of self-discovery that lies within each of us. I am reminded of the words of encouragement that have guided me along the way: "You go, girl!" And so, with gratitude in my heart and a sense of purpose in my step, I embrace the path that lies ahead, knowing that the greatest adventure of all is the journey within.

APPENDICES

APPENDIX A

FIFTEEN LESSONS FROM AROUND THE WORLD

These are the lessons I learned as I traveled the world. Each destination offered its own gift—some joyful, some painful, but all transformative.

1. Dream Out Loud

My trip began as a dream—an audacious leap of faith. Taking the first step toward a big dream is often the hardest, but daring to dream out loud is where transformation begins, where people and resources begin to align around the dream.

2. Purpose Starts with a Simple Yes

Some of the most impactful people I met didn't set out to start organizations. They simply responded to the needs in front of them. Purpose often begins there, saying yes to the invitation in front of you.

3. People Are Better Than No People

I learned that I need connection and community. Even as an introvert, the warmth of human connection and hospitality I experienced gave me strength. The friendships I made and the conversations I shared became the true treasures of my trip.

4. Let Go of Scarcity Thinking

My instinct to penny-pinch and hold on tightly to money came from growing up in poverty. I learned to trust that there would be enough—and that I could spend a little more to live fully. The trip helped me move from a survival mindset to a thriving one.

5. Be Curious

Asking questions, listening deeply, and showing genuine interest in others created meaningful connections everywhere I went. Being curious allowed me to build bridges across language and culture. Curiosity was also a window into being like children, full of wonder and playfulness.

6. The Pearls Are in the Pastures

The most beautiful moments often came not from man-made wonders but from the natural world—the quiet of the hills in Tuscany, the majesty of the Maasai Mara in Kenya, the stillness of the Swiss Alps. Beauty is often found in the natural world.

7. Trust Is Freedom

I learned to let go of rigid plans, embrace spontaneity, ask for help, and lean on others. Some of my best experiences—meals, friendships, and moments of awe—came from following the unexpected and allowing myself to be taken care of. Spiritual growth requires letting go!

8. You Can Be Both Strong and Soft

So many of the women I met had a strength and a softness, and it was beautiful. Strength isn't just about independence—it's also about allowing yourself to be cared for. I discovered the power of vulnerability and the beauty of allowing others to support me.

9. Hold the Beauty and the Brokenness

I saw poverty and struggle, but I also saw resilience and joy. Life isn't one or the other—it's both. Learning to hold those contrasts in the world and within myself without judgment was transformational.

10. Love Again, Even When It Hurts

Falling in love with so many people and places was great, but leaving people behind was hard. It hurts to say goodbye over and over. But I learned that even with loss and grief, I had to take the leap and open my heart again. When I thought I was done, opening my heart once more was worth it, and I am glad I did.

11. Presence Is Power

Being fully present—smelling the food, feeling the wind, hearing the voices—made the world come alive. Life became richer when I fully engaged with it. Present moment, wonderful moment!

12. Healing Requires Telling the Truth

I had to face the truth about my childhood—my parents' struggles, the instability I experienced, and the shame I carried. Owning that truth was essential for healing.

13. Embrace Uncertainty

Trying to control everything kept me from growing. When I surrendered to the unknown, to the messiness of life, to the chaos of uncertainty, and began to see the inevitable mishaps and disappointments as hidden opportunities, I discovered new strength and freedom.

14. Creative Expression Heals

Writing "Where I'm From" poems with others helped me process my own story and connect with others. Creativity became a form of therapy and connection.

15. Home Is **Not Just** *a Place*

I went searching for the world, but what I found was a deeper sense of home within myself. Home became the relationships I built and the sense of peace I carried inside.

APPENDIX B

REFLECTION QUESTIONS

Use these reflection questions to engage more deeply with the lessons in the book. Consider journaling your responses or discussing them with a book group. A more detailed discussion guide for individual reflection or book groups can be found at www.ebonywalden.com.

1. Dream Out Loud

What's one dream you've been holding back on because it feels too big or too risky?

2. Purpose Starts with a Simple Yes

What's one small need you've noticed in your community or among your friends or family that you could respond to today?

3. People Are Better Than No People

Who are the people that make you feel seen and supported? How can you cultivate deeper connections with them or build new ones?

4. Let Go of Scarcity Thinking

Where in your life are you holding on too tightly to resources, opportunities, or relationships out of fear of not having enough?

5. Be Curious

What's one question you could ask someone this week to better understand their story or perspective?

6. The Pearls Are in the Pastures

When was the last time you slowed down and fully appreciated the beauty of nature or a simple moment? When can you find time to do so this week?

7. Trust Is Freedom

Where in your life could you loosen control and trust that things will unfold as they're meant to? Who can you lean on?

8. You Can Be Both Strong and Soft

How can you allow yourself to be supported without feeling like you're giving up your strength?

9. Hold the Beauty and the Brokenness

How can you honor both the difficult and joyful parts of your story without judgment?

10. Love Again, Even When It Hurts

Is there a relationship or situation where you've closed off your heart? What would it take to open it again?

11. Presence Is Power

What's one way you can practice being more present in your daily life?

12. Healing Requires Telling the Truth

What's one truth about your life or your past that you need to face in order to experience deeper healing?

13. Embrace Uncertainty

What do you need to surrender in order to shift your mindset to see uncertainty, mishaps, disappointments, or change as opportunities rather than threats?

14. Creative Expression Heals

What creative outlet (writing, art, music, etc.) helps you process your emotions or tell your story?

15. Home Is Not Just *a Place*

Where or with whom do you feel most at home? What do you need to do to be more at home with yourself?

☞ Visit www.ebonywalden.com for a full downloadable Book Group Discussion Guide for a more in-depth exploration of the lessons and experiences in this book.

APPENDIX C

THE R-TO-R METHOD

The Remember to Reset (R-to-R) Method is my personal framework for healing and transformation that emerged from my travels. It encapsulates the process of making peace with my past. This method offers a pathway for moving through difficult experiences and finding clarity and strength on the other side.

1. Remember

Start by looking back. Remember your story—both the beautiful and the painful moments. Honor your truth and give yourself permission to hold the full complexity of your experience. This may require some prompts, journaling, or the assistance of a therapist.

2. Reckon

Reckoning means facing the truth without running away from it. It's about acknowledging how your past has shaped you and confronting any patterns or beliefs that no longer serve you. Reckoning requires honesty and courage. You might need to have some conversations with the people that caused you pain or write about the impact this has had on your life.

3. Reconcile

Reconciliation means finding peace. It's about letting go of resentment, forgiving yourself and others, and accepting what cannot be changed. It's about making peace with both the light and the shadow sides of your story. A conversation or a reconciliation ritual to release what does not serve you might be warranted.

4. Rest

Rest is the essential step of integration. Take time to breathe, reset your nervous system, and allow yourself to recover from the emotional and spiritual work or healing. Rest creates the space for new insights to emerge. Take time away or go on a retreat.

5. Reflect

Reflection is where clarity and meaning begin to emerge. What have you learned? How have you changed? What wisdom can you carry forward? Reflection allows you to distill the lessons from your experiences and see the bigger picture. Write out your lessons and keep them handy.

6. Reset

Reset is about doing things differently. After resting and reflecting, you have the chance to make new choices. What patterns or habits need to shift? What new intentions can you set? Resetting allows you to step into your next chapter with greater clarity and purpose. Find a therapist or friend to process and practice new habits with as well as to hold you accountable.

☞ *Visit www.ebonywalden.com*
for a downloadable journal guide
to apply the R-to-R Method to your own life.

APPENDIX D

"WHERE I'M FROM" POEM TEMPLATE

I'm from

A) Three items found inside or around your home growing up.

____

____

____

I'm from

B) Two sayings or phrases you heard often while growing up.

____

____

I'm from

C) Three names or nicknames of family and friends.

____

____

____

I'm from

D) Two heartbreaks, disappointments, or tragedies you experienced.

____

____

I'm from

E) Three people, places, or things found in your neighborhood.

____

____

____

I'm from

F) Three victories or joyful moments in your lifetime.

____

____

____

I'm from

G) Three styles of music or types of foods that were a tradition to you or that you enjoy.

____

____

____

That's where I'm from.

APPENDIX E

LET'S CONNECT

My hope is that the lessons in this book inspire you to travel and to embark on your own journey of transformation. If my story resonated with you, I invite you to take the next step:

- **Explore More:** Visit www.ebonywalden.com for additional resources, including extended reflection questions, a discussion guide, photography, and poetry inspired by the journey.
- **Join the Conversation:** Sign up for my Substack newsletter and join an online community of travelers and seekers at www.substack.com/@ebonywalden.
- **Work with Me:** If you're interested in workshops, speaking engagements, or coaching, visit www.ebonywalden.com for details.
- **Share Your Story:** You can also write your own "Where I'm From" poem. I'd also love to hear how this book has impacted you. Share your thoughts on social media using the hashtag #WhereImFrom and tag me @ebonywalden80 on Instagram.

Thank you for being part of this journey. My hope is that you continue to seek the pearls in the pastures and find home within yourself.

Scan the QR code below to visit my website:

ACKNOWLEDGMENTS

First, I want to thank the people who helped make The Poetic Justice World Tour a reality. Without your support, this journey—and this book—would not have been possible.

Thank you to Fred Perry for dreaming out loud. You were the spark that set this journey in motion. A huge thank you to Wilson Whitaker for helping me visualize my travel dreams by building the trip website and blog that allowed me to take the leap toward making the trip a reality. Thank you to All Souls Charlottesville for your unwavering support. You accepted donations on my behalf, and, more importantly, provided a home that nurtured my creative self before and after the trip. Your support helped me grow and heal and provided the bookends to this season of transformation.

To everyone who donated and helped me fundraise (friends, family, and coworkers)—you were part of making this journey possible. Your generosity carried me across continents and helped make this dream come true.

In writing this book, I am especially grateful to WriterHouse for supporting authors like me in their journey toward developing our craft and shaping our stories. To Sharon Harrigan—your teaching, guidance, and feedback helped birth this book. I would not have written it without your three classes on memoir writing. To my classmates in the two Memoir in a Year classes at WriterHouse between 2015 and 2017—thank you for workshopping this book with me. You were like midwives to this book, helping me shape and deliver it into the world. Thank you Amber Padilla, Basira Harpster, Cora Schenberg, Jennie Moody, Kathy Bleam, Leslie Middleton, Sarah Van Steenburg, Sera McNaughton, and Trudy Hale.

A special thanks to my first readers—Hope Mills Voelkel, Brandi Collins, Lacette Cross, and Maco Faniel—for your thoughtful feedback, encouragement, and honesty. Your insight helped me strengthen the heart of this book.

Thank you to Lisa Ellison for helping me get to the core of my story and for your encouragement. Your guidance helped me uncover the deeper truths beneath the surface.

Thank you to Pat Dobie for your expert editing and insightful feedback. You helped me refine and elevate this book.

A big thank you to Marci Alboher for being a fan of my writing and connecting me to so many people and opportunities over the years. Your support, friendship, and mentorship have been invaluable.

To Brooke Warner and the She Writes Press publishing family—thank you for believing in this work and giving it a home. Your support has meant so much to me.

And of course, to my family and close friends—thank you for listening to me ramble for years about writing this book. Your patience, love, and support gave me the strength to keep going. This book would not exist without the generosity, insight, and support of all these people. Thank you for being part of this journey.

AUTHOR BIO

Author photo © Brittany Fan

Ebony Walden is an author, filmmaker, and speaker who has traveled to fifty countries and all fifty US states. She is the founder of Ebony Walden Consulting, a racial equity–focused consulting firm, and the creator of *Black Beyond Borders*, a documentary series and podcast exploring culture, creativity, connection, and cuisine across the African diaspora. Ebony also writes *Beyond Borders,* a Substack newsletter on travel and transformation. She lives in Richmond, Virginia.